The Revival of Islamic Rationalism

In this book, Masooda Bano presents an in-depth analysis of a new movement that is transforming the way that young Muslims engage with their religion. Lead by a network of Islamic scholars in the West, this movement seeks to revive the tradition of Islamic rationalism. Bano explains how, during the period of colonial rule, the exit of Muslim elites from madrasas, the Islamic scholarly establishments, resulted in a stagnation of Islamic scholarship. This trend is now being reversed. Exploring the threefold focus on logic, metaphysics, and deep mysticism, Bano shows how Islamic rationalism is consistent with Sunni orthodoxy and why it is so popular among young, elite, educated Muslims, who are now engaging with classical Islamic texts. One of the most tangible results of this revival is that Islamic rationalism – rather than jihadism – is emerging as one of the most influential movements in the contemporary Muslim world.

MASOODA BANO is Professor of Development Studies in the Department of International Development and Senior Golding Fellow at Brasenose College, University of Oxford. She is the author and editor of several books, most recently *Female Islamic Education Movements: The Re-democratisation of Islamic Knowledge* (Cambridge University Press, 2017) and *Modern Islamic Authority and Social Change, Volumes I and II* (2017, 2018).

The Revival of Islamic Rationalism

Logic, Metaphysics and Mysticism in Modern Muslim Societies

MASOODA BANO

Oxford University

CAMBRIDGE
UNIVERSITY PRESS

CAMBRIDGE
UNIVERSITY PRESS

University Printing House, Cambridge CB2 8BS, United Kingdom

One Liberty Plaza, 20th Floor, New York, NY 10006, USA

477 Williamstown Road, Port Melbourne, VIC 3207, Australia

314–321, 3rd Floor, Plot 3, Splendor Forum, Jasola District Centre,
New Delhi – 110025, India

79 Anson Road, #06–04/06, Singapore 079906

Cambridge University Press is part of the University of Cambridge.

It furthers the University's mission by disseminating knowledge in the pursuit of
education, learning, and research at the highest international levels of excellence.

www.cambridge.org
Information on this title: www.cambridge.org/9781108485319
DOI: 10.1017/9781108756273

First published 2020

Printed in the United Kingdom by TJ International, Padstow, Cornwall

A catalogue record for this publication is available from the British Library.

Library of Congress Cataloging-in-Publication Data
NAMES: Bano, Masooda, author.
TITLE: The revival of Islamic rationalism : logic, metaphysics and mysticism in modern
Muslim societies / Masooda Bano.
DESCRIPTION: 1. | New York : Cambridge University Press, 2019. | Includes index.
IDENTIFIERS: LCCN 2019034884 (print) | LCCN 2019034883 (ebook) |
ISBN 9781108485319 (hardback) | ISBN 9781108706827 (paperback) |
ISBN 9781108756273 (ebook) | ISBN 9781108756273(ebook) |
ISBN 9781108485319(hardback) | ISBN 9781108706827(paperback)
SUBJECTS: LCSH: Faith and reason–Islam. | Islam–21st century.
CLASSIFICATION: LCC BP190.5.R4 B365 2019 (ebook) | LCC BP190.5.R4 (print) |
DDC 297.2–dc23
LC record available at https://lccn.loc.gov/2019034884

ISBN 978-1-108-48531-9 Hardback

In the loving memory of my mother, Zahida Amin
(1946–2019)

Contents

Maps

Tables

Preface

My earlier works have focused primarily on Muslim-majority countries. Interested in tracing the evolution of Islamic scholarly platforms in contemporary times, I was drawn to leading establishments such as al-Azhar University or Saudi Salafism as well as the rich informal networks of Islamic learning in the Muslim heartlands. It was thus while doing fieldwork with female Islamic study groups in Syria in 2010 that I first heard of Alqueria de Rosales, a madrasah in the mountains of Granada, which I was told had been recently established by some Spanish converts. Moorish Spain, due to its critical contribution to early Islamic scholarship, had always been a region of historical interest to me, and I therefore made a note to visit Rosales. Academic commitments meant that I could not find time until the summer of 2012 to actually make this visit, but it proved a journey very well worth taking. The discussions that I began during this visit with Abdus Samad (the head of Rosales), his family, the young Muslims attending a retreat there, and Dr Umar Faruq Abd-Allah, who by chance was there during those dates, motivated me finally to take Islam in the West seriously. Since then my fieldwork has expanded to include Islamic learning institutions in the United Kingdom, Europe, the United States, and Canada, and the results have been fascinating. In this volume, I identify a network of Islamic rationalist scholars working across the United States and Europe, which – though very much a product of the West – is deeply embedded in the Islamic scholarly networks in Muslim-majority countries and in my assessment has initiated the most important Islamic revival movement of the twenty-first century. I base this claim not on my fieldwork with this network in the West but on my prior work on Islamic knowledge production in Muslim-majority countries, which has enabled me to identify the contribution of the network to global Islamic scholarly debates.

To date normally referred to as 'the traditionalists', the scholars in this network are reviving the deeply philosophical and mystical dimensions of Islam, while placing equal emphasis on the *shari'ah*. Taking Hadith Jibril as the essence of Islamic teachings, these scholars are keen to focus on *Iman* (a rationalist *'aqidah*), *Islam* (a *shari'ah* that has been operationalised by logical methods developed under the four *madhhabs*), and *Ihsan* (deep mysticism). I therefore prefer to refer to these scholars as Islamic rationalists. They themselves might like to self-appropriate the term 'traditionalists', as it helps to assert their claim to represent the authentic Islamic scholarly tradition; but the reality is that other Islamic networks equally claim to be representing the authentic tradition. What is, however, distinctive about this network is that it is helping to revive rationalist readings in Islam, the Ash'ari-Maturidi school of *kalam*. It is these scholars' ability to familiarise young Muslim university students with the deeply philosophical and mystical dimensions of their faith that, I argue, is making them so popular among young Muslims not only in the West but also among societal elites even within Muslim-majority countries. The evidence that this book provides about the rapid spread of this movement among university-educated Muslim youth in the West, as also among affluent youth in Muslim-majority countries, shows that, contrary to popular assumptions, it is not militant Islam but Islamic rationalism that is set to become the popular face of Islam in the current century. Drawing on the evidence presented in this book, especially in the last two chapters, I argue that the current century, which opened with Islam being labelled as a religion of violence, will by its end be known as a century for the revival of Islamic rationalism; the Islamic militancy that we have witnessed in the first decade and a half has in reality acted as a trigger for this revival.

The significance of this book rests not merely in mapping an important Islamic revival movement of the present century; for me personally it is important because it represents the culmination of my scholarship over the last fifteen years on different forms and modes of Islamic knowledge platforms wherein I have demonstrated that whether Islamic knowledge stagnates or goes into a creative mode is a direct response to societal conditions. The political, economic, and social realities, which together form the societal conditions, have a direct bearing on how the texts are interpreted, what questions are asked of those texts, and which scholars and texts from earlier Islamic scholarship become popular. As I have discussed at great length in my previous monograph, *Female Islamic Education Movements: The Re-democratisation of Islamic Knowledge* (Cambridge University Press), colonial rule led to a decline of creativity within the Islamic scholarly establishment, because societal conditions became unconducive for it. The revival of Islamic rationalism is similarly a product of the changing societal conditions in which young Muslims in the diaspora, as well as in the urban centres of Muslim-majority countries, find themselves. Thus, in my assessment there are no grounds for the claim that there is something inherent in Islam that is anti-creativity, is radical or militant, or is necessarily hostile to individual freedoms, democracy, and women's agency. Such claims also fail to take account of simple historical reality: why has Islam inspired one of the world's most sophisticated civilisations, as well as regimes as narrow-minded as that of the Taliban? Islam has indeed a clearly identifiable core, which is its greatest strength, but around the core rulings there is much scope for adaptation to local realities.

Further, my second major analytical concern is to establish the role of elites in knowledge creation, as we simply cannot understand the causes of the stagnation of Islamic scholarship in the past two centuries, or fully appreciate the importance of this movement for the revival of Islamic rationalism, without understanding the critical relationship between elites and knowledge creation. The colonial period not only led to changes in the societal conditions in which 'ulama had to produce Islamic knowledge – they lost access to financial resources and faced intense competition from modern Western educational institutions, which now received state funds and awarded degrees that provided routes to upward mobility – but most critically it led to the exit of Muslim elites from the Islamic knowledge platforms. This also involved the exit of the leading Islamic scholarly families, who in order to maintain their elite status sent their younger generations to be educated in Western institutions. The result was that Islamic scholarship during the nineteenth and twentieth centuries was for the first time in Islamic history primarily delegated to the socially and economically marginalised, and often also the least intellectually able: in ethnographic studies of madrasahs, including my own, parents repeatedly acknowledge sending their weakest child to the local madrasah for schooling. The consequent stagnation in Islamic thinking during the previous two centuries should thus not be a surprise. The biggest contribution of the current movement for Islamic rationalism is that it is reversing this colonial legacy by motivating Muslim societal elites – culturally liberal and university-educated Muslim youth in the West and also increasingly in Muslim-majority countries – to engage seriously with the study of Islamic texts. It is this, as I show in the last two chapters of this volume, that is enabling the rationalist movement to have a real-life impact on Muslim communities and societies. The engagement of elites with any knowledge base brings intellectual capital acquired through their education in leading institutions, but equally elites bring social connections and influence that in turn shape socio-economic and political institutions. Their involvement also brings economic security to a knowledge platform, as they have the resources to support it. This book thus shows how changing societal conditions and the re-engagement of Muslim elites with Islamic texts are causing the rationalist movement to have a major impact not only on how Islam is being understood by educated Muslim youth, but also on how it is to be lived.

For the scholars and individuals featured in this book, I have primarily relied on analysing their writing and their speeches on audio recordings or YouTube videos, and on attending their events in a range of locations (including Cambridge, London, Chicago, New York, Berkeley, and Toronto) and asking questions during those seminars. I have also visited or spent time at Rosales, SeekersHub, Cambridge Muslim College, and Zaytuna College. Thus, this book is by no means an attempt to present the biographies of the scholars linked to this network, or to present a summary or defence of their views or positions. It presents my independent assessment of an Islamic revival movement that has had a meteoric rise in the last twenty years in terms of the influence that it is today exercising on the more affluent Muslim youth, and which in my assessment is set to play a critical role in changing perceptions and presenting a more intellectual and humanist face of Islam to the world in the twenty-first century.

Finally, it is a pleasure to acknowledge the generous support I have received from the European Research Council (ERC). Between 2014 and now, I have held a five-year ERC start-up grant (ERC grant agreement no. [337108]), funded under the European Union's Seventh Framework Programme [FP7/2007–2013], which enabled me to build a research team to study changes in contemporary Islamic authority. I will, in particular, like to acknowledge the contributions of Nathan Spannaus and Christopher Pooya Razavian, two of the researchers I engaged on this project, who have made active contribution to the analysis presented in Chapter 5. I am also very grateful to Beatrice Rehl, my editor at Cambridge University Press, for her enthusiasm for this project and to Maria Marsh for seeing potential in the initial idea.

A Note on Transliteration

The transliteration in this volume has been kept simple in view of the multidisciplinary nature of the expected readership. With the exception of the ' to indicate the Arabic letters 'ayn and ' hamza, diacritical marks have been avoided. Except for the word 'ulama, the plural form of Arabic words is indicated by addition of an *s* to the singular form. To avoid strain on the eyes and minimise distractions while reading, words that are frequently repeated (such as madrasah) are not italicised. Other non-English words are italicised only on their first occurrence. Non-English words used only once in the text are defined where they occur but are not included in the glossary.

Glossary

'Abayah	A robe-like dress worn by Muslim women
Adab	Islamic norms of behavior and comportment
'Aqidah	Islamic creed
'Aql	Intellect
Ash'ari	School of Islamic theology
'Asr	Muslim afternoon prayer
Bay'ah	Oath of allegiance to a Sufi shaykh
Bid'ah	Illegitimate religious innovation
Dar al-'ulum	House of the Sciences; a common title for an Islamic seminary or educational institution
Dars	Sermon; here specifically refers to Islamic lessons
Darurah	Necessity
Da'wah	Proselytizing, Islamic propagation
Dhikr	Reciting praises to God or to Prophet Muhammad
Fajr	Muslim morning prayer
Fard al-'ayn	Legal obligations that must be performed by all Muslims
Fatwa	A formal but generally non-binding statement on an issue or question related to Islamic law, given by a mufti (from ifta', 'to advise')
Fiqh	Islamic law or jurisprudence
Fiqh al-aqalliyat	Jurisprudence of minorities
Fiqh al-waqi'	Jurisprudence of reality
Fitrah	Human nature

Ghusl	Bath
Hadith	Reports describing the words, actions, or habits of Prophet Muhammad
Hajj	The annual Muslim pilgrimage to Mecca
Halal	Permissable in Islamic law
Halaqah	Teaching circle
Haqiqah	Spiritual truth
Haram	Forbidden by Islamic law
Hukm (pl. ahkām)	Positive Islamic laws derived from Islamic legal methodology
'Ibadah	Ritual practices such as prayer and fasting
Ifta'	To advise; the act of giving a fatwa
Iftar	Opening of the fast
Ihsan	State of utmost religious piety
Ijazah	Permission given to a student to teach the texts that were learned in the Islamic sciences
Ijtihad	The process of legal reasoning in which the jurist applies maximum effort in order to derive a ruling
Ikhwani	Of Muslim Brotherhood orientation
'Ilm al-kalam	Science of discourse; study of Islamic creed
'Ilmi	Islamic schools in Nigeria
Iman	Faith
Isnad	A chain of transmitters or authorities
Jum'ah	Friday congregational prayer
Kabar	Grave
Kalam	Islamic theology
Khawarij	Seceders; early sectarian group that revolted against the Caliph Ali ibn Abu Talib (d. 661/ 40)
Khilafah	Leader of the caliphate or Muslim ummah
Khutbah	Sermon given during the Friday midday service
Madhhab	Way; an Islamic legal school of thought
Madrasah	Place of study; an Islamic educational institution, higher religious school
Maghrib	North Africa region; also name of the the Muslim evening prayer
Ma'rifah	State of high sprituality
Masha'ikh	Plural of shaykh (Islamic scholars)
Mashriq	East
Maslahah	The common good

Maturidi	School of Islamic theology
Mawlid	Refers to the birthday of the Prophet
Minbar	Pulpit in the mosque
Mi'raj	Prophet Muhammad ascension to the heaven
Mu'amalat	Legal transactions such as marriage, leasing, and sales
Nafl	Optional prayers
Namaz	Obligatory five daily prayers
Naql	Copy; imitation
Nashids	Chats; Sufi songs
Naskh	Abrogation
Qat'i	A classification in Islamic epistemology for knowledge that is certain and definitive
Rabb	The Lord
Salaf	The first generation of Muslims
Salih	Pious; those on the right path
Shahadah	Testimony; declaration of faith in Islam
Shari'ah	God's eternal will for humanity that is considered binding; the ideal of Islamic law
Silsilah	Chain; spiritual geneology
Sirah	Biography of Muhammad
Suhbah	Friendship, companionship, comradeship
Sunnah	Established custom and cumulative tradition based on Prophet Muhammad's example
Surah	Chapter of the Quran
Tafsir	Clarification; Quranic commentary and interpretation
Tahajjud	Midnight prayer
Tahqiq al-manat	Ascertaining the reason, refinement of the cause
Tajdid	To make new, renovate; religious reform
Takfiri	One who excommunicates
Tanzih	God's transcendence
Taqlid	Following another's position or judgment in Islamic legal or religious matters
Taqlidi	The act of doing *taqlid*
Tarawih	Special night prayer in Ramadan
Tariqah (pl. turuq)	Way; a Sufi order
Tasawwuf	Sufism, Islamic mysticism

Tashbih	God's immanence
Tawhid	Oneness of God
'Ulama (alim singular)	Islamic scholars
'Umrah	Optional Muslim pilgrimage to Mecca that can be performed any time during the year; often referred to as lesser Hajj
Usul al-fiqh	Islamic legal theory (the 'roots' of fiqh)
Wali	Friend of God
Wudu'	Islamic ritual purification
Zakat	Obligatory charity, one of the five pillars of Islam
Zawiyah	Circle; a platform for study of Islam

I

Global Shifts and the Rise of Islamic Rationalism

In 1994, in the mountains of Granada, a family of Spanish converts opened a *madrasah* (Islamic school), Alqueria de Rosales, extending over 116 hectares of land. Abdus Samad (Antonio Romero), the head of the household, had taken his young wife and two children to Saudi Arabia in mid-1980s at the invitation of King Fahd to pursue Islamic education. Though formally registered as a student at Umm al-Qura University in Mecca, he acquired his actual knowledge of Islam (as he came to understand and practise it) in the *halaqah*s (study circles) led by non-Saudi shaykhs in the surroundings of Kabah as well as the Masjid-i-Nabawi. In these study circles, Samad was with a friend and fellow convert, Dr Umar Faruq Abd-Allah, an American; the two had first met in Granada in the early 1980s, when it was home to a growing community of Muslim converts. The close affiliation developed in the sixteen years spent in Saudi Arabia translates today into the hosting of a number of Islamic-knowledge retreats at Rosales. The oldest-established of these – a five-day course on al-Ghazali – is co-taught by Dr Umar and Tim Winter (Abdul Hakim Murad), another convert (an Englishman); the two had first met in Saudi Arabia. Tim Winter, himself a student then, is today an influential Islamic scholar in the United Kingdom. Connected to them is Hamza Yusuf, the president of the first Islamic liberal arts college in the United States, who today is a leading Muslim public figure in the West. Dr Umar, who credits his return to the United States in 2000 to Hamza Yusuf, had first met him during his time in Granada, where, as new converts, both were studying Islam; Granada is also where Tim Winter and Hamza Yusuf first met. Together these individuals, in their capacity as scholars or founders of important Islamic scholarly platforms in the

West, are part of a fast-expanding Islamic revival movement that is noticeable for inspiring young modern-educated Muslims in the West, but also some among their counterparts even within Muslim-majority countries, to undertake serious study of Islamic scholarly tradition.

A normal mapping of this network of scholars and institutions that they are establishing would have begun in the hills of Berkeley instead of those of Granada, simply because Hamza Yusuf, the most important nodal point in this network (as we will see throughout this volume), is based there. I have, however, chosen to introduce the key characters of this network in the order that I was first introduced to them. This is for two reasons: first, it is important to appreciate how young Muslims come to join this informal network of like-minded scholars and the institutions that they have founded through different nodal points; and second, it also helps to demonstrate how this network, while based in the West, is closely intertwined with many traditional scholarly networks in the Muslim-majority countries. It was in Damascus during the summer of 2010, when I was doing fieldwork with female Islamic study circles in Syria (Bano 2017), that I was first introduced to Rosales. Damascus, being a popular destination for the study of traditional Islamic sciences and the Arabic language, at the time hosted many Western converts. In particular, at Al-Fatih Institute, one of the two leading Islamic education foundations in Damascus, to which I was linked, connections with the Spanish Muslim community were strong. It was there that a young British undergraduate of South Asian origin, based in Damascus for a year-long intensive Arabic-language course, first brought Rosales to my attention. She talked about its effort to revive the Andalusian Islamic scholarly tradition, with its focus on rationalist and mystical scholarship in Islam that had produced figures such as Ibn Arabi and Ibn Rushd. I made a note to visit this institution. It was, however, only in the summer of 2012 that I finally managed to make my first visit.

My arrival at Rosales coincided with that of Dr Umar, who, though based in Chicago, commits to spending time at Rosales each summer. During this time he takes part in retreats and since 2014 he has in fact initiated a new week-long annual retreat programme, named *Zawiyah,* that he himself plans and leads, but chooses to host at Rosales.[1] Repeat

---

[1] The Zawiyah retreat takes the form of a week-long series of lectures organised around a specific theme: the 2017 retreat, for example, focused on *al-fitra* (our primordial nature). Dr Umar personally develops the curriculum for each Zawiyah retreat. This retreat is unlike the other examples that we will discuss in the next chapter: rather than repeating the

visitors to Rosales, however, get to appreciate that he is more accessible in the days that he spends there outside of these retreats, when he has more free time. During these days, he makes a special effort to prepare and deliver lectures in Spanish to cater to the local Spanish Muslim community – a commitment that he takes very seriously.[2] My arrival outside of the formal retreat days thus allowed for in-depth discussions with Dr Umar. However, I came to appreciate the real significance of this network when I returned in August of the same year to take part in the annual al-Ghazali retreat, which is the longest-running retreat at Rosales. More than seventy young Muslims, many of whom are graduates of (or current students of) leading Western universities, or upwardly mobile professionals, were among the participants; some also came from Muslim-majority countries.[3] These were confident young Muslims: confident of their religious identity, but also actively engaged with modern everyday institutions. Those whom I interviewed appreciated the calm surroundings offered by Rosales, which allowed for reflection and introspection; they took an active interest in the lectures, and most were very respectful of the scholars. Some of them had in the past also attended the Rihla programme – a three-week Islamic education retreat initiated by Hamza Yusuf under the Deen Intensive Foundation (see Chapter 2), at which Tim Winter and Dr Umar also teach.

The participants at the retreat thus had heard these scholars speak on many similar platforms; however, it took me more than three years and fieldwork across multiple sites in the United Kingdom, the United States, and Canada, and in Muslim-majority countries such as Egypt, Saudi Arabia, and Pakistan, to recognise the full expanse of this network and to appreciate that there is a deeper coherence to their approach. Though entirely independent of each other, these scholars and institutions are consciously coordinating their efforts to revive what they view as the authentic Islamic scholarly tradition: an understanding of Islam that

---

same programme each year, it aims to attract back the same students who have attended previous retreats by focusing on a new topic each year. This is a deliberate strategy to encourage the students to dwell deeper on specific themes each year. The focus of the first Zawiyah retreat was on Hadith Jibril, which, as we will see in Chapter 2, is central to the teaching of scholars within this Islamic rationalist network.

[2] It arises primarily out of a sense of obligation to support recent converts, but it also stems from the desire to increase Islamic teaching resources in the Spanish language in order to facilitate learning among Muslim populations in Latin America.

[3] In the 2012 retreat, for example, there were participants from Egypt, Pakistan, and Indonesia.

combines close adherence to classical Islamic legal scholarship as represented by the four Sunni classical schools of Islamic law (*madhhabs*), and appreciation of the strong rationalist foundation of Islamic theology, while also retaining a heavy emphasis on moral and spiritual training in search of deeper mysticism (*tasawwuf*). In defending this concept of Islam, these scholars are keen to link back to the work of classical Islamic scholars; the twelfth-century mystic and jurist Muhammad al-Ghazali features prominently in this list. It is due to this three-fold focus that these scholars are often labelled as traditionalists, or revivers of traditional Islam (Mathiesen 2013). I, however, argue that this label is inadequate to explain the essence of their appeal to young educated Muslims. My first reservation is that all Islamic groups, irrespective of their approach or method, claim to represent traditional Islam, because of the implicit association between the word 'traditional' and authentic practice.[4] My other reservation is that in Western media and policy reports on Islamic institutions, the word 'traditional' is often used interchangeably with 'conservative' or 'orthodox' Islam, which is understood to be irrelevant to modern realities. Such conceptions of traditional Islam run counter to the rationalist and mystical dimensions of Islam and its inbuilt ability to relate to changing times that these scholars are keen to highlight. I, on the other hand, argue for recognising the importance of this network in reviving *Islamic rationalism,* which in my view makes the distinctive contribution of this network most apparent, as will be illustrated in this volume.[5] The scholars in this network indeed claim to present traditional Islam, but what makes them distinctive is their effort to establish that in historical terms Islam presented a balance that could both appeal to the rationalist mind and also nurture the inner spiritual life, and it is this balance that enables Islam to stay relevant and responsive to the needs of the changing times.

Scholarship on Islam in the West to date remains largely focused on mapping the expansion of Islamic schooling networks, or Sufi *tariqahs* (Sufi orders), from the Muslim-majority countries to the diaspora communities in the West (Gilliat-Ray 2010; van Bruinessen and Allievi 2011).

---

[4] Mathiesen (2013) notes that the term 'traditional Islam' does not actually exist in Arabic. In self-appropriating this label, the Islamic rationalist scholars and those who have chosen to label them as such have tried to establish their claim to historical authenticity.

[5] In order to fully grasp this argument, it is, however, important to appreciate how Islamic rationalism differs from the more restricted notions of human rationality associated with Western philosophical tradition (Walbridge 2011) – a subject that we will discuss in detail in the next chapter.

Existing studies have thus focused on the practice of hiring imams for the American, British, or European mosques from among the graduates of Islamic universities or madrasahs in the Middle East, Saudi Arabia, South Asia, or North Africa (Gilliat-Ray 2010; van Bruinessen and Allievi 2011). Scholars have, however, failed to recognise that a major shift in power dynamics between Islamic institutions in the Muslim-majority countries and those emerging in the West is under way (Bano 2018a; 2018b).[6] The Muslim-diaspora communities in the West are no longer mere recipients of Islamic knowledge. They are increasingly becoming a base for the emergence of powerful Islamic scholarly networks. Scholars within these networks do indeed continue to seek their training from specialists in the Muslim-majority countries, but on return relate these teachings to the demands of modern realities in ways that are making their teachings more effective in encouraging young, educated, and socially liberal Muslims to fully embrace Islam. These scholars are not only attracting young Muslim university students and young profession-als in the West; they have also begun, as we will see in Part II of this book, to attract the attention of young Muslims from affluent and culturally liberal families within Muslim-majority countries.

It is important to note that the network of scholars under study is not the only one attracting young educated Muslims in the West; as we will see in Section 2 of this chapter, many other parallel networks are emerging where scholars in the West are relating Islam to modern reality in ways that are proving more effective in enabling young Muslims to appreciate Islam and adhere to its moral dictates than has been possible for the mosque-based imams recruited from overseas. However, this network is particularly noteworthy because of the profile of its followers: these scholars are appealing to educated and culturally liberal young Muslims from affluent families. These Muslims, due either to their afflu-ent family background or to their education in prestigious universities, acquire a degree of social capital that makes them particularly well placed to influence socio-economic and political institutions among Muslims in diaspora communities and within the Muslim-majority countries. These are the young Muslims who are able to influence societal institutions in the light of their convictions. However, due to it being well integrated in the modern socio-economic and political institutions that are largely

---

[6] Even studies that are focused on the new Islamic scholarly platforms emerging in the West (Grewal 2013; Korb 2013) do not fully explore their relationship with the older Islamic-authority platforms.

shaped by the Western secular framework, this is also the population that is at risk of moving away from Islam; or at least it lacks the conviction that Islam can provide a legal or moral framework for the modern world. These are the young Muslims who fail to relate to the highly conservative and rigid readings of Islam often promoted by the mosque imams in their neighbourhood; they are also embarrassed and perturbed by the violence promoted by extremists in the name of this religion.

This book is the first in-depth study of this network of scholars, whose individual members (in particular Hamza Yusuf and Tim Winter) are often profiled or interviewed in the Western media and consulted by Western governments, and who themselves increasingly act as spokespersons for Muslims. Their existence as a collective or as a community, their understanding of Islam, and the critical implications of their work for shaping the future of Islamic scholarly debates have, however, as yet remained unexamined. Existing studies of Islam in the West have begun to note the individual impact of some of these scholars, but they fail to connect the dots and recognise the links between them, and to see them as a movement. Scott Kugle's (2006) work is one exception, but he does not map this specific network; instead, concerned mainly with establishing Hamza Yusuf's role in introducing Ahmad Zarruq, a fifteenth-century Sufi-jurist, to young North American Muslims, he presents Hamza Yusuf as part of a loose network of Sufi-jurists who are gaining prominence in American Islam. Most importantly, existing studies of these scholars, even when cognisant of their growing influence, do not situate their methodological, theological, or philosophical approach within traditional Islamic scholarship. Consequently, many end up dismissing these scholars as representing a soft Islam (a 'pop Islam', appealing to young Westernised Muslims, which lacks scholarly rigour and depth, just as is often the case with the growing number of Sufi platforms in the West, which are attracted to Sufi's message of love but have little knowledge or appreciation of the Islamic legal dictates or ritual practices). This limited engagement with the actual methodological approach of these scholars has resulted in a failure to recognise that this network is emerging as an important Islamic revival movement in the twenty-first century that is helping young educated Muslims, especially from affluent families, to appreciate the creative spirit within Islam, and that it thereby has great potential to bridge the assumed gap between Islam and modern reality.

This book presents a rare in-depth account of this contemporary Islamic revival movement. Such an effort also provides a fascinating opportunity to map the intergenerational shifts in the attitudes of young

Muslims in the West as well as among some of their counterparts in the Muslim-majority countries, who are keen to discover both the intellectual and the deeper mystical dimensions of Islam. A study of this movement thus also directly relates to a broader conceptual concern in social science: namely the relationship between knowledge creation and societal conditions (Nonaka 1994; Nonaka and Toyama 2003; Ober 2008). The conceptual concerns addressed through a study of this network and its followers help us to address ongoing debates within social science about how texts acquire meaning. Are texts static, or do scholars and students bring their own experiences to their interpretation? How is a certain form of knowledge kept dynamic and responsive to the changing needs of society? What role, if any, does financial affluence within a society and that of the scholarly classes play in ensuring creativity within any field of knowledge?

Despite extensive research on Muslim societies since the events of 11 September 2001, the dominant narrative led by the media, Western think tanks, and policy documents often attributes Islamic radicalisation to Islamic texts; Islam is perceived and presented as a religion that is inherently violent and anti-modernity, whose foundational text, the Quran, makes numerous explicit references to jihad, denies women basic freedoms, and endorses dictatorial over democratic regimes.[7] A close study of this Islamic revival movement, however, helps to expose the limits of such assertions: it shows that a society with material affluence, political freedoms, and easy access to higher education is key to the revival of rationalist and philosophical strands of Islamic scholarship which were central to classical Islamic scholarly tradition but underwent a major decline during the colonial period in all Muslim societies (Robinson 2003; Saliba 2011; Bano 2017). There is a close association between societal conditions and textual interpretations. Further, a key conclusion of this book is that the engagement of the social elite with a scholarly tradition is critical to the flourishing of knowledge and creativity within that tradition. In this volume, the term 'elites'[8] is used loosely not only to refer to hereditary elites but to point towards those individuals who exert influence on social, economic, and political institutions because

---

[7] The Islamic emphasis on jihad can mean many things, including working to purify one's inner self (Malik 2006), but many of the Quranic references to jihad also explicitly refer to armed struggle.

[8] This interpretation is close to how Oxford dictionary defines the term, 'A group or class of people seen as having the greatest power and influence within a society,' accessed 15 December 2017, https://en.oxforddictionaries.com/definition/us/elite.

they hold government office, or lead major financial institutions, or lead prominent cultural, artistic, or literary platforms that influence societal attitudes, or because they control print and electronic media. This is so because for a field of knowledge to remain dynamic it is important that the state and society make demands on the scholars to provide answers to the challenges at hand; it is also equally important that a knowledge base continues to receive adequate financial patronage for it to be able to attract the best minds. (See Section 3 of this chapter for the conceptual foundation of these arguments.)

How societal conditions shape knowledge formation and transmission is an area of active research inquiry in different fields of social science (Nonaka 1994; Ober 2008), including the sociology of education; this association is, however, routinely ignored by Western policy makers and media outlets, many of whom attribute Islamic militancy or radicalisation to Islamic texts. In my book, *Female Islamic Education Movements: The Re-democratisation of Islamic Knowledge* (2017), I presented a detailed conceptual framework to illustrate how the societal conditions which ensured that the state elites as well as ordinary members of the public engaged with the study of Islamic texts were key to creating the Golden Age of Islam; I also argued that creating incentives for Muslim elites to engage with Islamic texts is key to reviving the intellectual spirit within Islam in modern times. In developing this framework, I drew on the work of a classicist, Josiah Ober, who in a bid to explain the success of democracy in classical Athens emphasised the need to mix different forms of knowledge in a society for it to find optimal solutions to collective societal challenges (Ober 2008). His primary concern was to establish the importance of non-technical knowledge, which he refers to as dispersed knowledge held by the people, instead of merely drawing on the knowledge of the experts in finding optimal answers to collective societal challenges. Equally, he established the importance of having incentives in society to encourage people to engage with a given knowledge base, in order for them to invest in this mixing of knowledge. Simply put, this argument is very close to Tariq Ramadan's view that to make Islamic *fiqh* (Islamic jurisprudence) relevant to modern reality, we need not just the scholars of text but also scholars of the context, as only then can socially relevant answers be found from within the Islamic framework (Ramadan 2009).

In *Female Islamic Education Movements*, I advanced a similar argument. Drawing on historical accounts of Islamic knowledge transmission, I traced how, in early Muslim societies, Islamic knowledge was always socially embedded; the fact that Muslims had political authority meant that Islamic law and moral code were the dominant framework. Consequently, it was not only the scholars of the text but also scholars of other sciences, and lay members of the public, who contributed to the evolution of both rationalist and transmitted sciences in Muslim societies, as the state and the society provided incentives for everyone to innovate in all fields, while at the same time respecting an Islamic frame of reference. This balance was, however, entirely disrupted during the period of colonial rule. Colonial rule replaced Islamic knowledge platforms with Western schools and colleges and replaced *shari'ah* (Islamic law) with common law, thus eroding incentives within Muslim societies to innovate within the Islamic framework. This led to the isolation of Islamic knowledge and the division of knowledge into Islamic and Western sciences, a division which historically did not exist.[9] Islamic educational platforms became marginalised, and Islamic law became largely irrelevant to the shaping of political and economic institutions; consequently, the state and society also stopped making demands on the Islamic scholarly classes to find answers to the demands of the time from within the Islamic moral and legal framework. The most significant damage to Islamic knowledge-transmission practices occurred as a result of the exit of the Muslim elites from the Islamic scholarly platforms. Islamic education and its scholars became more and more inward looking, losing the creativity and intellectual energy that were evident in earlier Muslim societies.

I concluded in that book that any intellectual revival in Islam requires a reversal of this colonial legacy and the creation of incentives within Muslim societies for all segments of society, especially the elites, to re-engage with the study of Islamic texts; and that it further requires the creation of incentives within society to apply the Islamic moral and ethical framework to modern challenges. I then moved on to demonstrate how female Islamic education movements that have emerged across the Muslim world since the 1970s are important for precisely this reason:

---

[9] Islam encourages the pursuit of knowledge and does not make any distinction between Islamic and secular knowledge. Thus, classical Islamic scholarship contributed to fields such as mathematics, medicine, and astronomy, which today are regarded as modern or Western subjects (Hodgson 1977a). For the religiously oriented, the Islamic sciences indeed had a more special status, but that did not mean neglect of the modern or rationalist sciences (Robinson 2001); in fact, as we will see in the next chapter, while Hellenist philosophical influences on Islamic scholarship did peter out by the end of the twelfth century, the rational mode of reasoning and argumentation became a cornerstone of all Islamic sciences (Walbridge 2011).

many of them are motivating educated, modern, and culturally progressive women from elite Muslim families to study Islamic texts. These women bring their contextual knowledge to the study of Islamic sciences and in the process create incentives for the scholars to demonstrate Islam's ability to provide answers to the demands of the time. The evidence presented in this book sustains the same framework. However, in this book I do not try to present the entire framework in detail again (readers are strongly encouraged to read chapter 2 in *Female Islamic Education Movements*, to understand the underlying assumptions that such a framework makes about human decision-making and processes of institutional persistence and change); here, instead, I focus on going deeper to explore three specific aspects of the broader framework developed therein: first, the importance of different forms of knowledge; second, the importance of engagement by societal elites in the creation and use of knowledge if a knowledge base is to remain creative[10] and dynamic; and, third, the relationship between societal conditions and knowledge creation. Existing debates in the social sciences about these important questions must be discussed in detail in order to understand the significance of this movement as I see it; before that, however, we need to define the core members of this network in some detail.

I CONNECTING THE DOTS: A MOVEMENT IN THE MAKING

Social movements remain a critical area of research in social theory because of their transformative potential. Movements work to bring change to the existing societal order, but this change is not always aimed at creating a new system; in fact, religious movements often work to revive what their members maintain was the authentic tradition but which has been lost in the modern world.[11] Thus, religious movements can often

---

[10] Some anthropologists working on Muslim societies have argued that this emphasis on highlighting the creativity within the Islamic tradition reflects a bias in favour of the Western liberal framework; in their argument, creativity can equate to deception, because it requires Islamic scholars to find ways to shape the tradition to fit the Western liberal framework – see Agrama (2012) and my critique of his work (Bano 2018a). In this book, we will see how for the scholars leading this Islamic rationalist movement, as well as the young Muslims who follow them, Islam's historic ability to be creative and responsive to the changing needs of the time is central to its appeal.

[11] Within sociological theory, scholarship on religion and social movements has been primarily focused on analysing how religion often acts as a powerful resource (see Burns and Kniss 2013). But, if we interpret social movements as consisting of loosely connected platforms that work together towards achieving a shared goal (Killian

be aimed at revival, not merely reform, of the tradition – the latter type being closer to a typical social movement, due to its focus on change. A movement, whether committed to reform or to revival, normally consists of a collection of entities which are independent and not hier-archically linked but have a largely shared conception of how things should be (Killian et al. 2013); this independence of key actors or organ-isations is what differentiates a movement from an organisation. The network of scholars mapped in this volume is precisely a movement in the same spirit. The actors that I map are all independent of each other – all preserve complete autonomy and are not linked in any hier-archical order – yet they do share a common vision of the need to revive Islam's rationalist foundation and its deep mystical essence, both of which, in their view, were central to classical Islamic scholarship and practice.

This movement for revival of what in my view is best referred to as *Islamic rationalism* involves a large pool of scholars and platforms; many of them are located in Muslim-majority countries, with whom, as we will see in Chapter 3, the scholars in this network are closely connected and to whom they credit their own learning. The volume is, however, mainly focused on mapping the network as it has evolved in the West, because it is these scholars, many of whom are converts, who are helping to popularise this reading of Islam to the young educated Muslims, not just in the West but also in the Muslim-majority countries. These scholars today have visible followings among modern, university-attending, and culturally liberal Muslims both in the West and among a growing number of their counterparts in the Muslim-majority countries. It is through these scholars that many of these young Muslims are discovering the scholars based in Muslim-majority countries, as well as the influential scholars and the classical texts in Islamic logic, *kalam* (Islamic theology), philosophy, and classical schools of Islamic law from the early periods of Islam. In fact, this movement is the result of an acute awareness among these scholars of the need to promote what they view as the authentic Islamic tradition among Muslim youth. These scholars share a widely held concern among educated and culturally liberal Muslims that the dominant Islamic platforms have lost the real essence of Islam, both its rationalist foundation and deeper mysticism, and have adopted a very limited

---

et al. 2018), religious movements, whether new or old, are a form of social movement (Beckford 1986).

reading of the texts which equates faith mainly with performance of specific ritual practices. The gradual learning about and appreciation of these two dimensions of Islam, as we will see in Chapter 4, had indeed been key to their own conversions and to sustaining their Islamic convictions over time.

That these rationalist scholars are making an independent yet coordinated effort to revive the balance that classical Islamic scholarship provided between reason and revelation is recorded in the proceedings of the meeting that they organised in Leicester, United Kingdom, in 1999. Attended by many of the scholars associated with this network, including Hamza Yusuf, Tim Winter, and Dr Umar Faruq Abd-Allah, the meeting was organised specifically to discuss a strategy for undertaking *da'wah* (Islamic propagation) effectively among Muslims in the West. Having returned to the West only recently, after spending many years studying classical Islamic texts with traditional scholars in different Muslim countries, these scholars were of the view that the Islam that was being taught by the traditional mosque or Islamic school networks in the West lacked its true theological and mystical depth. As Tim Winter notes in an interview with Akbar S. Ahmed for a Pakistani newspaper: 'The mosques (in the UK) are full, but the message in the mosques is not always ideal . . . There's a sense of disconnect, a hiatus, between the discourse of the leadership and what the masses actually need' (Ahmed 2017). Their shared vision is also visible in how they reference each other in their writings and speeches.

In the view of these scholars, the typical mosque imams or teachers in Islamic schools were failing to enthuse the young educated and culturally liberal Muslims, who have been trained in Western rationalist and liberal thought and were socially integrated in Western culture, about Islam, as they were failing to show the richness of Islamic scholarly tradition. This realisation, as we will see in Chapter 4, stemmed from the exposure that these scholars had experienced to different forms of Islam on travelling to Muslim countries, before settling for a form that, based on their own reading of the classical texts and personal spiritual journeys, most appealed to them as being the authentic Islamic tradition: a strong theology which appeals to reason, a deep metaphysical and mystical experience which purifies the soul, and a clarity in legal rulings that has been preserved by classical Islamic schools of law.

These scholars are thus reviving what can be viewed as the classical understanding of *Islamic rationalism* as associated with the legacy of al-Ghazali.[12] This approach recognises the limits of Hellenic philosophical influences which entered Islamic thought through the Mutazilites (a group within early Muslim society that advocated rational approaches), yet is also cognisant of the limits of extreme textual rigidity. It is the balance that resulted from this tension with the victory of al-Ghazali's approach to revive the Islamic sciences over those of pure philosophers that led to the founding of a strong rationalist basis to all Islamic sciences (Walbridge 2011). Al-Ghazali, who is regarded as an expert in philosophical as well as legal texts, retained the focus on reason, argument, and counter-argumentation in the development of Islamic sciences while nevertheless creating space for recognising the human mystical experience as a critical part of human reason. As Walbridge (2011) shows in *The Caliphate of Reason*, the struggle between al-Ghazali and the philosophers of the period did not lead to the closure of the doors of *ijtihad* (Islamic reasoning); rather it led to the absorption of rational thought as a foundation for all Islamic sciences. This is how I use the term 'Islamic rationalism' in this volume, whereby the use of reason to explore the concept of God is encouraged, while at the same time recognising that to make meaning of human existence we need not only the intellect but equally the soul. It is precisely this conception of Islam that I have come to associate with this network of scholars, the more I have heard them and read their work. Most importantly, as we will see in Part II of this volume, it is also precisely this conception of Islam that I have seen appreciated by their avid followers.

By tracing the multiple Islamic scholarly platforms to which these scholars were exposed on conversion, it is clear that they did not come to appreciate this specific understanding of Islam due to a lack of exposure to more textual or *hadith*-centric readings of Islam such as are attributed to Saudi Salafism or South Asian Deobandi networks (Bano 2018a). In fact, as students all the scholars mapped in this network were equally exposed to the more textual Islamic traditions which encourage more literalist readings of the texts, and a few of these scholars in fact learned most of their Islam while living in Saudi Arabia, but they did not find that narrowly textual readings of Islam met their spiritual or

---

[12] Tim Winter's PhD dissertation is on al-Ghazali; both he and Dr Umar teach on a popular week-long al-Ghazali retreat held at Rosales each year. Scholars in this Islamic rationalist network routinely reference al-Ghazali's work in their speeches and writings; SeekersHub offers courses on his major works; and he is a member of the perennial faculty of Zaytuna College.

intellectual needs. This search for Islamic knowledge and appreciation of the need for deeper mystical training while respecting the Islamic legal tradition and ritual obligations is key to explaining the appeal of this movement among educated and culturally liberal Muslims. What is unique about this Islamic revival movement is its emphasis on establishing that logic, mysticism, and respect for shariʿah are three equal and integral aspects of Islam. It is this balance among the three that these scholars are trying to revive in the everyday teaching and practice of Islam that sets them and their followers apart from many other Islamic groups, especially the more conservative traditions, such as Saudi Salafism or the South Asian Deobandi network, as well as the New Age Sufi networks mushrooming in the West. Mapped against the existing network of Islamic scholarly platforms which have a global presence, these scholars are thus closer to the al-Azhari tradition or the legacy of Ottoman *ʿulama* which is seeing a revival in the form of a much more proactive Diyanet (Presidency of Religious Affairs) in Turkey under the AKP (Justice and Development Party) (Bano 2018a). However, as we will see in Chapter 4, rather than these formal platforms, such as al-Azhar and Diyanet, which are state-regulated, these scholars eventually chose to learn their Islam from more informal networks of scholars and Sufi shaykhs.

On the basis of my fieldwork, I am of the view that while this movement consists of a global network of scholars, at the heart of its global revival are three key institutions: Zaytuna College in Berkeley, California, United States; Cambridge Muslim College in Cambridge, United Kingdom; and Alqueria de Rosales on the outskirts of Granada, southern Spain – and three key scholars: Hamza Yusuf, Tim Winter, and Umar Faruq Abd-Allah.[13] Surrounding this core circle is the next generation of scholars and institutions. These are individuals who have been inspired by this first generation and in fact on conversion were guided by them as to where to go to acquire Islamic knowledge. On returning to the West, some from within this second generation have initiated new platforms with visible followings of their own. These individuals, however, are always quick to show their deference for the scholars from the first generation and to acknowledge the inspiration that they continue to draw

---

[13] I do not include Abdus Samad, the founder of Rosales, among them, mainly because he himself does not teach, even though he is very knowledgeable. The institution that he has established, however, is an important base for spreading the teachings of these Islamic rationalist scholars among European Muslims and also among some from the Muslim-majority countries, who can more easily access a retreat in Spain than one in North America.

from them. Three important institutional platforms established by this generation are Ta'leef Collective, led by Usama Canon; SeekersHub, operating out of Toronto, Canada; and the recently opened al-Maqasid Institute in Pennsylvania. The most popular platform among these three is Ta'leef Collective, which operates out of San Francisco as well as Chicago. SeekersHub, which operates out of Toronto, is in particular focused on developing online courses that are followed by Muslim subscribers from across the globe. Al-Maqasid, led by Yahya Rhodus, who is closely associated with the Ba'alawi Sufi scholarly tradition from Yemen, is the newest of these three platforms. A physical space to establish the institute was acquired only in 2016, but Yahya Rhodus himself has been a visible member of this network for a number of years, having taught on many of the platforms linked to this network, including Zaytuna College, SeekersHub, and Rihla programme. In addition, there are other figures, such as Jihad Brown, who on conversion spent time overseas in the study of Islam and have been guided and inspired by scholars from the first generation. Although on their return they have not established new institutions, they are known to the followers of this network by virtue of their speaking engagements on many of the platforms linked to this network.

Profiles of these two generations, however, do not alone explain this Islamic rationalist network as a movement; to grasp its full scale, we need to look at the third generation of scholars that it is able to inspire.

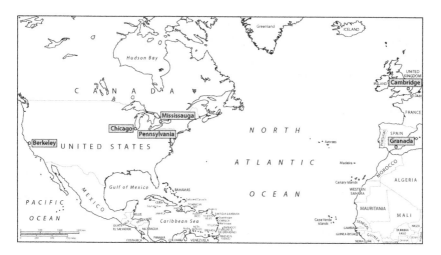

Map 1.1 Islamic Rationalist Scholars: Key Locations in the West

Members of this third generation are young Muslims who are still students in these institutions. These young people are either enrolled in a formal degree programme or simply engaging in informal study circles with these rationalist scholars; the latter group, enthused by the first two generations, are keen to pursue higher Islamic education in the hope of becoming either future academics in the field of Islamic Studies, or imams in mosques, or leaders within Muslim communities. Unlike the first two generations, these young Muslims consist not primarily of converts but of a growing number of young, educated, culturally liberal, and socially influential Muslims from within Muslim communities who are being inspired by these scholars to pursue serious study of Islamic tradition with a focus not just on fiqh but equally on the rationalist and mystical Islamic sciences. This third generation is thus much larger in number than the other two. This evidence of their strong following among young Muslims is what helps to establish that the movement has become mainstream; as I have found in my own fieldwork, it is not just the young but increasingly also their parents who turn up at the lectures of the scholars in question.

To understand the full scope of this network, it is important to understand the dynamics and activities of all three generations in some detail. Hamza Yusuf is clearly at the heart of this movement, as I see it. In my fieldwork, I have found him to have had a phenomenal influence in inspiring young Muslims to study Islam, as well as fellow scholars to undertake da'wah; he is also the one credited by most within the network with having an endless stream of ideas about the new institutional platforms that Muslims need to establish. To understand the scope of this network, it is thus appropriate to look first at the institutions that Hamza Yusuf has set up, for he has both established and inspired some of the most influential institutions within the network: institutions that are able to attract educated, young, and culturally liberal Muslims from among the affluent Muslim families in the West.

First Generation

Hamza Yusuf's most important institutional initiative is Zaytuna College, the first Islamic liberal arts college in the United States, which received formal accreditation in 2015. It was established in Berkeley in 2009 by Hamza Yusuf, Imam Zaid Shakir, and Hatem Bazian. The college is rooted in the Western liberal arts tradition, which can enable students to pursue a life of thought and reflection and, by allowing them to combine Islamic and Western scholarly traditions, aims to enable them to indigenize Islam in the West. Proud equally of their Western heritage and their Islamic identity, the leadership of Zaytuna maintains that Islam is no stranger to the Western tradition. In their view, historically both traditions learned from each other; they argue that there is a need for Muslims to revive the authentic Islamic tradition that is capable of engaging productively with modernity, rather than reacting to it. The College offers a bachelor degree in Islamic Studies, based on its own integrated curriculum, which provides a serious grounding in foundational Islamic texts as well as in those from the Western philosophical tradition. Its degrees are open to both men and women and are designed 'to educate students to become morally, intellectually, and spiritually accomplished persons who, having been rigorously trained in the Islamic and Western scholarly traditions, are ready to interact with and shape modern society by the light of principles that transcend it, being motivated constantly by the intention of finding the extent of human wisdom' (Zaytuna College 2018a). Zaytuna College has proven relatively successful in mobilising resources: its main building is on the famous Holy Hill, which hosts The Graduate Theological Union, a consortium of eight private independent American theological schools, and is next to the University of California Berkeley campus; many of its students receive financial support.

While in the long term Zaytuna College might prove to be the most important platform established by Hamza Yusuf, there are many other institutions that have helped to establish the influence of this network among young Muslims which are also to his credit. In fact, one of the reasons many are impressed by him is because he is known 'as a man of ideas, someone who loves to read, the intellectual who can approach any issue with a philosophical lens, and is inspirational in terms of giving those who are keen ideas for establishing new institutions to serve the Muslim community'.[14] Rihla, Sacred Caravan, and Sandala Productions are some of the other platforms that he has initiated, apart from inspiring many others, such as Ta'leef Collective and the Revival of the Islamic Spirit, which operates out of Canada.[15] The Rihla programme, which was

---

[14] A respondent in Toronto, August 2016.

[15] *Deen Intensive Foundation*, accessed 17 December 2017, www.deenintensive.com/; *Sacred Caravan*, accessed 17 December 2017, www.sacredcaravan.com/; *Sandala Productions*, accessed 17 December 2017, https://sandala.org/.

initiated under the Deen Intensive Foundation, has played a major role in spreading the teaching of this network of scholars among the young Muslim university students. The Deen Intensive Foundation initially started organising short Islamic retreats in the United States and Canada beginning from 1995; in early 2000s, it launched the three-week annual Rihla retreat which today is one of the most influential intensive Islamic education programmes organised by an Islamic platform in the West. During this three-week intensive programme participants study Islamic logic, fiqh, hadith, and other Islamic sciences. The retreat is usually organised in a Muslim country or at a location where there are at least remains of an Islamic past, such as Andalusia in Spain; the retreat was held twice at Rosales, which is on the outskirts of Granada. Other main venues have been Morocco, Konya and Istanbul in Turkey, and most recently Malaysia. Since it is organised as a retreat, students also have the chance to interact with the scholars over meals and hold discussions after formal sessions.

Given the number of young people who have taken part in the Rihla programme since its inception, it could be argued that as of now it is Rihla, more than Zaytuna College, that has helped to spread the real influence of Hamza Yusuf and the rationalist network as a whole. As explained by a close associate of Hamza Yusuf who played an active role in establishing the Deen Intensive retreats and in organising the first Rihla programme, what is now known as the Rihla programme was held for the first time in early 2000s on the invitation of the Moroccan government. The Deen Intensive Foundation also operates an online television network, with an annual subscription fee of US$119. It offers subscribers copies of the actual Rihla course study packs from successive years, as well as recordings of all the lectures, including the question and answer sessions. During the three-week annual Rihla programme, subscribers can access all the teaching sessions online: the learning thus is not confined to those who can physically attend the Rihla programme.

Another important platform established by Hamza Yusuf is the Sacred Caravan 'Umrah programme. Now in its second decade, this programme is organised every year as a ten-day *'umrah* (lesser Hajj) retreat. For most of the initial years, Hamza Yusuf himself led this retreat; in recent years, due to his growing commitments, Dr Umar has on occasions replaced him. Another core member of the Sacred Caravan 'Umrah programme is Feraidoon Mojadedi, who teaches Islamic poetry, particularly the works of Rumi, and works closely with Hamza Yusuf on developing the plan for each year. The Sacred Caravan programme is important because those who join this annual retreat are older Muslims, as the retreat package is not cheap.[16] Also, it features people not only from the United States and the United Kingdom but also from Muslim-majority countries. In the 2016 Sacred Caravan programme that I attended, most participants were above the age of 50, and while most came from the United States, there were also some from the United Kingdom, Pakistan, and Malaysia. The group, which comprises between 50 and 60 individuals, gets to spend four or five days each in the holy cities of Mecca and Medina. The scholar leading the group gives a number of afternoon lectures on a specific topic, apart from leading the group in the actual performance of the ʿumrah. The material provided by the organisers includes a book especially produced for Sacred Caravan entitled *Visiting the House of God*. This compilation by Hamza Yusuf draws on Dr Mostafa Badawi's *The Pilgrim's Guide to Important Sites in Makka and Madina* and provides a summary of the key rulings related to *hajj* and ʿumrah from all four Sunni madhhabs and also advises on the main prayers that should be recited during this period. This book is produced by Sandala Production, another of Hamza Yusuf's initiatives. Smaller in scale than the other three initiatives covered above, Sandala Production acts as a publishing house and promotes sales of a variety of Islamic goods.

While Hamza Yusuf has himself established the institutions listed above, among those he has inspired others to open a particularly influential one is the Revival of the Islamic Spirit (RIS). This platform is operated by a network of young Canadian Muslims who were inspired by Hamza Yusuf in the mid-to-late 1990s, when he first began to appear on the speaking circuit of leading universities in North America. The RIS mainly takes the form of an annual Islamic convention in Toronto which brings together leading Islamic scholars from across the globe. Two of the young Muslims who initiated this platform have since then acquired recognition as emerging scholars in their own right, but still they draw heavily on advice from Hamza Yusuf in determining the theme of the annual convention.[17] This annual convention has become the most influential annual Islamic gathering in Canada. Equally influential and also inspired by Hamza Yusuf is Taʾleef Collective, which has done the most to illustrate the practical implications of the teachings of this network to promote tolerance. Led by Usama Canon, one of Hamza Yusuf's earlier students,

---

[16] The Sacred Caravan ten-day ʿumrah package, including flights from the United States, costs US$3,600 per participant.
[17] A number of my respondents in Toronto highlighted this point.

Ta'leef Collective emerged from reflections on the needs of new coverts to Islam, who often fail to find adequate support from within the Muslim community. Though remaining focused on this core mission of supporting new converts, Ta'leef is today a flourishing institutional platform operating out of San Francisco as well as Chicago, promoting a culture in which Muslims of all orientations and backgrounds, not solely converts, feel equally welcomed. It organises a diverse set of activities, ranging from seminars, lectures, and week-long retreats to community-building activities such as potluck meals, barbecues, and Ramadan *iftar*s (opening of the fast).

While the above network of institutions is directly led or inspired by Hamza Yusuf and are located in North America, in the United Kingdom Cambridge Muslim College (CMC) operates under the same philosophy. Established in 2009 by Tim Winter, the structure of its educational programme is, however, quite distinct. Until very recently, it has retained its focus primarily on teaching graduates from British Islamic seminaries, namely the dar al-'ulums, in order to complement their religious learning with a sound knowledge of the local realities. Rather than trying to initiate an Islamic education programme, it aimed to complement and complete the education of graduates from the existing dar al-'ulums. This was in response to the popular concern that, due to the closed culture of these dar al-'ulums, their graduates are failing to relate to the society in which they are required to teach and take up Islamic leadership positions. The focus of CMC's main one-year degree programme has therefore all along been on helping to improve these students' understanding of the realities of contemporary British society so that they can better relate their Islamic knowledge to the realities of the time. With this one-year degree programme now well established, in 2016 the college launched a four-year Islamic Studies programme (CMC 2018a). The CMC describes its main goal as becoming 'a recognised centre of excellence offering a BA and MA in Islamic Studies, taught by a team of Islamic scholars in conjunction and collaboration with the expertise available at the University of Cambridge' (CMC 2018b) and it is making steady progress towards that. Tim Winter, arguably also because he occupies a formal faculty position in Cambridge University, has not directly embarked on opening as many institutions as has Hamza Yusuf, but he actively contributes to many of the institutional platforms within this network by taking part in the retreats organised by other institutions and giving seminars and lectures: for example, he regularly features in the Rihla annual retreat and also co-leads the al-Ghazali retreat held every summer at Rosales.

Dr Umar, the third key figure from the first generation, has, unlike the other two, not established a new institution; but he has been playing a critical role in supporting the activities of all the above-noted institutional platforms and also those established by the second generation. Most importantly he has played an important role in making Rosales visible in both Europe and the United States. As noted above, due to the close association developed between Dr Umar and Abdus Samad, the two have worked together to plan many of the activities at Rosales. While Rosales also is working towards developing a proper degree-based teaching pro-gramme, it is yet to launch it. The delay is mainly due to weak in-house ability to do the teaching. Since Abdus Samad himself does not teach, for the implementation of its academic programme the institution remains reliant on visiting scholars who come to lead specific retreats. Here the support of Dr Umar has been instrumental. Apart from teaching on retreats organised by Rosales, since 2014 Dr Umar has hosted his Zawiyah retreat at Rosales, which brings a large number of young Americans to Rosales for a week. Rosales thus is an important component of the multiple bases that Dr Umar is using to spread the teachings of this Islamic rationalist network: his seminars and gatherings in Naperville, Chicago, which is his home base, the Rihla programme, the Sacred Caravan, SeekersHub seminars, and Ta'leef Collective gatherings in Chicago.

Second Generation

Among the second generation, it would be appropriate to start by looking at the work of Ta'leef Collective, given the visibility that this platform and its main founder, Usama Canon, have acquired within this network. Ta'leef Collective informally started its activities in 2007 as an outreach programme of Zaytuna College, before becoming registered as an inde-pendent non-profit organisation in 2009.[18] Its mission is to support young Muslims and assist newcomers to Islam. Its 'mantra' is 'Come as you are, to Islam as it is' (Ta'leef Collective 2018). Its core emphasis is on encouraging people not to discriminate against or judge others or the purity of their faith. It holds regular seminars and lectures, as well as

---

[18] In a number of interviews Usama Canon has explained how he was advised by Hamza Yusuf to launch such an initiative, and how many of the activities that developed under Ta'leef Collective initially were originally part of the outreach activities of Zaytuna College.

week-long spiritual retreats. However, what it calls its community-care programmes are central to its mission; through them it promotes its message of tolerance and acceptance of diversity within the Muslim community. It is through these activities that it hopes to instil the message among its members that however objectionable should someone's actions appear to oneself – such as those of a gay Muslim, or a Muslim covered in tattoos, or one not dressed in accordance with Islamic requirements of modesty – one does not have the right to judge them. Ta'leef's co-founder is Mustafa Davis, who is a childhood friend of Usama Canon and a fellow convert; he, however, takes a less active role in leading Ta'leef's activities and works as a documentary maker. Both became close to Hamza Yusuf on conversion in mid 1990s, before travelling overseas to pursue Islamic studies. Ta'leef adherents have, however, recently have had to deal with some sad news: in late September 2017, Usama Canon, who had turned forty that year, announced that he had been diagnosed with Lou Gehrig's Disease and that he would take sabbatical leave from Ta'leef Collective starting in December 2017. Ta'leef will thus become the first case to test how these institutions will survive beyond the life cycle or continued guidance of their founding figures.

Yahya Rhodus, another early student of Hamza Yusuf, is also today a prominent figure from the second generation. He moved to California at a time when Usama Canon and Mustafa Davis were also there, and the three became quite close. He has acquired a visible following of his own because of the teaching he has done at many of the institutions in question, including Zaytuna College, where he taught between 2008 and 2010 after he had returned from studying Islamic sciences overseas. He had spent a few years in Damascus before moving to Yemen, where he was particularly inspired by Dar al-Mustafa in Tarim, a madrasah influenced by the Ba'alawi Sufi tradition from Yemen; the Ba'alawi scholars claim direct descent from the Prophet himself (see Chapter 3). Recently, he has established a formal institution, al-Maqasid Institute, in Pennsylvania, which is expected to become a branch of Dar al-Mustafa by gradually moving towards offering a four-year Islamic degree programme. Al-Maqasid's stated mission is four-fold: 'Our Vision is to facilitate the realization of Iman (faith), Islam (worship), and Ihsan (character) through immersion in the prophetic inheritance. Our Mission is to cultivate holistic learning environments rooted in knowledge ('ilm), devotion (suluk), and service (da'wa) by providing full-time, seasonal, online, and community programs' (al-Maqasid 2018). It offers 'Knowledge: text-based, traditional teaching; Devotion: purification of the heart; worship and litanies; Service: channeling God-given abilities to some type of service' (al-Maqasid 2018). While the launch of the formal degree programme will require some time, the Institute has meanwhile started holding regular seminars, short retreats, and informal teaching of specialised books. In 2017 it led a complete Ramadan Program, which consisted of daily *tarawih* prayer, daily classes led by Yahya Rhodus on Imam al-Haddad's book *The Aphorisms,* and the hosting of community iftars on Tuesdays and Saturdays. Its classes are made more widely accessible via livestream, and registered students receive access to class materials. Yahya Rhodus also makes regular appearance at SeekersHub in Canada, which is another influential platform within this network.

Established by Shaykh Faraz Rabbani, the only case of a Muslim from birth among the scholars discussed so far, SeekersHub is distinctive in two ways: first, its primary focus is on offering free online Islamic studies courses, although it also offers in-house educational programmes; and second, Faraz Rabbani is a formal student of Nuh Keller, instead of studying under any one of the three figures identified as core to this Islamic rationalist network. Yet, as I will argue, despite these differences SeekersHub and Faraz Rabbani are important parts of this network of traditional scholars who are popularising Islamic rationalism among educated young Muslims in the West.[19] Of South Asian heritage and born and raised in Canada, Faraz Rabbani, who did an undergraduate degree in business and economics, was inspired to pursue formal study of Islamic sciences, first in Damascus and then in Jordan, as well as Pakistan, after hearing Hamza Yusuf and Nuh Keller speak at the same 1996 student conference in Toronto where those leading Revival of Islamic Spirit had first heard these scholars. Faraz Rabbani was among those who at the end of the conference took formal *bay'ah* (vow of allegiance) with Nuh Keller – a fact that is key to differentiating Nuh Keller from this network, and an issue whose importance for an understanding of the appeal of this movement will become clear in the next chapter.

Faraz Rabbani then followed Nuh Keller to Damascus and Amman. It was on Nuh Keller's advice that Faraz Rabbani returned to Canada at the end of his training to open SeekersHub. I was first introduced to SeekersHub in 2012 by Dr Umar, who described Faraz Rabbani as a like-minded scholar who is working towards promoting a similar

---

[19] SeekersHub split into two factions in 2018, leading Faraz Rabbani to establish SeekersGuidance. This new platform now performs the activities which, at the time of the fieldwork, were carried out under the banner of SeekersHub.

conception of Islam; since then my attendance at its seminars in Mississauga, where it is based, and study of its online courses have in my assessment upheld Dr Umar's assessment. SeekersHub's online courses cover the three-fold focus that is core to the teaching of this network: an understanding of Islamic fiqh by studying the four Sunni madhhabs, an appreciation of the rationalist basis of Islamic theology, and a deep focus on tasawwuf. This is reflected in the list of online courses offered by SeekersHub. Along with its online courses, SeekersHub also aims to build close-knit communities of learners. At the SeekersHub main office in Mississauga, regular educational activities take place for local students. An informal Islamic Studies programme has already been launched, with plans to turn it into a proper recognised Islamic seminary programme over time. It also hosts many community activities, such as the Thursday evening prayer gatherings, seminars, and a very full iftar and prayer programme during Ramadan. At locations where it has a number of subscribers for its online courses, it encourages them to gather at one location to facilitate mutual learning.

Third Generation

The description of the numerous institutions established by the scholars from the first two generations demonstrates the scope of the Islamic rationalist network; but this evidence alone does not sustain my claim that this network has initiated an important Islamic revival movement with a rationalist bent, attracting students from educated, liberal, and affluent backgrounds. My assertion is based on the evidence presented in the second half of this volume on the emergence of a third generation of scholars and leaders within Muslim communities who are being taught and inspired by the scholars from the first two generations. This third generation consists partly of those enrolled in the formal degree programmes offered by some of these institutions, but equally of those who only attend the informal activities, retreats, or seminars organised by these scholars or these institutions. As would be expected, only a few of those who attend these retreats pursue serious Islamic education. The main objective of these retreats is to help young Muslims embody some of these teachings in their everyday living, irrespective of their professional orientations or educational background; it is not to make them all specialists in Islamic sciences. But a few from among those who regularly attend the seminars or retreats organised by these scholars do become inspired to pursue more serious Islamic education, even if they do not enrol in a formal degree programme of Islamic studies. Thus, two categories of serious student are emerging within the third generation: those enrolled in the formal degree programmes offered by some of these institutions and those who do not formally enrol but regularly follow these scholars by attending their lectures, listening to their recordings and YouTube lectures, and reading their work and the work of the scholars they recommend. As we will see in Chapters 6 and 7, it is the number of the potential scholars, public figures, and social leaders that are emerging within the third generation that shows how this network has indeed succeeded in initiating an Islamic revival movement to re-engage with what they view as traditional Islam and what I refer to as Islamic rationalism. It is the steady expansion of this third generation of followers that provides evidence that this network has become mainstream: it is not merely confined to a few converts but has developed strong roots among Muslims in the West and among some even in Muslim-majority countries.

It is worth noting here that among the first-generation scholars a few other prominent American scholars could arguably be included: two such figures are Imam Zaid Shakir, who co-founded Zaytuna College, and the university-based academic, Sherman Jackson. I have, however, not mapped them as part of this network as they have slightly distinct approaches. Zaid Shakir, for instance, is much more directly involved in leading social activism on the ground than Hamza Yusuf or other members of this network. Sherman Jackson, on the other hand, acts more as a university academic and remains focused on communicating mainly through his writings and lectures, rather than trying to demonstrate by his own conduct how to live by Islamic values, as do the scholars in this network. As we will see in the next chapter, for scholars within this network, a key feature of what they understand as traditional Islam involves modelling for students how to discipline one's body and soul to follow the Islamic moral and ethical code. Academics such as Sherman Jackson are thus better viewed as sympathisers who share these scholars' approach to Islam but have distinct teaching approaches.

Another question that merits attention at this point is the absence of female scholars within the Islamic rationalist network as I have mapped it. Although some female scholars are appearing on platforms described above,[20] they as yet have not developed visible followings; in my

---

[20] Saara Sabbagh, for example, taught a course on purification of the heart during the 2017 Rihla programme but she is as yet a relatively unknown name.

fieldwork, none of those in the third generation, including the female students, named any of the emerging female scholars as their inspiration. But in this respect the experience of this network is not unique. In order to put this issue into perspective, it is important to remember that while in early periods of Islam there is evidence of women acting as teachers, some of whom even taught male students (Nadwi 2013), this tradition of female scholars specialising in Islamic sciences such as the study of hadith largely fizzled out between the fourteenth and twentieth centuries;[21] during that time women have not been involved in the formal study or teaching of Islam. However, in the past three to four decades we have witnessed the emergence and spread of movements promoting the formal study of Islam among women (Bano 2017). Some women preachers with a reformist agenda have also emerged who have attempted to lead mixed-gender prayers (Hammer 2012),[22] but they have failed to develop a following within mainstream Muslim populations; the women's Islamic education movements that are spreading fast are those that respect a more traditional understanding of the texts (Bano and Kalmbach 2012; Bano 2017).

This network is thus not an exception in having no established female scholars. However, since many of the enrolled students in these institutions are women, within the third generation there is a strong probability that the trend will change. Recently, Zaytuna College has been promoting lectures by some of its female graduates who are now pursuing higher education in theology departments in the United States. Similarly, in recent annual Rihla retreats, women teachers have been included, as a departure from the all-male faculty in the earlier years.

2 WHY DOES THIS MOVEMENT MERIT SCHOLARLY ATTENTION?

To appreciate the significance of this Islamic rationalist movement, it is necessary to situate its emergence within the existing landscape of Islamic learning platforms in the West. This contextualisation is important

---

[21] Within the Sufi tariqahs, women did remain more active, even during this period, than those belonging to the mosque- and madrasah-based networks (Bano and Kalmbach 2012).

[22] Amina Wadud, an African American convert, attracted much media publicity after leading mixed-gender prayers in New York in 2005 (Hammer 2012). More recently, in Berlin and Denmark, some female preachers have made similar attempts (Guardian 2016; Nelson 2017).

because, as in the case of all successful movements, its emergence and spread is not just a story of commitment to certain fixed textual beliefs; rather it is a story of winning over young Muslims because of the ability of the scholars leading it to demonstrate the usefulness and relevance of Islamic beliefs to the everyday realities faced by young modern Muslims. Intergenerational comparisons within Muslim communities in the West show how these communities are undergoing many changes that are also affecting how the younger generations engage with the very notion of religion, and with Islamic dictates more specifically.

In 2010, there were an estimated 44 million Muslims in Europe, constituting 5.9 per cent of the total population (PRC 2017); in the United States, the total number of Muslims is estimated to be 3.3 million (PRC 2018). At 1 per cent of the total population (PRC 2018), Muslims in America constitute a much smaller share of the citizenry, yet their presence is equally pronounced. The first-generation Muslim immigrants built mosques and madrasahs out of their commitment to transmit Islamic knowledge to their children, and they recruited imams trained in Islamic institutions in Muslim-majority countries (Gilliat-Ray 2010; Ahmed 2011; van Bruinessen and Allievi 2011). This heavy reliance on imams from Muslim-majority countries has meant that influential Islamic scholarly traditions in the Muslim world, such as al-Azhar Mosque and university complex in Egypt, Diyanet (Directorate of Religious Affairs) in Turkey, Deoband in South Asia, and Saudi Salafism, have expanded successfully in the West (Bano 2018a). The improvement in economic conditions of some second- and third-generation Muslims, compared with their parents' generation, and their more liberal attitudes have, however, put this practice of inviting imams from overseas under pressure. Born and raised in the West, many second- and third-generation Muslims are more integrated in the Western liberal democracies than were their parents' generations (Cesari 2002). This shift in economic conditions, educational levels, and social attitudes is particularly pronounced in the United Kingdom and Europe, where the first-generation immigrants came primarily as labourers (Abbas 2005; Bano 2018b); this was unlike the United States, where from the beginning immigration policies restricted immigration to more educated and professional immigrants (Ahmed 2011). These young Muslims find it difficult to appreciate the imams from overseas. Not knowing the language and culture of their host societies, most imams fail to relate to the questions raised by the young (Bano 2018b); there is also a major communication barrier, due to the imams' often limited command of the language of the host country

(Bano 2018b). Consequently, many young Muslims are deserting mosques, due to their inability to appreciate the teachings at the mosque. In my own interviews, I have found that many young Muslim men might continue to attend Friday prayers out of a sense of ritual obligation, but they do not expect the imam to be able to provide meaningful guidance on the everyday choices that they have to make in the Western context.

This shift in sensibilities of the second- and third-generation Muslims born and educated in the West is indicative of the pressure that the established Islamic platforms in the West face in retaining their authority; the challenges faced by Islamic authority platforms in the Muslim-majority countries are, however, no different. With improved access to university education and easy access to TV networks, the internet, and mobile technology, the sensibilities of the young Muslims even in the Muslim-majority countries have become highly influenced by Western culture and the secular liberal values. As Eickelman (1992: 643) has argued, the impact of higher education and mass communication, especially since the last quarter of the twentieth century, has had a profound impact on how Muslims engage with their faith:

> What is my religion? Why is it important to my life? and, How do my beliefs guide my conduct?, while seen as generating a uniform or monolithic response by many scholars, are in fact distinctly modern questions ... For something like religion to be objectified in people's consciousness, it must be discussed, and this entails discourse. If, for reasons of political intimidation or social deference, people do not discuss it directly, then it is discussed publicly for them by 'experts' with whom they may or may not agree.

Western culture has made deep inroads in the shaping of the attitudes and values of Muslim youth from the upper and upper-middle income brackets in most Muslim-majority countries, especially in the urban areas.[23] As I have outlined in a two-volume project on modern Islamic authority platforms, this shift in the sensibilities and aspirations of young Muslims in the West, as well as those within the Muslim-majority countries, is having major implications for the Islamic authority platforms (Bano 2018a; 2018b). These changed lifestyles, attitudes, opportunities, and challenges faced by the young create pressure on Islamic platforms to provide answers to the changing needs of the time if they are to retain

---

[23] See more detailed analysis of the evidence available on the changing subjectivities of young Muslims around the globe in Bano (2018a).

young Muslims within their fold of adherents and enjoy continued support (Bano 2018a; 2018b).[24]

One example of how even the liberal Islamic scholarly platforms are being labelled as conservative, rigid, and supportive of ISIS is the pressure put on al-Azhar, the oldest continuously running centre of Islamic learning, noted for preserving classical Islamic scholarly traditions, by secular voices in the media under the al-Sisi government in Egypt (Bano 2018a). Other Islamic centres of learning face similar pressures. The fact that highly rigid readings of Islam are failing to retain followers among the young is evident in the transformation underway even within Saudi society (Bano 2018a). The state long criticised for promoting a highly restrictive reading of Islam is today increasingly giving in to calls for individual autonomy and social freedom. This is manifest in growing educational and employment opportunities for women and the state's recent decision to remove the controversial ban on women driving and allow opportunities for entertainment through opening up of cinema houses and hosting of musical concerts. This is not to argue that these conservative Islamic platforms have no followers; indeed, many young Muslims continue to gravitate towards these platforms, as is also evident in the ability of the dar al-'ulums in the United Kingdom to continue to recruit new students (Gilliat-Ray 2010; van Bruinessen and Allievi 2011). The objective of documenting the changing attitudes of young Muslims, however, is to highlight that while conservative platforms might have some adherents, their authority is increasingly being rivalled by new institutions. Many young Muslims are in search of platforms which can relate Islamic teachings to modern times, and some on failing to find such moderate platforms are even at the risk of losing their faith. The evidence of the latter comes in different forms.

First, most of the scholars within the network of scholars under study, as well as many other prominent Islamic scholars in the West, have explicitly addressed this concern in their lectures. These scholars are keen to highlight that they routinely encounter young Muslims who are disenchanted with the perceived rigidity of their religion and are on the verge of moving out. Second, academics based in Western universities who study

---

[24] Assertions about Saudi money supporting Salafi movements around the globe remain highly exaggerated (Bano and Keiko 2015); it is ultimately local donations, especially from the affluent patrons, that sustain the Islamic mosque-madrasah network – unless the institution is funded by the state, as is the case for al-Azhar University, for Diyanet, or for official Saudi scholars (Bano 2018a).

Muslim communities or Islamic thought have started to comment on this trend. Writing in the international edition of the *New York Times*, Faisal Devji (2017) notes the growing trend among Western Muslims of conversions away from Islam. He makes some interesting points about the nature of these conversions. First, he notes that the decision to convert indicates a new trend among Muslims, compared with conditions in the past when those who were not religious might have simply shown indifference: 'The Muslims among whom I was raised in East Africa included many who refused to pray or fast and were openly critical of religion. It would never occur to them to renounce Islam and proclaim atheism as a new identity or mission, which would have catapulted them back into a theological narrative.' Second, noting the existence of a group that calls itself ex-Muslim and since 2007 has been operating in a number of countries, including the United States, Canada, Britain, France, Germany, and New Zealand, Devji (2017) argues: 'By retaining "Muslim" in their name, ex-Muslims are recognizing the theological character of their renunciation.' He also notes that ex-Muslims often come not from secular Muslim backgrounds but from those who are devout but on exploration of the text find many of their questions left unanswered. Noting that this movement away from Islam is not solely a phenomenon among Muslims in the West, he notes a 2012 WIN/Gallop International poll which shows that 5 per cent of Saudis identified as atheists, and that close to 22 per cent of respondents in the Middle East expressed doubts about religion.

While it is true that most of the examples that Devji (2017) quotes in support of his argument draw on isolated cases or on media reports in which reported cases of conversion collectively amount to no more than a few hundred, as I have also argued elsewhere, the highly restricted strands of Islam, in my experience, appeal only to a few (Bano 2018a). In my own fieldwork, I have rarely come across young Muslims who have denounced Islam, but many do indeed have questions about the ability of the Islamic scholarly classes to provide answers to the needs of the time. Most Muslims whom I have seen enthused about their religion regard Islam as a civilisation which inspired creativity in all aspects of human existence, and not just a narrow set of theological beliefs. This aversion to a very rigid reading of Islam is also evident in the emergence of new mosque initiatives in the West, which are offering extremely liberal interpretations of Islamic texts. One example is the new Berlin mosque initiative, where a female imam is pushing the boundaries in ways that remain unacceptable to mainstream Muslims, even those who normally would be considered liberal (Nelson 2017). That such radical liberal initiatives, which clearly violate the established consensus in Sunni Islam, are finding an audience, even if small in number, is indicative of the disillusionment of some with highly restricted readings of Islam.

It is in the light of this inability of the existing mosque-madrasah platforms to appeal to more modern, educated, and socially integrated Muslims that we have to study the emergence of the new scholarly platforms in the West, of which the movement under study is one. Some of these movements talk about reform of Islam, and others about revival of the authentic Islamic tradition. Elsewhere, I have grouped these new initiatives into three categories: neo-traditionalists, neo-legalists, and neo-conservatives (Bano 2018b). Neo-traditionalism (under which the scholars in the Islamic rationalist network were placed) is an approach which interprets the Islamic scholarly tradition as being inherently adept at coping with change and diversity; its focus is on reviving a respect for rich Islamic scholarly tradition as preserved by the four Sunni madhhabs, while simultaneously cultivating an appreciation for tasawwuf through working on 'cleansing of the heart'. Learning the *adab* (Islamic norms of behaviour) and being in the *suhbah* (company) of scholars is central to this approach. The methodology proposed by the neo-legalists is totally different from that of the neo-traditionalists. Here the emphasis on suhbah as well as tasawwuf is entirely absent. Instead, the focus is purely on finding answers to contemporary challenges by attempting to bridge the gap between Islamic law, contemporary realities, and modern sciences. Tariq Ramadan's work on Islamic ethics and work at the International Institute of Islamic Thought (IIIT) best represent this approach (Spannaus 2018a; 2018b). The neo-conservatives, on the other hand, are leading institutions that are an extension of the two most conservative Islamic scholarly platforms, namely Deoband and Saudi Salafism, but whose initiators are trying to adapt their traditional reasoning to modern realities (Razavian 2018c; Razavian and Spannaus 2018). From within the Deoband tradition, examples include Ebrahim College in London and Darul Qasim in Chicago (Razavian and Spannaus 2018); from within the Saudi Salafi tradition, Yasir Qadhi, a prominent Salafi reformer in the United States, is a good example (Razavian 2018c).

The growing popularity of these new Islamic scholarly platforms emerging in the West, which differ in their methodology but agree on the need to make young Muslims appreciate the relevance of Islam to modern reality, illustrates the vacuum left by the traditional mosque imams. Two factors make the neo-traditionalist network particularly noteworthy among these three categories: one, its approach is more comprehensive, due to its focus not just on the law and ethics of Islam but on reviving serious engagement with Islamic scholarly tradition in its entirety; two, its method is more rigorous, whereby the focus is not just on giving lectures but on helping young Muslims to embody the Islamic moral and ethical framework. Thus, both the content of what they cover and how they cover it is distinct from the other two approaches. Ultimately, however, what makes this network particularly noteworthy is the profile of its followers: the scholars in this network are able to enthuse educated, culturally liberal, and financially affluent young Muslims about Islam. Given the societal elites' ability to shape social institutions, the potential within this network to revive Islamic rationalism and to inspire young Muslims to actually influence socio-political and economic institutions in its light is significant. To understand why I argue for recognising the importance of this movement in shaping the future of Islam, due to its ability to influence young Muslims who are from within the societal elites, it is important to outline the conceptual basis of the reasoning that provides the framework for the empirical evidence that is presented in the subsequent chapters.

3 TYPES OF KNOWLEDGE, SOCIETAL ELITES, AND SOCIAL CONDITIONS: THE THEORETICAL FRAMEWORK

To fully understand both the emergence of the Islamic rationalist movement and its potential to influence understandings of Islam, not just among Western Muslims but also among those in the Muslim-majority countries, it is important to draw on the debates within social theory on the types of knowledge, the role of elite engagement in keeping a knowledge dynamic, and the relationship between innovation and routinisation of learning and societal conditions. Understanding the complexity of knowledge-creation processes is important, because only then do we appreciate how knowledge formation is a process that is highly socially embedded. A field of knowledge is shaped not just by certain ideas or dictates, but by scholars' personal experiences, and their immediate knowledge of the context has a direct bearing on the interpretation of the text. Further, elite engagement is key to keeping a field of knowledge dynamic. This relationship exists for a number of reasons: elites act as potential patrons, but also are the ones who have the power to influence and shape socio-economic and political institutions. It is only through the engagement of elite groups and individuals, especially those controlling state institutions, that learning is transformed from a field of knowledge into formal rules and regulations, thereby providing a society with action-guiding rules – a process to which Ober (2008) refers as *codification of knowledge*.[25] As I also illustrated in *Female Islamic Education Movements*, in pre-colonial Muslim societies the fact that the state was governed under shariʿah meant that laws were codified in accordance with the Islamic legal and moral framework. This process of codification required scholarly classes to relate Islamic rulings to modern reality, while simultaneously creating incentives within the society to work within the Islamic frame of reference. It is important to consider each one of these relationships in some detail, in order to understand the significance of this movement: first, the relationship between different forms of knowledge; second, the role of societal elites in knowledge formation; and third, knowledge formation and its relevance to societal conditions.

Relationship between Tacit and Technical Knowledge

Every field of knowledge has its technical language and its experts who command specialist expertise in it. In Western academia, most fields of knowledge have historically operated in isolation. Recent years have, however, seen growing support for interdisciplinary research. This shift in approach reflects the growing recognition that cross-fertilisation of ideas across different disciplines can bring creativity; economists, for example, are today increasingly borrowing insights from behavioural scientists (Baddeley 2017). In the case of religious knowledge, maintaining neat disciplinary boundaries has, however, always been a challenge: most religions aspire to shape the moral and legal framework underpinning every socio-economic and political institution. This all-encompassing nature of religious knowledge requires it to operate in close association with the other fields of scientific knowledge. The recognition that religious knowledge needs to stay attuned to developments in other fields of knowledge and as a result be responsive to the changing social

---

[25] Ober (2008) argues for recognising the importance of incentives in leading a society to invest in the creation of certain forms of knowledge. These incentives, he argues, are created through a three-step process: coordination, assimilation, and codification of knowledge. Ober is primarily concerned with highlighting the importance of lay knowledge, that is, knowledge held by the people, which is also of importance in this volume. But, in highlighting the importance of the codification of knowledge in creating incentives for society to further invest in it, he ends up emphasising the role of the state (and thereby the elites) in shaping investment in a given field of knowledge.

reality has also been at the heart of all religious reform projects. In contemporary times, Tariq Ramadan's Islamic reform project aims to do precisely that by bringing together the scholars of Islamic text and of modern sciences (Ramadan 2009). An influential Muslim thinker and scholar, Ramadan maintains that in recent centuries the gap between Islamic and what was traditionally called rational sciences has become so wide that it is not possible for Islamic scholars of fiqh to fully understand the complexity and technical knowledge of each field. His effort thus aims to bring together scholars of the fiqh and those of modern sciences in the hope that they might jointly resolve the apparent gulf between Islamic ethics and present-day realities. This, he argues, needs to be done in all fields, such as environmental studies, bio-ethics, and economics.

That knowledge can be of different types, and that religious knowledge needs to evolve in line with other fields of knowledge in order to stay relevant, is one aspect of the debate; the other aspect focuses on recognising the complexity of the knowledge-production process (Ober 2008). Scholars from across the social sciences have highlighted the importance of non-technical knowledge in finding optimal answers by emphasising the importance of the knowledge of everyday realities. This form of knowledge has been referred to as lay knowledge, knowledge of everyday reality, or tacit knowledge. An important distinction is maintained between knowledge acquired through direct experience (*tacit* or *lay knowledge*) and knowledge that is acquired through a formal learning process (*communicable* or *specialist knowledge*). Introduced by Michael Polanyi (2009), the concept of tacit knowledge has had popular appeal because of its implicit suggestion that '*we can know more than we can tell*', as much human learning happens unconsciously through being part of a given environment, context, and culture. Knowledge expressed in words and numbers represents only one form of it. For Polanyi, tacit knowledge has a personal quality and it is hard to formalise and communicate it. Polanyi, an anthropologist, was however not the only scholar to highlight the important of tacit knowledge. Friedrich von Hayek, a Nobel Prize winner in economics, similarly noted the importance of knowledge of everyday realities and market conditions for economic decisions to be accurate. Hayek's (1945) influential paper, *The Use of Knowledge in Society*, argued for recognising the importance of lay knowledge for optimal economic planning: 'Today it is almost heresy to suggest that scientific knowledge is not the sum of all knowledge. But a little reflection will show that there is beyond question a body of very important but unorganized knowledge which cannot possibly be called scientific in the sense of knowledge of general rules: the knowledge of the particular circumstances of time and place' (Hayek 1945: 521). He maintained: 'And the problem of what is the best way of utilizing knowledge initially dispersed among all the people is at least one of the main problems of economic policy – or of designing an efficient economic system' (Hayek 1945: 520). Similarly, Douglass North (1990), another Nobel Prize winner in economics, has highlighted the role of tacit knowledge to emphasise how informal institutions, norms, values, and beliefs play a role in shaping formal institutions. Ober (2008) similarly notes the importance of lay knowledge in explaining the successes of classical Athens: the state put in place incentives for people to combine lay and specialist knowledge to find optimal answers to critical societal challenges.

These studies argue that technical knowledge, though highly prized, is not of itself enough to yield socially useful or acceptable answers; until that knowledge is blended with lay knowledge of the realities, technical experts can end up making highly flawed decisions. Today, we see this critique of technical knowledge most visibly applied in the field of international development, where technical experts routinely fail to put in place adequate reforms (Escobar 1995; Gow 2008), due to their lack of tacit knowledge of the local realities; solutions proposed prove either impractical or unable to appeal to the local people. Tacit knowledge thus consists of the sub-conscious knowledge that we have of our immediate reality, culture, and history, by virtue of our mere existence. This knowledge of everyday reality is important in ensuring that a technical field of knowledge remains creative and responsive to societal needs. The reason this debate is important for understanding the significance of the Islamic rationalist movement is that, as I will illustrate in this book, the main strength of its scholars is that they have tacit knowledge of the reality as shared by young educated Muslims. The reason they are able to popularise traditional learning among young educated Muslims more effectively than the scholars from whom they themselves learned is that the scholars leading this network come from the same socio-economic and educational background as the young Muslims they are trying to guide. They are thus able to relate to how the young educated Muslims think, how they speak, what they aspire to, what kinds of social gathering and platform appeal to them, and so on. Since the colonial period, the typical Islamic scholar in a Muslim-majority country, on the other hand, comes from an economically and socially marginalised class (Bano 2012b; Pierret 2013) and thus lacks the tacit knowledge to relate to modern-educated youth and the societal elites who are embedded in a totally different global and secular worldview from the localised and the narrowly shaped view of the typical madrasah teacher.

Elites and Knowledge Creation

I have argued above that tacit knowledge is key to understanding why Islamic rationalist scholars are able to make Islam relevant to modern reality in the eyes of young educated Muslims; in this section I will spell out my argument for suggesting why their growing following among Muslims from educated and affluent backgrounds indicates their ability to influence societal institutions in future decades. From research on elites we are in a position to deduce three key links between elites and knowledge formation: elites provide financial patronage; they often bring important intellectual capital, due to the privilege of being better educated; and most importantly they have social capital and are able to utilise lessons from a field of knowledge to shape socio-economic and political institutions.[26] While the role of elites in supporting a field of inquiry through extending financial support does not need much academic evidence, given that all leading Western universities draw on the generosity of their affluent patrons, it is important to share some evidence on the links between elites and enhanced intellectual and social capital.

Within education studies, the relationship between the socio-economic profile of a child and his or her educational outcomes has been a long-established area of research interest (Gambetta 1987; Lareau 1987; Howard and Gaztambide-Fernandez 2010). There is evidence to show that children from middle-income and upper-income families perform better than their peers because of a number of factors. First, they get more support at home, either because their relatively better-educated parents can personally provide them with additional support, or because they can hire additional teaching support. Second, their parents have better social networks and have more influence, so they can make more

---

[26] Bonds (2011), in his paper on the role of corporate and military elites in shaping environmental policy, notes four ways in which elites shape knowledge and its utilisation. In addition to identifying their role in funding research, and then ensuring utilisation of that knowledge, he also identifies two other roles that they play: elites suppress information that may threaten their interests; and they can fund experts willing to attack and discredit potentially damaging research.

demands on the teachers and the school management. Focusing on parental networks, Horvat et al. (2003) used ethnographic data to examine social-class differences in the relations between families and schools. They note that the middle-class parents in their study tended to react collectively, in contrast to the working-class and poor parents. The middle-class parents were uniquely able to draw on contacts with professionals to mobilise the information, expertise, or authority needed to contest the judgments of school officials. Similarly, using the concepts of cultural and social capital, McNeal (1999) provides a theoretical framework to explain why there should be differential effects of parental background across cognitive outcomes (for example, achievements in science) and behavioural outcomes (for example, rates of truancy and dropping out).

Finally, just as elites and upper-middle-income students bring their social networks and creative energy, elites as graduates or adherents of a knowledge base play an even more important role in its growth, as they help to shape socio-economic and political institutions in the light of that knowledge. As government officials they define the constitution and laws of the state; as social elites they shape cultural expression; as economic entrepreneurs they shape the nature of economic activity and contracts. This ability of the elites to shape institutions makes them critical as trend setters and shapers of social attitudes; it also makes them critical agents of institutional persistent or change (North 1990; Acemoglu and Robinson 2000; 2009). The role of elites' involvement in social movements is thus well recorded. They have the social networks, the knowledge, the connections, and the ability to deal with influential actors within a society, be it the state, the media, or a social institution. Due to their ability to make a field of knowledge socially relevant, they also have the indirect impact of creating incentives for future research and inquiry in that field. When a field of knowledge has social relevance, its scholars are under pressure (and have the incentives) to stay responsive to the emerging questions. It is this complex relationship between elites and a field of knowledge that makes their engagement so critical to generating creativity within that field.

In interpreting these results it is important to be clear about who we consider to be elites. 'Elites' are normally understood as hereditary elites, who inherit certain privileges and prominent status in society from one generation to the next. But in this volume the term is being used more broadly. I am using the term *elite* as it is manifesting itself in the twenty-first century, when hereditary wealth is increasingly being replaced by educational and professional success to confer elite status.

Acknowledging the role of universities in producing elites, an article in the *Economist* (2015) argued as such: 'today's rich increasingly pass on to their children an asset that cannot be frittered away in a few nights at a casino. It is far more useful than wealth, and invulnerable to inheritance tax. It is brains.' Similarly, as Meyer (1977: 55) noted in a paper published in the 1970s:

> in modern societies education is a highly developed institution. It has a network of rules creating public classifications of persons and knowledge. It defines which individuals belong to these categories and possess the appropriate knowledge. And it defines which persons have access to valued positions in society. Education is a central element in the public biography of individuals, greatly affecting their life chances. It is also a central element in the table of organization of society, constructing competencies and helping create professions and professionals.

That universities today are the main route to acquiring elite status is well recognised. Even within Muslim countries the role of university education in determining upward mobility is clear.[27] As we will see throughout this book, it is due to this power of modern universities, especially leading Western universities, to create global elites that the Islamic rationalist network (by virtue of engaging with university-educated Muslims who are destined to be important figures in their societies or communities) has the potential to exert a wide-ranging impact and influence on institutions in Muslim societies.

Societal Conditions and Knowledge Creation

A certain amount of affluence is essential for societies to support vibrant educational systems: the challenges faced by education bureaucracies in most developing countries bear witness to that (UNDP 2014). The colonial period dramatically changed the socio-economic and political structures within Muslim societies, thereby having a direct impact on both the content of Islamic education and the mode of Islamic knowledge transmission. There is evidence that in pre-colonial Muslim societies Islamic knowledge was not interpreted to mean solely the knowledge of Islamic sciences; instead all forms of knowledge, philosophy, mathematics, medicine, astrology, history, and sociology were seen as part of the Islamic

---

[27] Even in the case of Saudi Arabia, students sent to the American universities in the 1960s were, on their return, given prominent positions within the government ministries and thus became influential figures in their society.

knowledge base. Also, because the state was being run in the name of Islam, irrespective of the level of devoutness of the incumbent ruler, the overall frame of reference for shaping societal institutions came from the Islamic legal and moral framework. This created incentives for all, including the elites, to innovate in all areas of socio-economic and political development, while respecting the basic Islamic framework (Saliba 2011; Bano 2017). It meant that Islamic knowledge platforms attracted Muslims of all dispositions, not just those who were interested only in becoming imams (Hodgson 1977a). This is why most of the prominent Muslim scholars over the centuries were not necessarily mosque imams or even heads of madrasahs, as is normally the case today, but were leading figures in all fields of life, or specialists in non-Islamic sciences (Saliba 2011). Thus these scholars had knowledge of different fields of inquiry as well as knowledge of the secular realities of the institutions that they were often leading.

Further, because the Islamic frame of reference was the dominant framework in these societies, questions linked to Islamic dictates routinely inspired research in other fields, and vice versa. Islamic law of inheritance is, for example, noted as having created incentives for Muslims to invest in the study of algebra. Muhammad Al-Khwarizmi's *Al-Kitāb al-mukhtaṣar fi ḥisāb al-jabr wa'l-muqābala* (The Compendious Book on Calculation by Completion and Balancing), which became a foundational text of algebra, devoted chapters to using algebra to solve problems related to Islamic inheritance rules (Encyclopaedia Britannica 2018). Similarly, Abu Bakr Muhammad ibn Abdallah ibn Ayyash al-Hassar (Selin 1997), a mathematician from the Maghrib specialising in Islamic inheritance jurisprudence during the twelfth century, developed the modern symbolic mathematical notation for fractions.

Apart from creating incentives for expressions of creativity within an Islamic frame of reference, Muslim political authority also ensured financial patronage for Islamic education platforms. Madrasahs were either patronised by the state or were richly endowed by affluent patrons. Thus, during the pre-colonial period, not just pure sciences but Islamic arts and culture also flourished (Hodgson 1977a). This equilibrium, however, was disrupted during colonial rule. First of all, the loss of Muslim political authority led to erosion of state patronage for the Islamic knowledge platforms (Bano 2017). Further, the establishment of Western educational institutions ensured that the formal degrees issued by these institutions, rather than the education acquired in the madrasahs, became the primary route to upward mobility (Robinson 2003; Bano 2017). The immediate impact of this was that students from elite families and upper-income groups deserted the Islamic education platforms, because Islamic knowledge no longer shaped the socio-economic and political institutions; instead, Muslim elites needed to master Western knowledge if they were to retain their privileged status in the changed societal context. The result, in the light of the above discussion on elites and social knowledge, was as expected: Islamic education platforms lacked financial resources and with the passage of time were unable to attract the best minds from within Muslim societies (Eickelman 2007; Pierret 2013; Bano 2017); the few bright students that they did attract, being from a poor or low-middle income socio-economic background, lacked the social networks and resources to make Islamic knowledge socially influential. This led to the isolation of Islamic knowledge during the colonial period.

To understand the full magnitude of this shift, it is important not merely to note how the Muslim elites disengaged from the Islamic knowledge platforms, but equally to highlight how, having been educated in Western schools and universities, many of the new Muslim elites became highly critical of Islamic knowledge platforms. Western education systems also developed appreciation for Western liberal values. Göle (1997: 50), for example, illustrates in some detail how in the case of Turkey the Republican elites that replaced the Ottoman rule and the Ottoman religious elite

were the product of this new way of writing, reading and speaking. They used the Latin script, spoke 'pure,' 'original' Turkish, without a local accent, mastered Western languages (French being gradually replaced by English after the 1950s), and referred themselves to Western sources in science and literature.

Similar was the experience with elites produced under the colonial periods in other colonial contexts.

As Desai (1950:918) wrote about Indian elites during the colonial period,

We might say that the way of looking at the world or the scientific attitude was the formal aspect. The substantive aspect was made up of beliefs, values, views and ideas on technology, economic system, system of government and organisation of society. In brief, we can say that Western society, its history and culture were the main items of the knowledge content of the new educational system, and the difference between the new intellectuals and traditional intellectuals could be understood in terms of their respective orientations. The former were Western-oriented while the latter were oriented in Indian tradition. It is generally presumed that all those who took to the new education also approved of Western society and culture, and that consequently as a class the new intellectuals were the most potent and active agents of Western society and culture in India or of Westernisation in India.

Thus, with the concentration of political authority in the hands of Muslim elites who took inspiration from the Western liberal framework rather than from local religion and culture, the tacit knowledge consisting of the everyday experiences of the Islamic scholarly classes became very different from that of these societal elites and upwardly mobile Muslims from middle-income families attending Western educational institutions. This has resulted in an inability on the part of the Islamic scholarly classes to influence the societal elites, or even the upper-middle-income Muslims who were now educated in Western colleges and universities. Pierret (2013), for example, notes how the Islamic scholars in Syria in the twentieth century saw the Western-educated youth as being most at risk of losing their religious orientation; he also notes how as a result some of the prominent Islamic scholars particularly made an effort to attract young Muslim college students to Islamic circles as they were the ones who would go on to fill senior positions in the state and society. I have myself recorded the socio-economic marginalisation of Islamic scholars in madrasahs in Pakistan, and to some extent even in northern Nigeria, in my earlier work (Bano 2008; 2009; 2012b; 2017). Even when trying to respond to the changing societal context and growing Western influences, which many of the Islamic scholars did, they have been unable to impress upon the social elites and the educated Muslims their ability to find answers from within the Islamic tradition in response to the changing modern realities. Their limited exposure to modern education; their lack of command over English or French, which in post-colonial Muslim societies is the sign of good education and elite status; their limited exposure to modern economic and cultural institutions; and their often rural background severely restrict the ability of these scholars to impress modern-educated and upwardly mobile young Muslims who are very much connected to the global culture through the internet, cable TV networks, and the latest mobile technology.

Part I of this volume focuses on establishing how a critical reason for the success of the Islamic rationalist scholars in attracting university-educated, socially liberal Muslim youth to serious study of Islam is their shared tacit knowledge of the young people's realities, having been born in Western middle-income families and being able to combine that knowledge with the technical knowledge of Islamic sciences, having invested many years in the study of Islamic sciences, linked both to fiqh and to tasawwuf, in Muslim-majority countries. This ability to share a tacit knowledge of the realities of the educated and socially liberal Muslim youth, while reviving a strand of Islam that combines rationalist and mystical dimensions which appeals to the rational approach that these young Muslims have developed as students in Western universities, is thus key to the success of these scholars. Part II of the volume in turn shows how it is important to understand that the rise of this movement is indicative of contemporary societal shifts in Muslim-majority countries as well as changing demographics of the second- and third-generation Muslims in the West whose experiences, aspirations, and tastes differ from those of their parents' generation. Further, given that the scholars leading this movement are Western converts to Islam from a Christian background, a study of this movement also provides an insight into the limits of Western modernity and the comparative appeal of Islamic theology to some.

4 METHODOLOGY

As noted at the outset, the genesis of this project can be traced to my introduction to Rosales during my fieldwork in Syria in 2010. However, I became clear about the importance of this Islamic rationalist network after attending a few of the retreats and the interviews with young Muslim university students across the Netherlands, France, and Germany in addition to the United Kingdom and the United States that I started to conduct in 2012. Hamza Yusuf was identified by these young Muslims as being very popular across these different settings; the influence of Tim Winter was also evident. I therefore initially started my fieldwork by participating in the retreats held by these institutions and attending any seminars or lectures by the scholars from the first generation. At the same time, I started to hold interviews with the participants of these retreats, seminars, and lectures. It was through these initial interviews and fieldwork that I slowly came to identify the scholars and platforms that I present as being part of the second generation.

The fieldwork with this network of scholars has been conducted in the United States, the United Kingdom, Canada, Spain, and Saudi Arabia, where I joined the Sacred Caravan 'Umrah programme in 2016. Given their popularity, these scholars travel extensively, and thus it has been possible to listen to them at their home base as well as in other locations. I have returned to Rosales each summer since 2012 to take part in the retreats and conduct interviews with Dr Umar, Abdus Samad, and the participants in the retreats. Within the United States, the main fieldwork has been done in Chicago, where I was able to observe some of the activities of Ta'leef Collective, and where on my first visit in 2014 I conducted in-depth interviews with Dr Umar, who resides in Naperville, a suburb of Chicago. In California, I have visited both Zaytuna College and Ta'leef Collective and interviewed the followers of both. In the United Kingdom, I have paid a number of visits to the Cambridge Muslim College and conducted interviews with the senior staff and former and current students. In Canada, I spent time at the SeekersHub office at Mississauga and interviewed some of its young students; I also conducted important interviews with students linked to this network of scholars in Edmonton. I also took part in the Sacred Caravan 'Umrah trip to Mecca and Medina in 2016; this journey, which is normally led by Hamza Yusuf, was led in that year by Dr Umar. Thus, to most of these institutions, I have made repeated visits between 2012 and 2017, or I have heard the scholars speak at a number of different locations. This means that I was by chance at Zaytuna College on the day it inaugurated its new building on the Holy Hill and was able to listen to Hamza Yusuf's opening speech, and then again by chance I was there in 2016 when it launched its new book store.

Thus, this book mainly draws on ethnographic fieldwork and interviews, but it also equally draws on the rich information and resources available on these scholars on the internet and YouTube. The lectures by these scholars are routinely uploaded on YouTube at times by their own institutions and at other times by their keen followers. Further, there are many websites listing their published works; some are maintained by the scholars themselves, but others are maintained by some of their enthusiastic followers: the website entitled *The Unofficial Biography of Hamza Yusuf*[28] is one interesting example. Also, many of these scholars, especially Hamza Yusuf and Tim Winter, have over the years been interviewed many times about the reasons behind their conversions and their journeys since then. Thus, much of the information required on their profiles was already available in these interviews. Further, all the institutions established by these scholars maintain active websites, where their lectures are uploaded routinely, and the institutional activities are properly recorded. Another useful resource was the Deen Intensive online TV channel; for an annual charge of $119, it provides unlimited access to all

---

[28] Website link: http://shaykhhamza.com/biography/; accessed on 1 May 2018.

the Rihla course material and recordings of the lectures from current as well as previous years. The information available on these scholars was extensive; their visible presence on the Web and the number of downloads for many of their videos and lectures in themselves helped to verify the extent of their influence. Thus, this book is my understanding of this network of scholars, their approach and their impact; it is by no means a biography of these scholars or a summary of how they view themselves.

Finally, my earlier research on Islamic scholarly platforms in Muslim-majority countries has also played a critical role in helping me to appreciate the importance of the movement in question. It is due to my earlier research on Islamic scholarly platforms that in Chapter 3 I am able to map the currents of Islamic scholarly debates in the different contexts in which these scholars studied; it is also due to my work on Islamic scholarly platforms in Muslim-majority countries that I argue that these Islamic rationalist scholars are making an impact even there, even though they are physically based in the West. During my fieldwork in a number of Muslim-majority countries, I have been able to ask respondents about their awareness of these scholars, which, as illustrated in Chapter 7, has helped to establish their wide reach.

5 THE STRUCTURE OF THIS BOOK

The remaining chapters of this volume are divided into two parts. In line with the conceptual framework set out in this introduction, Part I focuses on understanding how the success of the Islamic rationalist scholars in inspiring educated Muslim youth rests in their ability to combine specialist knowledge of Islamic sciences with that of Western philosophy, and their tacit understanding of the reality of living as an educated Muslim in a secular society. Part II focuses on the followers of this movement to show how the changing socio-economic realities of the second- and third-generation Muslims in the West, as well as of the educated youth in the Muslim-majority countries, are key to understanding why Islamic rationalism is gaining prominence in the twenty-first century, as opposed to the more conservative and literalist Islamic traditions that took root among many Islamic educational institutions during the colonial period.

Chapter 2 introduces these scholars' approach to traditional Islam and highlights how exploring the rational basis of Islamic theology and the rational methods underpinning the Islamic sciences is just as critical to their understanding of Islam as is the study of tasawwuf and shari'ah. Further, the chapter shows that to understand their approach it is important to focus not only on the content of their teaching but also on their method. The chapter illustrates the emphasis placed by these scholars on learning from scholars who can demonstrate an uninterrupted chain of knowledge transmission from the very first generation of Muslims. Further, Islamic learning to them does not simply imply study of the Islamic texts; rather, it equally involves learning to discipline the self through spending time with the Sufi shaykhs who embody the Islamic moral code. The chapter thus highlights the emphasis placed by the rationalist scholars on maintaining suhbah with respected scholars and Sufi shaykhs; it also shows how the retreats that these scholars organise aim to inculcate within the students an appreciation for being in the company of people with a high moral character. The chapter also discusses how a conscious decision by these scholars not to position themselves as Sufis, and Hamza Yusuf's presumed reservations about the practice of bay'ah, common among formal Sufi tariqahs, have played a key role in enabling this movement to gain acceptance within mainstream Muslim communities.

Chapter 3 focuses on mapping the geographical locations and the religious milieu in the Muslim-majority contexts in which these scholars secured their Islamic knowledge. The chapter is equally focused on highlighting the changes witnessed by traditional Islamic scholarly platforms in the Muslim world during the colonial period. The chapter illustrates how during the colonial period many Islamic educational platforms adopted a more formal degree-based programme, replacing the older informal mode of Islamic knowledge transmission. Traditional Islamic teaching methods focused on study of a major book, rather than covering a fixed curriculum; further, the *ijazah* (permission given by the teachers), rather than a formal degree, marked the successful completion of the learning process. Faced with competition from the modern schools and universities with their formal curricula and set examinations, many of the Islamic educational institutions and madrasahs replaced the informality of the original system with these formal rules. Yet, despite these changes, Islamic educational platforms became marginalised during this period, due to a declining patronage base and their loss of relevance to the way the state, society, and the economy were organised by the colonial authorities. The chapter thus presents the continued challenges faced by Islamic education platforms in Muslim-majority countries today and their perceived lack of social relevance, before introducing the specific locations and scholarly networks from which the scholars within this Islamic rationalist network learned. The chapter helps to illustrate how these scholars had an appreciation for the more informal and traditional networks which had best preserved the traditional mode of Islamic teaching; this is illustrative of their own starting dispositions, but it is also key to understanding why on return to their home countries they could establish credibility to speak in the name of Islam.

While Chapter 4 demonstrates these scholars' detailed knowledge of the Islamic sciences, it also presents an analysis of their socio-economic background and their training in Western educational institutions prior to their conversions, and it maps their motivations for conversion to show that they share a tacit knowledge of reality as experienced by young university-educated Muslims. The chapter illustrates how all the scholars in this network come from middle-class families, and that most had training in Christian theology and were propelled by basic existential questions to explore the meaning of life. There is a shared narrative of how the Christian concept of the Trinity failed to answer their spiritual and theological questions, and how the continuous search for answers led them to explore other religions: a process that eventually exposed them to Islamic theology, which proved particularly appealing with its clear emphasis on one God. Further, the chapter records how almost all these scholars came mostly from a humanist background, with interests in the arts, music, literature, and civil rights movements. It is thus not surprising that the understanding of Islam that appealed to them is the one that blends a rationalist outlook with deep mystical spirit, while also respecting the shari'ah.

Chapter 5 maps the real-life implications of the teachings of these Islamic rationalist scholars. The chapter examines the positions that they take and the justifications they provide for their positions on issues that affect the everyday actions of Muslims, such as questions relating to gender, economics, science, arts, and the environment. By focusing on the writings and speeches of these scholars, the chapter illustrates how their conception of Islam makes it possible for their young followers to be proud of their Islamic heritage and yet also be active members of the modern secular society in which they live. The chapter highlights the emphasis placed by these scholars on utilising Islam's inherent ability to adapt to the reality of the time. In advocating this, however, they are clear that certain core principles are fixed and remain non-negotiable; their position on homosexuality, as discussed in this chapter, is illustrative of this. This emphasis on being creative and adaptive while being clear about the core principles of Islam that are non-negotiable is, as I illustrate in the chapters in Part II, another critical factor that has helped them to win credibility within mainstream Muslim communities. In advancing such a balance, these scholars also end up presenting a critique of Western modernity which is in reality also shared by some prominent Western philosophers who argue that Western modernity has led to the loss of the spiritual dimension in human existence; there is, for example, much in common in their views on modernity with those expressed by Charles Taylor (2007) in *A Secular Age*.

Chapter 6, the first chapter in Part II, shifts the focus to the followers of the Islamic rationalist movement, especially those who are training to become future scholars or are taking up leadership positions within Muslim communities. The chapter presents detailed profiles of many of the followers to identify the factors that make these young university-educated and socially liberal Muslims gravitate towards these scholars. The chapter shows that, as argued in Part I, the unique ability of these scholars to combine specialist knowledge of Islamic sciences with philosophical debates in the Western scholarly tradition and their tacit knowledge of the reality of growing up as a religiously oriented young person from a middle-income family in a secular society make these scholars particularly effective in communicating with educated Muslim youth. Further, the fact that all the first-generation scholars are white converts also plays an important role; the arguments in defence of Islam become more convincing and inspiring for the followers when they see a white man from a well-to-do family, with a good command of the Western philosophical tradition and Christian theology, convinced of the rational foundation of Islam and appreciative of its ritual and deeper mystical practices. The chapter also shows how most of the followers of these scholars will count as members of societal elites, as they represent the upper-income groups within the Muslim communities and are keen to influence the popular understanding of Islam – thus relating back to the argument about elites and social influence.

The final chapter records the evidence of the influence of these scholars among affluent Muslim youth in the Muslim-majority countries before moving on to show how some of the young followers of this Islamic rationalist network have already started to initiate dynamic projects which promise to highlight the creativity energy within the Islamic tradition. The chapter presents evidence that, coming as they do from influential backgrounds, the followers of this network are well positioned to shape the public face of Islam in the coming decades, both in the West and within Muslim-majority countries. Their efforts may lead to a widespread revival of the study of philosophical and mystical texts from classical

Islamic scholarship which has been largely neglected by Muslims in the past two centuries; they are also popularising the rationalist foundation of Islam in the West, thus harbouring the potential to correct the radical and militant image that is associated with it today. The chapter also records some of the criticisms that these scholars face from some of their own students; in particular, these scholars' discomfort with political Islamists creates dilemmas for some of their brightest students and also puts these scholars at odds with reformist Islamic scholars, such as Tariq Ramadan (Ramadan 2004; 2009), equally popular among the young. These challenges, however, cannot distract our attention from the creative energy that this movement has injected into contemporary Islamic scholarship by reversing the colonial legacy and inspiring educated Muslim elites to re-engage with the Islamic texts.

PART I

SPECIALIST VERSUS TACIT KNOWLEDGE

2

What Is Islam?

'Umar ibn al-Khattab narrates:

As we sat one day with the Messenger of Allah (Allah bless him and give him peace), a man in pure white clothing and jet black hair came to us, without a trace of travelling upon him, though none of us knew him.

He sat down before the Prophet (Allah bless him and give him peace) bracing his knees against his, resting his hands on his legs, and said: 'Muhammad, tell me about Islam'. The Messenger of Allah (Allah bless him and give him peace) said: 'Islam is to testify that there is no God but Allah and that Muhammad is the Messenger of Allah, and to perform the prayer, give zakat, fast in Ramadan, and perform the pilgrimage to the House if you can find a way.'

He said: 'You have spoken the truth,' and we were surprised that he should ask and then confirm the answer. Then he said:

'Tell me about true faith (iman),' and the Prophet (Allah bless him and give him peace) answered: 'It is to believe in Allah, His angels, His inspired Books, His messengers, the Last Day, and in destiny, its good and evil.'

'You have spoken the truth,' he said. 'Now tell me about the perfection of faith (ihsan),' and the Prophet (Allah bless him and give him peace) answered: 'It is to worship Allah as if you see Him, and if you see Him not, He nevertheless sees you.'

The hadith continues to where 'Umar said:

Then the visitor left. I waited a long while, and the Prophet (Allah bless him and give him peace) said to me, 'Do you know, 'Umar, who was the questioner?' and I replied, 'Allah and His messenger know best.' He said,

'It was Gabriel, who came to you to teach you your religion.'

(*Sahih Muslim*, 1.37: hadith 8)[1]

---

[1] As produced in Keller (1995).

This hadith, referred to as Hadith Jibril, is recognised as *sahih* (authentic) by all Sunni groups; its importance is recognised in many commentaries, including those produced by scholars associated with the Salafi tradition. It is, however, paramount in the teaching of most Sufis. The constant effort to reach the state of *Ihsan*, where one's inner self is so purified that one worships Allah as if one sees him, is to the Sufis the very essence of tasawwuf. This hadith is also central to the teaching of all the scholars in this network. Dr Abd-Allah's annual Zawiyah retreat, which, unlike the other retreats organised by the Islamic rationalist scholars, introduces a new topic each year to steadily build up a student's knowledge of Islam, devoted the first retreat to study of Hadith Jibril.[2] Tim Winter, Hamza Yusuf, and other scholars within the Islamic rationalist network similarly refer to this hadith routinely in their lectures and writings. For these scholars, this hadith captures the essence of Islam; in other words, what they understand to be the authentic Islamic tradition. *Islam* signifies the importance of respecting the shari'ah/fiqh; *iman* the importance of purity of one's *'aqidah* (creed); and *ihsan* the importance of embodying Islamic ethical and moral character.

It is when we understand the importance of these three dimensions of Islam, and the resulting emphasis that these scholars place on the one hand on simultaneous respect for shari'ah and tasawwuf, and on other on having strong creedal belief while encouraging logical reasoning, that we realise why their teachings are particularly appealing to modern-educated and more intellectually oriented Muslim youth. Their focus on developing sound knowledge of shari'ah through study of one of the four Sunni madhhabs gives their approach a methodological rigour and protects them from being labelled as yet another of the New Age Sufi groups which are criticised for being too lax in meeting Islamic ritual obligations. Yet their simultaneous focus on tasawwuf enables this group of scholars to emphasise the benefits of engaging in many Sufi practices to discipline the self in order to mould the body and the soul to live by the dictates of shari'ah. Finally, their focus on highlighting the purity of Islamic 'aqidah, while recognising its strong rationalist foundations, makes their understanding of Islam very appealing to Muslims who are intellectually oriented. In order to understand on what grounds these scholars claim

---

[2] The other retreats run by scholars in this network, as we will see in this chapter, mainly repeat the same content each year. They thus are designed to attract new students each year, while Zawiyah retreat aims to attract the same students back for more in-depth study of a specific aspect of Islam each successive year.

to represent traditional Islam, it is thus important to first briefly consider how the Ash'ari-Maturidi school of theology, which these scholars follow and which encouraged a rationalist defence of Islamic theology, came to be considered as the Sunni orthodoxy from the twelfth century onwards; it is equally important to appreciate how it carved out a moderate course between the purely philosophical and the purely textual approaches to the study of Islamic sciences.

My own fieldwork leaves me convinced that those who come to these scholars are not attracted to them because they are aspiring to join an exclusive Sufi tariqah, as there are many other formal Sufi shaykhs in the West who head traditional Sufi tariqahs that such individuals can join;[3] nor are they aiming to become specialists in shari'ah, as attending courses at a dar al-'ulum or a course run by a fiqh scholar[4] could also serve that purpose. Those who follow the Islamic rationalist scholars do so because, while appreciating the value of both tasawwuf and shari'ah, they are particularly excited to be presented with a rationalist defence of the Islamic tradition which appeals to intellect and reason. For almost two centuries, Muslims in most contexts have been receiving education in a system inherited from the West which during the colonial period came to replace the Islamic education system in all Muslim countries. This adoption of the Western education system has also helped to assert the supremacy of Western civilisation in promoting philosophy, humanism, and intellectual reasoning. Islam, on the other hand, is widely presented in popular discourse as essentially anti-reason, inherently violent, and lacking in the rich humanist endeavours capable of cultivating arts and aesthetics. While my own fieldwork, and limited but steadily growing scholarship on contemporary Muslim youth, suggests that most young modern-educated Muslims do remain internally convinced of Islam's ability to inspire critical reasoning, very few have any direct exposure to the deeper intellectual debates that historically marked Islamic scholarship. The education that Muslims receive in the regular schools and universities does not expose them to the complexity and richness of Islamic sciences, and neither does their traditional Islamic education.

---

[3] Many Sufi orders operate in the West and tend to attract favourable reviews in the media as they are seen to promote a tolerant and mystical version of Islam.

[4] In the United Kingdom and the United States, there are many dar al-'ulums, especially from the South Asian Deobandi tradition, where students can acquire specialist knowledge of shari'ah (see Razavian and Spannaus 2018).

Studies of Islamic knowledge transmission in contemporary times reconfirm that, whether based in the Muslim-majority countries or living in the diaspora, Muslim parents remain committed to transmitting basic Islamic knowledge to their children (Hefner and Zaman 2007; Zeghal 2007; Bano 2012b); but this teaching is normally focused exclusively on learning to say one's daily prayers, read the Quran in Arabic, and occasionally read its translations or longer commentaries (*tafsir*), and learn basic hadiths. There is limited provision for learning about the historical richness of Islamic sciences. Compared with this limited exposure to Islamic scholarly tradition, studying with the network of rationalist scholars helps young Muslims to appreciate the richness of classical texts in all fields of Islamic sciences, including philosophy, law, and tasawwuf. This does not mean that these scholars themselves necessarily specialise in the teaching of classical texts in Islamic philosophy, or that classical texts are what they primarily teach; the ability even of young university-educated Muslims to fully grasp the complexity of debates underlying Islamic sciences, such as kalam, remains limited, as is equally the case for Western philosophical texts. What, however, is critical in understanding the appeal of these scholars to young Muslim university students is their ability to make constant references to the richness of classical Islamic scholarly tradition, and, in particular, to allude to the sound reasoning underlying the evolution of early Islamic scholarly debates.

It is the ability of these Islamic rationalist scholars to demonstrate intelligent engagement with Western philosophical texts, and then illustrate through specific examples that Islamic theology and law can withstand Western philosophical critiques, that makes them particularly effective in convincing young Muslims of the value of their religion. I build this argument on the basis of my fieldwork with the students of these scholars and participants at their retreats and events (see Part II). It is due to this intellectual engagement that I argue that the real contribution of these scholars is best captured by emphasising their role in reviving Islamic rationalism and their efforts to demonstrate that this was the mainstream Sunni orthodoxy until the eighteenth century. This explains my preference for referring to them as Islamic rationalists. Yet it is understandable why they themselves prefer to be labelled as traditionalists: their entire project is dedicated to demonstrating that this ability to combine faith and reason has been at the heart of Islam's appeal from the very beginning. If the objective of the label is to assert their claim to represent Sunni orthodoxy, then indeed the label 'traditionalist' is more meaningful, as it helps to justify these scholars' claim to represent authentic Islamic tradition; but seen from the perspective of their appeal to the mainstream Muslim population, what is most striking is their ability to assert the rational basis of mainstream Sunni orthodoxy. I prefer the 'rationalist' label because this book is concerned not only with mapping their approach but equally with mapping why they are successful in attracting modern-educated well-to-do Muslims, and assessing the implications that the spread of this movement has for shaping popular discourse on Islam in the future. It is my contention that they are important to study because they are bringing Islamic rationalism back to the centre of the popular understanding of Islam.

This chapter will thus first briefly map the rise of the discipline of *'Ilm al-kalam* (Science of Discourse; literally: 'speech' or 'discussion'), a field of Islamic scholastic theology[5] that evolved in the eighth century to address questions about Islamic doctrine (Walbridge 2011: 50), and the gradual emergence and consolidation of the Ash'ari and Maturidi schools of Islamic theology, which from the twelfth century became recognised as representing orthodox Sunni Muslim theology. These schools of Islamic theology presented a balance between two polarising camps that emerged within early Muslim communities: those who, inspired by the Hellenistic philosophical tradition, argued for exposing religious truths to logical inquiry, and those more bound to the text and keen to adopt its literal meaning, whether or not a given ruling met the demands of reason (Walbridge 2011). It is therefore important to consider briefly how the Ash'ari and Maturidi schools of theology evolved, and how Abu Hamid al-Ghazali (1057–1111) played an important role in ensuring that this approach became the Sunni orthodoxy from the twelfth century until the start of its decline in the eighteenth century, when rationalist sciences in general became marginalised in the madrasah curriculums. The chapter will then illustrate how the rationalist scholars are trying to develop among Muslims an appreciation of the richness of the Islamic intellectual heritage by focusing their teachings on the three component parts of Hadith Jibril. The chapter also describes how these scholars expose their students to scholars and major books from classical Islamic scholarship and discusses why classical scholars such as al-Ghazali remain central to their teachings. The last section illustrates how the emphasis placed by Islamic rationalist scholars on reconnecting to the classical Islamic

---

[5] Scholastic theology focuses on an intellectual way of approaching God. It arose in Christian theology as scholars tried to find a logic to justify different religious dictates (Walbridge 2011).

scholarly tradition has implications not just for the content of their teaching but also for their preferred method of teaching.

I 'ILM AL-KALAM: ISLAMIC RATIONALISM

Muslims today normally interpret the 'Islamic sciences' to mean study of the Quran and hadith. When focusing on the Quran, there is an appreciation of the science of *tawjid*, which focuses on the proper vocalisation of Quranic syllables, and of *tafsir* (exegesis) of the Quran. When it comes to the science of hadith, most Muslims who receive a basic level of Islamic education are aware that a rigorous method of hadith verification evolved early on in Islamic history, leading to six authoritative hadith compilations between the seventh and tenth centuries. Beyond that there is, however, little awareness, even among educated Muslims, of the richness of Islamic sciences, how they evolved, and what methods classical Islamic scholars utilised to define what is a valid Islamic ruling. It is a little-known fact that even Greek Hellenistic philosophy was once central to the debates of Islamic scholars, and that, although interest in it eventually declined, its influence was absorbed into all the Islamic sciences by adoption of logical deduction as a key method (Walbridge 2011). For children born into a Muslim family today, Islamic education starts from the very early years; but in terms of time devoted to it or the importance accorded to it, it remains secondary to education received in modern schools, due to what is perceived as its limited worldly utility.[6] Islamic teaching thus remains narrowly focused on learning to recite the Quran in Arabic, say the five prayers, perform other ritual obligations, and understand basic Islamic *adab* (etiquettes). The fact that among the early Muslims there were some who claimed to be absolutely committed to Islam but still openly debated the notion of God or the status of the Quran as the divine word of God is not a subject discussed in present-day Islamic schools. As noted by many scholars, Muslim societies have been effective in transmitting to the next generations a general pride in Islam and its ability to inspire a great civilisation which contributed to scientific advancement, the arts, and philosophy. In my own fieldwork with young Muslims across different countries, I find that scholars such as Ibn Arabi and al-Ghazali, associated with the deeper philosophical and mystical debates,

---

[6] Only those who attend madrasahs full time devote more time to Islamic education. The ratio of full-time madrasah students is, however, very small compared with those attending modern schools in all Muslim contexts (for data on Pakistan, see Andrabi et al. 2005).

remain alive in the consciousness of many liberal, modern-educated Muslims. Yet their specific contributions and the relevance of their scholarship today is little understood. In understanding the contribution of the Islamic rationalism movement, it is thus important to briefly trace the evolution of Islamic sciences, especially ʿIlm al-Kalam, which laid the foundation of a rationalist theology in Islam.

The Prophet Muhammad left the Muslim community with the Quran, in which God himself takes the responsibility for its protection,[7] and also his hadith and *Sunnah* (examples from his conduct).[8] Yet having these resources did not mean that early Muslims had a homogeneous understanding of their faith; rather, differences over interpretations of Quranic verses and hadiths began to emerge from the time of the first four Caliphs. It is these differing interpretations of these core texts, and not necessarily a lack of faith in Islam or simple material opportunism, that led to the emergence of early factions in Islam, the assassinations of the last two of the four Rightly Guided Caliphs, and the break-up of the Muslim community into Sunni and Shia within the first century of Islam. The *Khawarij* ('those who have exited') challenged Ali not necessarily to gain political power but because they found Ali failing to implement God's mandate as they interpreted it. These tensions and debates emerging within the early Muslim community not only shaped the political currents of the time: they were equally reflected in the conflicting debates marking the intellectual milieu of the early Muslim community, which was rapidly expanding. Competing scholarly camps were emerging; two groups that became particularly strong and directly opposed to each other were the Muʿtazilah theologians and the hadith-focused literalist scholars.

The Muʿtazilah referred to themselves as *ahl al-ʿadl waʾl-tawhid* (the people of justice and monotheism), thus proclaiming undivided belief in one God: 'Their chief theological concern was to protect the unity, transcendence, and justice of God' (Walbridge 2011: 51). This group emerged in the eighth century in Basra, the capital of the Abbasid dynasty. Muʿtazilites were keen to debate the basic tenets of the Islamic ʿaqidah on rationalist grounds. They were rivalled by the more textual scholars, who

---

[7] Verse 15:9 states, 'Surely, We have revealed the Quran, and surely, We will Preserve it'; Verse 41:42 similarly asserts, 'No falsehood will come to it, in the present or in the future; a revelation from One who is Wise and Praiseworthy.'

[8] The Quran itself instructs Muslims to follow the Sunnah of the Prophet. Verse 33:21 states, 'Indeed in the Messenger of Allah (Muhammad SAW) you have a good example to follow for him who hopes in (the Meeting with) Allah and the Last Day and remembers Allah much.'

focused primarily on hadith and argued for following a ruling listed in the Quran or hadith whether or not its logic could be established. Contrary to what one might assume, given the dominant profile of Islam in the media today, during this early period it was the rationalist currents and the Mu'tazilite theologians who became very influential, enjoying strong backing within the Muslim elites.

To give an impression of the nature of this tension, it helps to understand how the subjects of the creation of the Quran and the attributes of God became central to this debate. For many Mu'tazilites who were inspired by the Greek Hellenistic tradition,[9] there was a question about whether the Quran was humanly created or the word of God, and whether it was eternal; they also questioned the nature of God's relationship with the universe. These questions emerged because the Quranic references to God and prophecy were 'vivid but not philosophical or theological' (Walbridge 2011: 65). Questions such as the following had begun to be raised by early Mu'tazilites, starting from the eighth century (although more sophisticated responses to them emerged only between the tenth and twelfth centuries):

> From the philosopher's point of view, the Qur'ān had left many critical questions unanswered: Was God part of the universe, as Aristotle and the *Timaeus* would seem to indicate, or was He beyond being, as the Neoplatonists would have it? What sorts of things did God teach through prophecy that men did not know? Were they things that man could know on his own but through ignorance or neglect had not figured out for himself, or were they things that in principle were beyond human knowledge and that thus could only be known by revelation? What was it about prophets that made them prophets? Did they differ from other human beings in some fundamental way, and if so, how? And how were scriptures, and particularly the Qur'ān, to be understood? Obviously, not everything in the Qur'ān can be taken literally, but how, then, were its symbols to be interpreted, and what in the Qur'ān could be understood symbolically? And what of the practical teachings of prophetic religion, the specific laws and rituals? How did they relate to human law and rational ethics? (Walbridge 2011: 65–66)

The debate on the nature of the Quran became so central and contested between the two camps that it ended up informing the very name of the discipline of kalam (speech). Mu'tazilites maintained that the Quran cannot be eternal, because logically if it were eternal it would be of equal status to God, thus violating His oneness. The Hanbalis (one of the four

---

[9] For an analysis of how Hellenistic influences entered Islamic theological debates in the eighth century through the translation of Greek philosophical texts, see Walbridge (2011: 115–118).

schools of Islamic law), who were the Mu'tazilites' main opponents and argued for strong adherence to the Quran and hadith texts, countered that the Quran is obviously eternal because it is God's perfect and timeless message, as it is described in scripture. Today, no Islamic teaching platform entertains debates such as these,[10] yet some among the early Muslims openly debated these questions, and under Caliph Ma'mun of the Abbasid dynasty the societal elites in fact favoured the rationalists. Imam Hanbal (780–855), who posed the strongest resistance to the Mu'tazilite scholars, was in fact imprisoned.[11] This pure rationalist current which accorded supremacy to philosophical truth over theology eventually could not develop strong roots among the Muslim masses. Consequently, many early orientalist scholars contended that the defeat of these rationalist philosophical currents in Islam led to the closing of the 'gates of ijtihad' and the stagnation of Islamic intellectual tradition from the twelfth century onwards. Yet, as subsequent scholarship has convincingly illustrated, while the Hellenistic rationalist currents could not embed themselves in the mainstream of Sunni Islamic scholarship or community, the confrontation between these early proponents of Greek philosophical influences and the hadith-centric scholars led the way to the adoption of logic as the key to the development of all Islamic sciences. This move towards a middle course is credited to the rise of the Ash'ari and Maturidi schools of kalam, which came to represent Sunni orthodoxy across the Muslim lands between the twelfth and eighteenth centuries (Walbridge 2011), and which also influenced the development of Islamic sciences, including the evolution of the madhhabs. It is important to briefly introduce the main scholars who influenced these debates, as we will later see how these very scholars are routinely invoked by the Islamic rationalist scholars that are under study in this volume.

The Ash'ari school of kalam takes its name from Abu al-Hasan al-Ash'ari (874–936), who was a native of Basra. Educated in

---

[10] I argue this on the basis of my exposure to madrasah curricula in a range of Muslim-country contexts (Bano 2008; 2012b; 2018a). A specific example to support this assertion also comes from a survey that I recently designed for young Muslim university students in the West. In response to the feedback from respondents during the pilot, a question to this effect was dropped, as the respondents felt that the question seemed inappropriate and risked producing bias against the survey.

[11] In 817 the Caliph al-Ma'mun instituted a policy (known as the *Mihna*) which endorsed official persecution of high-ranking 'ulama who held the belief that the Quran is eternal. Ibn Hanbal was briefly imprisoned and tortured during the *Mihna* for failing to adopt this position; this made him a symbol of popular resistance to the policy. The policy ultimately failed and was abandoned in 848.

Mu'tazilism, he later became committed to defending Hanbali-traditionalist theological positions.[12] But his Mu'tazilite background remained, and instead of relying primarily on hadith as the justification of these views, Ash'ari argued for them logically. This is what is called the 'great synthesis' of Ash'arism: the combination of theological positions supported by common consensus and a literal reading of scripture, justified and supported by rational argument characteristic of kalam (Walbridge 2011). To illustrate how it worked in practice, we can revisit the question on the Quran. As opposed to the two positions outlined above, Ash'ari acknowledged the logical validity of the Mu'tazilite position, but argued that these descriptions of the Quran show that it is eternal, but its eternality does not make it equal to God, because it is only co-eternal with Him and is not eternal independently. Likewise, with questions of free will, the relationship between faith and action, and the nature of God's attributes, the early Ash'ari scholarship used rational methods to defend essentially traditionalist positions.

While occurring within the sphere of Islamic theology, these debates simultaneously influenced the evolution of Islamic fiqh sciences. The Ash'ari method of reasoning particularly appealed to followers of Shafi'i – one of the four main Sunni schools of Islamic law (Walbridge 2011). When working with the Quran and hadith to define Islamic legal positions, the Shafi'i scholars were increasingly drawing on analogical reasoning, leading to the emergence of the science of *usul al-fiqh* (laws of jurisprudence). Shafi'i scholars in Iraq, Syria, and Iran began adopting Ash'ari kalam, and soon the two schools became very tightly linked. Similarly, Malikis in North Africa attached themselves to the school, though not as closely. In Iraq, Hanafism was associated with Mu'tazilism, which continued until the eleventh and twelfth centuries. Eastern Hanafis, however, had, like Hanbalis, developed their own theological school on the basis of their founder's beliefs, which took the form of the Maturidi school of kalam. Named after Abu Mansur al-Maturidi (853–944) of Samarqand, this school came to dominate in South and Central Asia, Inner Eurasia, and later the Ottoman Empire, and it became almost inseparable from Hanafism (Walbridge 2011). Maturidism, even more so than Ash'arism, combined rationalism with traditionalism in its theological approach, and this synthesis served as a prime impetus in the

---

[12] As a young man, Ash'ari was inspired by the Mu'tazila school; but, reportedly after a dream in which the Prophet Muhammad weighed in favour of Ibn Hanbal against the Mu'tazila, Ash'ari renounced Mu'tazilism – although its influence remained.

formation of coherent Sunni identity, the name for which (*ahl al-sunnah wa'l-jama'ah*) was formulated by Maturidis. Although a rivalry soon developed between Maturidism and Ash'arism, each of which considered itself the most orthodox school, they in large part recognised the other's validity and eventually arrived at a shared understanding of Sunni kalam that excluded the more extreme beliefs of both Mu'tazilism and Hanbalism (Walbridge 2011).

In the early eleventh century, advances in Islamic thought under the influence of the prominent Islamic philosopher and theologian Ibn Sina (980–1037) further shaped the Sunni kalam; Maturidism and Ash'arism were equally affected. The post-Ibn Sina kalam definitively resolved many of the earlier tensions concerning attributes of God or the nature of the Quran. For instance, the question of the eternality of the Quran, so problematic for earlier theologians, was decisively solved by Ibn Sina's revision of the three modalities of existence, developed by Aristotle (Walbridge 2011). Ibn Sina reasoned: everything is either necessary of existence – it must exist – or possible of existence – it may or may not exist – or impossible of existence – it cannot exist. Eternality had been God's primary characteristic, recognised as such even in Greek philosophy, but under the influence of Ibn Sina it was replaced by necessity. As a result, the objection that the Quran cannot be eternal because it would violate God's oneness was removed; God's oneness became linked with His being the only necessary being, so the Quran could be eternal because it is only possible of existence, and therefore of lesser status than God (Walbridge 2011). This new approach solved the issue so definitively that within a century or so it had ceased to be mentioned in theological works at all. (The fact that these debates are not covered in the Islamic education that Muslim children or adults receive today is thus not surprising; why, however, an awareness of these debates plays a critical role in further convincing intellectually oriented Muslims of the superiority of their religious tradition is an issue that will be addressed in Part II of this volume.)

Among Ash'aris, those scholars who incorporated Ibn Sina's philosophical concepts came to be called *al-muta'akhkhirun*, the 'later ones', to distinguish them from the earlier scholars of the school. Abu Hamid al-Ghazali is one such figure. Born near Tus in north-eastern Iran, Ghazali was educated locally in Nishapur in Shafi'i fiqh and Ash'ari kalam; he was also educated in Sufism. Ghazali left Nishapur for the court of Nizam al-Mulk (1018–1092), a powerful vizier in the Seljuq Empire, who had established a number of madrasahs across the region, the most important of which was in Baghdad. At this time the Seljuqs were promoting Shafi'i-Ash'arism,[13] and in 1091 Ghazali was made the head teacher of fiqh and kalam of the Baghdad Nizamiyya. In 1095, however, Ghazali underwent a crisis of conscience, and he quit his position in Baghdad. He spent the next year or so wandering through the Middle East, living as an ascetic. He travelled to Damascus, Jerusalem, and then Medina and Mecca, before returning to Tus in 1096. Wary of political entanglements, Ghazali refused any official teaching position, choosing instead to teach in his own small mosque and focus on Sufi ritual. In 1106 he relented accepting a position at the Nizamiyya madrasah in Tus.

Ghazali's impact on both Shafi'ism and Ash'arism, and on Sunni Islamic thought in general, was profound. He helped to further refine Shafi'i legal theory, contributed to the use of philosophical concepts in Sunni kalam, and at the same time wrote some of the most powerful treatises on the importance of mystical experience (Walbridge 2011). In *Munqidh min al-dalal* (Deliverance from Error), he argues that he found all of his knowledge of law and theology meaningless without mystical awareness. His *Ihya' 'ulum al-din* (Revival of the Religious Sciences), seen as his most important work, argued for Sufi-inspired morality as a necessary component of any form of religious knowledge. Although some argue that it was Ghazali's critique of the Islamic philosophers, inspired by Greek philosophy, in his book *Tahafut al-falasifa* (The Incoherence of the Philosophers) that contributed to the defeat of Hellenistic philosophical influences within Islamic scholarship and marked the beginning of the stagnation of Islamic thought, it is now well recorded that Ghazali critiqued the Greek interpretations of certain philosophical concepts, not the validity of those concepts themselves (Walbridge 2011). In fact, as Walbridge (2011) notes, Ghazali's critical engagement with the work of philosophers shows that he was himself among the finest of philosophers. He became very widely regarded in the history of Sunni scholarship, and even many non-Shafi'i or Ash'ari 'ulama' relied upon him and his works as an authority.

Ghazali represented the forefront of the Ash'ari school at the time of his death, and his ideas shaped the work of the prominent Islamic writers for centuries, particularly in Iran and the Islamic *mashriq* (east). Scholars such as Fakhr al-Din Razi (d. 1209, Herat), 'Adud al-Din Iji (d. 1355,

---

[13] They had previously promoted Hanafi-Mu'tazilism (Walbridge 2011).

Shiraz), Iji's students Saad al-Din Taftazani (d. 1390, Samarqand) and Sayyid Sharif Jurjani (d. 1419, Shiraz), and Jalal al-Din Dawani (d. 1501, Shiraz) were all deeply influenced by Ghazali. Through them, many of his ideas were introduced into Central and South Asian Maturidi kalam. Beyond the Islamic world, Ghazali was known as Algazel in Europe, and a number of his works were translated at least in part into Latin, as part of the early Renaissance incorporation of Islamic learning into European thought that also included Ibn Sina (Avicenna) and Ibn Rushd (Averroes, 1126–1198). Ghazali's influence in Europe was most significant in the theological and philosophical works of St Thomas Aquinas (1225–1274), who studied Ghazali while at the University of Naples. Aquinas is one of the major figures in Latin scholastic theology, which incorporated into Catholicism Platonic and Aristotelian philosophical concepts that had already been formulated into a monotheistic framework by Islamic scholars such as Ghazali. The wide breadth of his works and the range of approaches found therein enabled him to influence many different fields of inquiry (Walbridge 2011). He was both a philosophical theologian and a defender of Sunni orthodoxy, a devout mystic and a literalist legal scholar, a member of the most illustrious court of the time and one who rejected wealth and influence to wander as an ascetic.

The reasons kalam as a science received declining attention in the study of Islam from the eighteenth century onwards are contested. As mentioned before, one position blames it on a declining tolerance for reason within traditional Islamic scholarly platforms, with the defeat of the Hellenistic philosophers leading to eventual stagnation of Islamic sciences. The other position, which is today more influential and more grounded in evidence, places the emphasis on changing societal conditions of Muslim societies, with a decline in Muslim political authority. The onset of colonial rule revoked the status of Islamic knowledge platforms as being the main providers of education, which, as outlined in Chapter 1 of this volume, had serious consequences for the future of Islamic education in Muslim societies. We will revisit some of these concerns in the next chapter. For now, the remaining part of this chapter illustrates how the scholars under study communicate to their students and to broader audiences an awareness of the richness of classical Islamic scholarly tradition and its strong rationalist foundation.

As can be expected, these scholars do not address these complex philosophical debates in their routine lectures, given the mixed calibre of their audiences; but they do make routine references to them. Further, through their lectures and writings they encourage Muslims to re-engage with the work of these great scholars from the classical Islamic tradition. They also guide their students to read books by Western scholars who trace these complex intellectual debates in Islam. A former student of Zaytuna Institute,[14] now a PhD student at Columbia University in New York, had Walbridge's *God and Logic in Islam: The Caliphate of Reason* with him as he waited for me in a quiet café (appropriately named Think Café) on the 11th Avenue in New York – our agreed-upon meeting place. As can be discerned from the heavy references made to this text in the analysis presented in this section, in the book Walbridge presents a very detailed account of the nature of early philosophical debates in Islamic theology and the gradual adoption of the rationalist method of reasoning across all Islamic sciences. The book presents the complexity of philosophical debates marking early Islamic scholarship and thus is a dense text; but, as this former student of Zaytuna Institute emphasised, 'this book is recommended by Hamza Yusuf to all Zaytuna students as essential reading, as he argues it summarizes the Zaytuna's approach'. Walbridge has spoken at Zaytuna's annual convention ceremony and is on the advisory board of Zaytuna College journal, *Renovatio*. Similarly, both Hamza Yusuf and Tim Winter routinely refer to the work of William Chittick, renowned for his translations and interpretations of classical Islamic philosophy and mystical texts.

2 REVIVING ISLAMIC RATIONALISM THROUGH STUDY OF HADITH JIBRIL

That the contemporary scholars featured in this study belong to the Ash'ari school of theology is clear in their writings and in the references they make to the scholars from this tradition: Tim Winter and Yahaya Rodhus specialise in the study of Ghazali and teach courses on his major works; Hamza Yusuf teaches courses on Islamic logic during the Rihla, in which he engages with major works of early Ash'ari scholars; and Dr Umar routinely refers to Ibn Sina's analysis of God's existence being necessary during his lectures on 'aqidah.[15] The way these scholars translate these teachings for the mass of their audience is, however, not by

---

[14] Zaytuna College was originally founded as an Institute in 1996.
[15] I personally have heard him make frequent references to it in his teaching sessions on 'aqidah at a number of retreats that I have attended.

necessarily covering complex philosophical texts (these are confined to the teaching of specific courses, which normally only their more serious students will choose to study in depth), but by constantly referring to these works and connecting them to contemporary debates. It is here that their frequent reliance on Hadith Jibril as an entry point to cover these debates becomes important; it helps to teach the essential components of orthodox Islam as these scholars see it, in a way that is easily followed by a diverse audience. By focusing on how these scholars communicate the three-fold emphasis on Islam, iman, and ihsan in Hadith Jibril, their conception of what is traditional Islam, and the centrality of an Islamic rationalist theology that recognises the importance of intellect as well as mystical experience, becomes clear.

Islam

When it comes to their understanding of Islam, unlike what might be expected of a scholarly movement that places heavy emphasis on the importance of tasawwuf, the scholars in this network are very clear about the importance of following the five central pillars of Islam as outlined in the shari'ah and clearly spelt out within Hadith Jibril itself.[16] When Jibril asks the Prophet what is Islam, he replies: 'Islam is to testify that there is no God but Allah and that Muhammad is the Messenger of Allah, and to perform the prayer, give zakat, fast in Ramadan, and perform the pilgrimage to the House if you can find a way.' Advising their students to perform the ritual obligations such as praying five times a day, giving zakat, fasting in Ramadan, and performing the Hajj are thus central to their teachings. In the retreats that I have attended, I have seen many young Muslims who struggle to establish consistency in daily prayer ask these scholars if some intellectual or mystical line of reasoning within Islam can allow for laxity in performing ritual obligations provided that one subscribes to the basic belief; their response is always in the negative. During the retreats, these scholars always break the sessions for prayers at the designated time and join the congregation in prayer. If the retreats are held during Ramadan, they maintain a full teaching schedule and perform the prayers in the mosques, while fasting. In my own observation, their

---

[16] This emphasis on shari'ah helps to protect these scholars against the usual critiques of Sufi groups, namely that they are too lax in their performance of obligatory rituals and practices.

ability to sustain this demanding schedule and demonstrate the bodily discipline required to hold a post-*fajr* (morning prayer) teaching session after reciting the *tahajjud* (midnight prayer) acts as a great inspiration for those attending the retreats. I have had young followers of these scholars mention with great deference that these scholars hardly sleep for more than a few hours per night; to them it is indicative of their strict self-discipline and extensive bodily and spiritual training.

Just as in the case of fulfilling one's basic ritual obligations, the rationalist scholars are very clear on the importance of respecting Islamic legal reasoning when searching for an answer regarding any aspect of everyday life; however, they discourage self-interpretation, advising Muslims to respect the body of shari'ah as developed by the four Sunni madhhabs. The centrality of madhhabs in the teachings of these scholars is explained in detail in Tim Winter's 'Understanding the Four Madhhabs: The Problem with Anti-Madhhabism' (Winter 2014b). In this paper, Winter argues that the Muslims' greatest achievement over the centuries has been the ability of the Islamic tradition to preserve its internal intellectual cohesion despite the clash of different political factions and dynasties. This, he maintains, is an unusual success for a religious movement, as other traditions, including Christianity, have suffered from such divisions. Islam, he contends, was exposed to similar risks in its very first century, with the rise of Shiism, the emergence of Kharijis, and the birth of dynastic rule, but 'something of historic moment occurred' when the Sunni community united itself behind four Islamic schools of law (Winter 2014b). The emergence of these madhhabs, he maintains, helped to overcome the challenge posed by people drawing on Sunnah without having a method to test its validity.

Winter notes how the science of Islamic jurisprudence (usul al-fiqh) was developed to provide 'consistent mechanisms' for resolving any conflicts in a way which ensured that the basic ethos of Islam was not violated (Winter 2014b). Arguing that the term *ta'arud al-adillah* (mutual contradiction of proof-texts) is one of the most sensitive and complex of all Muslim legal concepts, he notes: 'The ulama of *usul* recognised as their starting assumption that conflicts between the revealed texts were no more than conflicts of interpretation, and could not reflect inconsistencies in the Lawgiver's message as conveyed by the Prophet (pbuh). The message of Islam had been perfectly conveyed before his demise; and the function of subsequent scholars was exclusively one of interpretation, not of amendment' (Winter 2014b). Winter further notes that, due to a shared conviction that Islam is a complete religion which has only to be interpreted for each time and not amended, the scholars from these four schools of law developed specific methodological tools to agree upon how to interpret the Quran, check the validity of the Sunnah, and settle any dispute or conflict within these two foundational sources.

This article is important because it helps to illustrate how, in a very concise and accessible manner, Winter explains to the reader not just the importance of the madhhabs but also the logical methods of reasoning that Islamic legal scholars evolved to settle differences of understanding in the text. He explains that any apparent difference in what was said on a given issue in the Quran or hadith was to be resolved through three steps: one, the text was to be linguistically examined to ensure that the contradiction did not arise due to an error in interpreting the Arabic; two, the scholars had to draw on a range of textual, legal, and historiographic techniques, to see if a textual source fell into the category of *takhsis*, that is, concerning special circumstances only, and hence forming a specific exception to the more general principle being discussed; three, the status of reports had to be assessed, whereby a Quranic verse overruled a hadith related by only one *isnad* (chain of transmission accompanying the hadith), as would a hadith supported by many isnads. If conflict were to persist, then the jurist had an obligation to assess whether one of the texts was subject to *naskh* (formal abrogation) by the other. Winter explains the concept of naskh by referring to the case of gradual prohibition on wine consumption in the Quran. He notes how in the Quranic verse it was first discouraged, then subsequently condemned, and later finally prohibited. Sometimes this progression, he explains, is easy to trace (*naskh sarih*); at other times it requires extensive research (*dimmi*). As he notes: 'The former is easily identified, for it involves texts which themselves specify that an earlier ruling is being changed ... The other type of *naskh* is more subtle, and often taxed the brilliance of the early ulama to the limit. It involves texts which cancel earlier ones, or modify them substantially, but without actually stating that this has taken place' (Winter 2014b).

This summary of Winter's efforts to explain to the ordinary Muslim reader the rigorous and logical methodology underlying Islamic classical scholarship on law helps to illustrate the way in which the Islamic rationalist scholars tailor their message for a broader audience. They keep their writings, their lectures, and their sermons accessible to a modern-educated Muslim who has had no exposure to formal study of Islamic sciences; yet, while keeping it simple, they also manage to communicate the complexity of the Islamic sciences and their strong foundation in logic.

It is this balance between bringing out the richness and complexity of Islamic sciences while communicating concepts in an accessible manner that makes these scholars popular. As we can see in this same article, Winter goes on to pin-point the specific methodology evolved by Imam Shafi'i to resolve conflicts in source-texts. He notes how Shafi'i's system of minimising mistakes in the derivation of Islamic rulings from the mass of evidence, which came to be known as usul al-fiqh, proved highly influential in accurately deriving the shari'ah from the revealed sources. But here Winter is also keen to emphasise that the method developed by Imam Shafi'i, as in the case of other formal academic disciplines of Islam, was not an innovation in the negative sense, but a working out of principles 'already discernible in the time of the earliest Muslims' (Winter 2014b). Winter credits the development of usul al-fiqh for ending the conflicts over the interpretations of shari'ah that marked the earlier two centuries. Abu Hanifa, Malik ibn Anas, al-Shafi'i, and Ibn Hanbal, who founded the four madhhabs, as Winter argues, developed 'sophisticated techniques for avoiding innovation, their traditions were fully systematised only by later generations of scholars ... But within each *madhhab* leading scholars continued to improve and refine the roots and branches of their school ... This type of process continued for two centuries, until the Schools reached a condition of maturity in the fourth and fifth centuries of the Hijra' (Winter 2014b).

He further notes how, as the madhhabs matured, an attitude of toleration and mutual respect among the scholars of the four schools became the norm. This mutual tolerance is again credited to Imam al-Ghazali, who, as Winter notes, established the practice among the Sunni 'ulama whereby even when they strictly followed one madhhab (*taqlid*), they did not regard the other madhhabs as wrong. Defending the importance of following the madhhabs and consulting scholars who specialise in Islamic sciences instead of interpreting the text for oneself, Winter notes:

Scholarship takes a lot of time, and for the ummah to function properly most people must have other employment ... The Holy Quran itself states that less well-informed believers should have recourse to qualified experts: 'So ask the people of remembrance, if you do not know' (16:43) ... And in another verse, the Muslims are enjoined to create and maintain a group of specialists who provide authoritative guidance for non-specialists: 'A band from each community should stay behind to gain instruction in religion and to warn the people when they return to them, so that they may take heed' (9:122). (Winter 2014b)

Noting the pitfalls involved in interpreting the text without consulting a scholar, Winter notes that without good command of Arabic a large portion of hadith remains inaccessible, as not all have been translated into English (Winter 2014b): 'To attempt to discern the Shariah merely on the basis of the *hadiths* which have been translated will be to ignore and amputate much of the Sunnah, hence leading to serious distortions.' This respect for the madhhabs and the detailed methods they evolved to engage with Islamic sources makes these scholars very critical of the Salafis as well as the twentieth-century Islamic reformers such as Muhammad Abduh and Rashid Rida, whom many credit with trying to make Islam meet the challenges of modern times. Unimpressed by their efforts, Winter comments that 'dazzled by the triumph of the West [Muhammad Abduh and Rashid Rida] urged Muslims to throw off the shackles of taqlid ... Today in some Arab capitals ... it is common to see young Arabs filling their homes with every *hadith* collection they can lay their hands upon, and poring over them in the apparent belief that they are less likely to misinterpret this vast and complex literature than Imam al-Shafi'i, Imam Ahmad, and the other great Imams' (Winter 2014b). Winter concludes by asserting that the late Said Ramadan al-Buti's, one of the most prominent Islamic scholars in Syria in recent times, was right that non-madhhabism is the greatest *bid'ah* threatening the Islamic Shari'ah.

In this short article, Winter thus gives to his readers a very inspirational account of the methodological sophistication of early Islamic legal scholarship, its relevance for all times, and the need for its revival to protect Muslims from the simplistic approaches of the Salafis and modernists. In this article, Winter thus in very simple language illustrates what Walbridge (2011) explains at the level of more philosophical debates about the adoption of rational methods in the development of Islamic science, citing the specific case of Islamic law. Much of the actual teachings of these rationalist scholars is thus focused on the study of classical Islamic legal texts. This effort to revive knowledge about the madhhabs and their importance to young Muslims (most of whom have no clear concept of what a madhhab means, let alone the specific method of reasoning that each madhhab evolved) is one of the major contributions of these scholars and a basis of their claim to be representing traditional Islam. This coherence of the classical Islamic scholarly tradition and logical foundations is an issue that also arises when these scholars explain the appeal of Islam over Christianity.

Thus, when it comes to the first of the three components of Hadith Jibril, namely *Islam*, the rationalist scholars are first of all keen to highlight the need for Muslims to re-engage with the madhhabs and to appreciate the logical methods developed by early Muslim scholars that are still just as relevant today, to make the shari'ah inform contemporary challenges. Second, by emphasising the importance of madhhabs, these scholars argue for recognising the role of 'ulama and Islamic jurists in interpreting Islamic law, just as one would expect in any field of academic inquiry. Third, by highlighting the legitimacy of all four madhhabs instead of building a defence of one, they encourage pluralism, internal debate, and tolerance within the Muslim community, which to them is the essential appeal of Islam. Most of these scholars themselves follow Malaki or Shafi'i tradition, but they are equally respectful of the Hanafi and Hanbali schools.

Iman: 'Aqidah

Developing a better understanding of what is iman, the second component of Hadith Jibril, which emphasises the essentials of Islamic 'aqidah, similarly remains central to the teachings of the rationalist scholars. In teaching 'aqidah, their first key concern is to emphasise to young Muslims that conviction concerning the 'aqidah is at the core of the faith, and that a weak 'aqidah in turn leads to weak actual practice of Islam. As discussed in some detail above, their emphasis on developing a strong 'aqidah, however, does not call for a blind conviction; in line with the Ash'ari-Maturidi school of kalam, they are instead keen to demonstrate how Islamic 'aqidah can withstand critical reasoning. Further, an equally important aspect of their teaching on 'aqidah is to argue for focusing on the essentials of 'aqidah and for leaving the non-essentials out. These scholars are conscious that including too much in the 'aqidah empowers some to call others *kafirs* (non-believers). This is a problem attributed by these rationalist scholars to some of the extremist Wahhabi scholars, who in their view include less important matters in the 'aqidah and then label those who do not agree with their position on these matters as kafir. This emphasis on restricting the 'aqidah to the essentials is again reflective of the importance that the Islamic rationalist scholars believe Islam ascribes to tolerance; just as they argue for accepting the legitimacy of all four madhhabs, they argue for confining the 'aqidah to the essentials.[17]

---

[17] Hamid (2013) similarly notes that a minimal definition of orthodoxy was a major point of agreement among the traditionalist Islam network in which he includes scholars such as Tim Winter, Hamza Yusuf, Dr Umar Faruq Abd-Allah, Zaid Shakir, and Nuh Keller. He argues that this broad approach was agreed upon in order to reduce chances of dispute about core elements of the 'aqidah as the network was coming together in the mid-1990s.

Just as one of Tim Winter's articles was useful in explaining the rationalist scholars' understanding of shari'ah and their appreciation of the logical foundation of the madhhabs, another of his articles, 'Reason as Balance: The Evolution of 'Aql', is important in highlighting how he and his fellow scholars understand Islamic rationalism. The article helps to illustrate their conviction that real human *'aql* (intellect) requires not just rational intellectual reasoning but also the inner spiritual dimensions that are regulated by the heart; it is this emphasis that separates Western rationalism from Islamic rationalism. As he argues: 'Contrasting itself with some evolved forms of the earlier religions, the new faith [Islam] announced itself as neither purely legalistic nor purely spiritualising' (Winter 2010: 1). It is this neglect of the inner dimensions that makes him particularly critical of the modernist reformers in the twentieth century, such as Muhammad Abduh and Rashid Rida, who, he argues, due to their focus on showing Islam as a progressive force when faced by Western pressures, attempted to show 'the Quran as the quintessence of *'aql*, or intellect'. Such an approach, he contends, made these scholars particularly critical of all forms of tasawwuf and Sufism, which to some of them appeared as an 'escape from the city of reason to the wilderness where God can be found' (Winter 2010: 2).

He instead argues that most Muslims experience Islam not simply as a set of arguments, 'but as a dithyramb which irresistibly transforms the soul' (Winter 2010: 3). To advance his argument, Winter (2010: 5) notes how the Quran acts as healing, as a balm for the heart:

The scripture seems to imply that our tragedy is an ignorant alienation from the Real, wherein lies all wholeness and appropriateness, and that only Heaven can send down the rain which revives the hearts. Whether it saves through its calligraphy or its cantillation, the Book does not seem to be saving through reason; it does not deny it, but it insists on 'descending upon your heart' (2:97), for its Author is not reached by the faculties of perception (6:103).

Noting that reliance on reason alone can be seriously misguiding, leading to errors such as pride, he refers to the example of Iblis (Satan), who uses his reason to defy God's command to prostrate himself before Adam. Reason, 'the steed of the formal theologians', he notes, 'is a noble part of God's creation, but is desperately slow and limited' (Winter 2010: 6). The Quran, Winter (2010: 6) notes, 'seems to be the authentic root of two disciplines whose mutual relations are controversial: formal systematic theology (*kalam*) and Sufism (*tasawwuf*).' He refers to the Prophet's own mysticism, exemplified in vital episodes of his life, such as the Ascension (*mi'raj*); elaborating on it, Winter (2010: 8) notes that it 'was not a kind of affective rapture disconnected from the rest of *'aql* or *fiqh*; it was simply one of its dramatic expressions and outcomes.' Noting that this was the original wisdom, Winter (2010: 8) adds that this 'ultimately found expression in the seemingly curious Ash'arite belief in physical soul'. In primal Islam, he concludes,

> the Mu'tazilite theologians who emerged towards the end of this period seem to have been the first to have proposed such a tension (*'aql* against *naql*, or tradition) ... In primal Islam, the word *'aql* thus had a supple, comprehensive meaning ... Such examples could be multiplied; yet it is clear that the new religion valued reason and intelligence highly, in a versatile and intuitive way that implies a broader definition than the contemporary understanding of 'intellect.'
> (Winter 2010: 8)

He notes how Sachiko Murata and William Chittick have reflected exhaustively on this inner Islamic metabolism, identifying kalam with the principle of drawing inferences about God as Transcendence (*tanzih*); and Sufism as Immanence (*tashbih*). He emphasises how these two scholars have made wonderful contributions by showing how the 99 names of God themselves capture this balance by including both the Names of Rigour and the Names of Beauty. Scholars who work on such philosophical and mystical dimensions of Islam are also frequently invited to Zaytuna's term-time seminar series, which are open to the public.[18]

Thus, Winter (2010: 7–8) notes: 'As though to refute those who characterise Muslim theology as denying the rationality of God, he [Ghazali] insists that formal rules of logic have an objective validity which must characterise God's power and acts. As his own career implies, however, he regards experience, or what he calls "tasting" (*dhawq*) as superior; although it can never challenge the truths known in theology; rather it supplies a more authentic proof for them.' Winter (2010: 10) further adds:

---

[18] Alexander Key, Assistant Professor at Stanford, who specialises in classical Arabic literature, was, for example, one of the speakers hosted at Zaytuna College in November 2017. He talked about his book, *Language between God and the Poets: Ma'na in the Eleventh Century*, which explores how, in the eleventh century, scholars were intensely preoccupied with the way that language generated truth and beauty. The book shows how scholars such as Ibn Sina and others developed a conceptual vocabulary based around the words *ma'na* and *haqiqah* to build theories of language, mind, and reality that answered perennial questions: how to structure language and reference, how to describe God, how to construct logical arguments, and how to explain poetic affect.

As Ghazali reminded his generation, the purpose of every form of revealed law was to remind its practitioners of God, and this 'reminder' (*dhikr*) required a consciousness that was inseparable from reason. *Fiqh*, later restricted to the sense of ritual and positive law, in its original Prophetic sense denotes intelligence itself ... Far from rejecting reason as a path to truth, Ghazali is advocating it, but a reason that, as with the *'aql* of the first Muslims, is detached, versatile and sober, rather than schematic, proud and indifferent to other indispensable dimensions of human totality.

In sum, the logical basis of Islamic 'aqidah remains important in the teaching of these scholars, but the notion of intellect is not one limited to the rationality of one's thought process. Instead it equally encompasses the inner experiences of one's soul. It is this balance that differentiates Islamic rationalism from how rationality is understood in the Western scholarly tradition.

Ihsan: Tasawwuf

Given what has so far been explained about the approach of these rationalist scholars, it should not be a surprise that tasawwuf, or an explicit focus on the working or purification of one's soul, is critical to their reading of ihsan, the third and final component of Hadith Jibril. As spelt out in Hadith Jibril, ihsan requires cultivating such purity of the inner soul that one is always aware of being in the presence of God. Developing such a purity of belief and action is, however, recognised to be a major challenge. Many might recite all five daily prayers and carry out the necessary rituals, including fasting and giving zakat, yet only a few ultimately reach such purity of faith. It is this effort to make one's each and every thought and action conform to Islamic moral and legal dictates that in the eyes of these scholars makes tasawwuf and Sufi teaching practices very important parts of Islam. In line with Ghazali's own experience, these scholars found tasawwuf to be the key to developing their own conviction in Islam. To understand why these scholars consider tasawwuf to be an important Islamic science, Nuh Keller's article, 'The Place of Tasawwuf in Traditional Islamic Sciences', is particularly useful.

In this article, Keller (1995) emphasises the importance of tasawwuf and Sufi practices by directly engaging with a core critique of Sufism advanced by its critics, namely that such a label did not exist in the Prophet's time. Keller in response draws on Ibn Khaldun's *Muqaddima* to argue that the term might not have existed but the practice did. He argues that formalisation of tasawwuf as a proper field of Islamic science developed in later centuries, as was the case with most Islamic sciences such as tafsir, Quranic exegesis, or *'ilm al-jarh wa ta'dil*, 'the science of the positive and negative factors that affect hadith narrators acceptability', or *'ilm al-tawhid*, 'the science of belief in Islamic tenets of faith' (Keller 1995). He notes how all these sciences developed after the death of the Prophet and were critical to the successful preservation and transmission of Islam. Drawing on Hadith Jibril, Keller (1995) emphasises how it is beyond any doubt that tasawwuf requires submission to the rules of sacred law. But this submission to the sacred law, he notes, equally requires tasawwuf. Asking why that is the case, Keller (1995) elaborates:

For the very good reason that the sunna which Muslims have been commanded to follow is not just the *words* and *actions* of the Prophet (Allah bless him and give him peace), but also his *states*, states of the heart such as *taqwa* 'godfearingness,' *ikhlas* 'sincerity,' *tawakkul* 'reliance on Allah,' *rahma* 'mercy,' *tawadu* 'humility,' and so on.

He then goes on to explain how tasawwuf is a science aimed at nurturing these states of piety and that it basically consists of 'dedication to worship, total dedication to Allah Most High, disregard for the finery and ornament of the world, abstinence from the pleasure, wealth, and prestige sought by most men, and retiring from others to worship alone' (Keller 1995).

Drawing on Ibn Khaldun again, Keller (1995) further argues that working to attain these inner stages of piety was the general rule among the Companions of the Prophet and the early Muslims, but with the rise of Islamic empires as Muslims became more attracted to this-worldly diversions, 'those devoted to worship came to be called *Sufiyya* or *People of Tasawwuf*'. Keller (1995) argues that Ibn Khaldun had noted that tasawwuf, which means total dedication to Allah Most High, was the general rule among the Companions of the Prophet and the early Muslims. Keller therefore asserts that the origin of the Sufi practice thus lies in the prophetic Sunnah. The sincerity to Allah that Sufi practice aims to cultivate, Keller argues, 'was the rule among the earliest Muslims, to whom this was simply a state of being without a name'. Muslims in subsequent generations, however, had thus to make systematic efforts to attain this level of purity; as Keller (1995) notes: 'and it was because of the change in the Islamic environment after the earliest generations, that a discipline by the name of Tasawwuf came to exist'.

The Islamic rationalist scholars thus emphasise the importance of tasawwuf by highlighting the need to purify one's inner self; they argue that Sufism is supported by evidence from within the prophetic Sunnah.

However, it is important to recognise a key difference between the approach of the scholars leading this rationalist network and that of Nuh Keller. As mentioned in Chapter 1 of this volume, Nuh Keller did actively appear alongside Hamza Yusuf on some platforms in the 1990s at the outset of their effort to promote da'wah in the West; however, soon their paths diverged, in view of their followers I have interviewed, due to their differing positions on the practice of taking *bay'ah* (oath of allegiance to one's shaykh). It is very important to appreciate that the scholars in this rationalist network do not operate as a Sufi tariqah. Hamza Yusuf is perceived to have deeper concern about the practice of bay'ah and does not encourage his students to take bay'ah, while Nuh Keller operates as a proper Sufi shaykh from the Naqshbandi Sufi order and takes bay'ah. During interviews in Toronto with individuals who had attended a joint retreat held by Nuh Keller and Hamza Yusuf in 1996, it became clear that this differing position on bay'ah led to open tension between the two scholars at the end of that retreat, when it came to light that Nuh Keller had taken bay'ahs from some of the student participants. Faraz Rabbani, who runs SeekersHub, was one of these young students. Hamza Yusuf was reportedly very upset, and this led to a serious discussion between the two scholars concerning their respective views of da'wah in the West.

Hamza Yusuf's main concern with bay'ah, as understood by those who were present at this retreat, is that it can lead to exploitation of young individuals, as the shaykhs may exercise excessive power over them. Thus, while being strongly committed to tasawwuf, Hamza Yusuf is not supportive of encouraging formalised Sufi tariqahs; or at least of being seen as promoting them. In view of some, Hamza Yusuf's reservation about taking bay'ah stems partly from his and Dr Umar's experience with Shayhk Abdalqadir as-Sufi Murabitun, an English Sufi convert from Norwich who was very influential among the Spanish Muslim community during the 1980s. It appears that Hamza Yusuf and Dr Umar had taken bay'ah with him during that time. Hamza Yusuf does not like to talk about the time spent with Shaykh Abdalqadir, but my fieldwork with members of the Spanish Muslim community in present-day Granada makes it clear that Shaykh Abdalqadir became a very divisive figure within this community, leading to its eventual break-up; Dr Umar and Hamza Yusuf were among the members who fell out with him. That experience could have played a role in making Hamza Yusuf apprehensive about promoting formal Sufi tariqahs or encouraging young Muslims to take bay'ah.

Ultimately, however, the reasons for his reservations about the formal-isation of Sufi tariqahs are less important. What is more important is to appreciate how this decision has played a key role in enabling the ration-alist scholars to attract Muslims from many different backgrounds. Some scholars within this network, such as Dr Umar, do take bay'ah in private, but they do not make it very public; I had, for example, attended many retreats with him but it was only when I visited him in Naperville, Chicago, where he lives, to conduct a series of longer interviews that I learned that every Sunday he holds a gathering where he also takes bay'ah from those seeking his guidance. Tim Winter also does not take bay'ah. During an interview with me, he was very clear that he does not feel qualified to take responsibility for someone's spiritual growth. The fact that these scholars do not take bay'ah, and a few who do prefer not to make it very public, is in my assessment key to the success of this movement: it has allowed Muslims from different orientations to gravi-tate towards it.

For the scholars in this rationalist network, tasawwuf thus remains critical to attaining the status of ihsan; it remains central to achieving inner harmony and inspiring all forms of beauty in human experience. Mystical poetry, good manners in engaging with everyone, and displays of fine aesthetics in the way one dresses and decorates personal and public space all become an extension of the spiritual harmony and inner beauty extending from the state of ihsan. It is therefore not surprising that both Tim Winter and Hamza Yusuf have often referred to the importance of appreciating beauty in one's surroundings and the role of poetry and the arts in nurturing the Islamic spirit; both have made this point with reference to the physical beauty of Turkish mosques and the quality of the Quranic recitations of the imams therein. As Tim Winter (2013) notes in his article, 'Ramadan in Istanbul': 'Some entirely secular souls will come to hear the Tarawih as they might attend the opera; and many have found God as a result.'

It is this subtle balance, whereby a logical defence of shari'ah, ration-alist theology, and deeper spirituality all come together to highlight Islam's ability to satisfy the intellect as well as the soul, that encompasses the importance of this movement. It is due to this balance that the scholars whose work is referenced from the classical Islamic scholarly tradition are neither the narrowly rationalist philosophers inspired by the Hellenistic debates nor rigid textualists; rather this movement draws on scholars, such as Imam Ghazali, who combined it all: law, theology, and tasawwuf.

3 ZAYTUNA'S PERENNIAL FACULTY: THE ROLE MODELS

In Section 2, I have drawn on writings, lectures, and interviews with this network of scholars to highlight their understanding of what they view to be the essence of authentic Islamic tradition; in this section, we will look somewhat more closely at the profile of the classical Islamic scholars whom they promote, as well as some of the contemporary scholars in the Muslim world with whom they actively associate. To develop this list, it is best to start by considering Zaytuna College's perennial faculty. This consists of a list of thirty medieval Islamic scholars who serve as models for Zaytuna. The table listing these thirty scholars on the Zaytuna College website is preceded by the following lines: 'A people disconnected from their past will never move confidently into the future. At Zaytuna College, we believe we must acknowledge and remain connected to the giants who have laid the intellectual and spiritual foundation upon which we aspire to build' (Zaytuna College 2018b). The full list of these scholars and their profiles as captured by Zaytuna College administration is presented in Table 2.1.

It is not surprising that Ghazali remains central on this list. We have addressed above the reasons he has been so important in influencing classical Islamic scholarly tradition, and how his work is central to the movement that aims to revive Islamic rationalism. Hamza Yusuf routinely talks about the importance of Ghazali as having 'this innate ability to transcend time and place'; he also notes the influence of Ghazali on Christian and Western thought. Further, he repeatedly reminds his listeners of the applicability and relevance of Ghazali's teachings to Muslims' current circumstances (Yusuf 2011b). In discussing the continued relevance of Ghazali, Yusuf emphasises the combination in his writings of the inward and outward elements of Islam, and the necessity for a Muslim to master both. Yusuf states that Ghazali, more than most scholars, understood the significance of these, to the point that even Ibn Taymiyya, who according to Yusuf took the opposite approach, relied upon Ghazali as an authority because of the value of his scholarly contributions, despite their differences (Yusuf 2011b).

The *Ihya'* remains very important to Yusuf, because it is a culmination of Ghazali's extensive works in law and theology as well as his experiences as a Sufi following his crisis of conscience in Baghdad. For Yusuf, this is the ultimate contribution of Ghazali. In a 2011 lecture entitled 'The Critical Importance of Al-Ghazali in Our Times' (Yusuf 2011b), delivered at a meeting of local Islamic organisations in Louisville, Kentucky, Yusuf

Table 2.1 *Zaytuna College Perennial Faculty*

1	**IMAM ABU DAWUD (d. AH 275, Basra)** Imam Abu Dawud (Sulayman b. al-Asha'ab b. Ishaq al-Azdi) was a master hadith scholar who collected many hadiths. He traveled in search of hadith throughout the Muslim world. He is the compiler of one of the seven major hadith collections, *Sunan Abu Dawud*.
2	**QADI ABU BAKR B. AL-'ARABI (d. AH 543, Fez)** Qadi Abu Bakr b. al-'Arabi (Muhammad b. 'Abd Allah b. Muhammad b. al-Mu'afiri) was a Maliki judge, hadith scholar, historian, and mujtahid; he traveled to the eastern Islamic world and studied with al-Ghazzali. His works include *Awasim min al-qawasim* and *Aridat al-ahwadi*, a commentary on Imam Tirmidhi's book. His exegesis on the Qur'an is entitled *Ahkam al-Qur'an*. He is commonly confused with the Andalusian Sufi Muhyi al-Din ibn 'Arabi.
3	**IMAM IBN HAJAR AL-'ASQALANI (d. AH 852, Cairo)** Imam Ibn Hajar al-'Asqalani (Ahmad b. Ali b. Muhammad) was originally from Asqalan (Palestine); early in his career he was interested in poetry and literature, later he turned to hadith and became a hadith scholar, encyclopedist, and historian. Though it was unusual at the time, his books became famous during his life. He was handsome, well to do, well traveled, and married scholarly women. He served as a judge in Egypt, and wrote a commentary on al-Bukhari, entitled *Fath al-Bari*, as well as histories and books on the hadith sciences, including biographies and assessments of accuracy of the chains of transmission. Al-Sakhawi, his student, wrote a grand biography of him, *Jawahir wa durar*.
4	***IMAM AL-BUKHARI* (d. AH 256, Khartang)** Imam al-Bukhari (Muhammad b. Ismail b. Ibrahim b. al-Mughira, Abu 'Abd Allah) is the undisputed hadith master, compiler of the famed Sahih, and considered by Muslims to be the most authentic source for prophetic traditions. Many believe his work is second in importance only to the Qur'an. Al-Bukhari was an orphan; by the time of his death he had memorized hundreds of thousands of hadith and traveled throughout the Islamic world in his efforts to verify chains of hadith transmission. He is said to have prayed two rak'as for guidance before writing any hadith in the Sahih; he wrote many other books, including two well-known histories: *al-Tarikh al-kabir* and *al-Tarikh al-saghir*, and a work on literature: *al-Adab al-mufrad*.
5	**IMAM SHAMS AL-DIN AL-DHAHABI (d. AH 748, Damascus)** Imam Shams al-Din al-Dhahabi (Muhammad b. Ahmad b. 'Uthman, Abu 'Abd Allah) was a historian, an expert in Qur'anic recitation, and a scholar of textual criticism of hadith. He wrote the twenty-three-volume *Siyar alam al-nubala'*, which is known for its accurate descriptions of

Table 2.1 (*cont.*)

	scholars, and a thirty-six volume history, *Tarikh al-Islam al-kabir*. Imam al-Dhahabi went blind seven years before his death.
6	**IMAM ABU HAMID AL-GHAZZALI (d. AH 505, Tus)** Imam al-Ghazzali (Muhammad b. Muhammad b. Muhammad b. Ahmad, Abu Hamid) traveled far and wide in search of knowledge. He was appointed professor in the prestigious Nizamiyah college in Baghdad, capital of Abbasid caliphate. He then left his teaching position for a life of asceticism. Al-Ghazzali was a Shafi'i jurist and perhaps the Islamic world's most famous Sufi author, popular until today for his very readable and clear works on Islam. His most famous work is *Ihya 'ulum al-din*. He wrote *Tahafut al-falasifah* as a refutation of metaphysics.
7	**IMAM 'ABD ALLAH B. ALAWI AL-HADDAD (*d. AH 1132, Hadramawt*)** Imam al-Haddad ('Abd Allah b. Alawi b. Muhammad) was a Sufi and author of many books, including poetry, and the following: *Aqidat al-tawhid*, *Da'wat al-tamma wa tadhkirah al-ammah*, *Tabsirat al-waliy*, and *Masa'ilat al-sufiyah*. He was blinded by chicken pox in his childhood; later in life, when oppressed by rulers of Tarim, he moved to al-Hawi. One of his students, Ahmad b. 'Abd al-Karim al-Shajjar, collected his sayings into a book entitled *Tathbit al-fu'ad*.
8	**IMAM IBN RAJAB AL-HANBALI (d. AH 795, Damascus)** Imam Ibn Rajab al-Hanbali ('Abd al-Rahman b. Ahmad) was a hadith scholar and jurist. He wrote a commentary on Imam Nawawi's al-Arba'in, making them fifty hadith and calling it *Jami' 'ulum wa al-hikam*. He also wrote important works on jurisprudence and an influential book on Hanbali methodology.
9	**IMAM RAGHIB AL-ISFAHANI (d. AH 502, Isfahan)** Imam al-Isfahani (Abu al-Qasim al-Husayn b. Muhammad b. al-Mufaddal) was the author of *al-Mufradat fi gharib al-Qur'an*, a dictionary of uncommon terms in the Qur'an; he was known for his sharp intellect and quick mind.
10	**IMAM IBN 'ATA' ALLAH AL-ISKANDARI (d. AH 709, Cairo)** Imam Ibn 'Ata' Allah al-Iskandari (Ahmad b. Muhammad b. 'Abd al-Karim) was a Sufi imam and second in succession to al-Shadhili. He was the author of *al-Hikam al-'Ata'iyah*, a significant work in the Shadhiliyah order. He adhered to the Maliki school with Shafi'i leanings, and taught at al-Azhar.
11	**IMAM IBN QAYYIM AL-JAWZIYAH (d. AH 751, Damascus)** Imam Ibn Qayyim al-Jawziyah (Muhammad b. Abu Bakr b. Ayyub) was one of the most famous students of Ibn Taymiyah; he was imprisoned with his shaykh in the citadel of Damascus. He is the author

Table 2.1　(*cont.*)

	of many works on theology, jurisprudence, and Sufism; he wrote *Zad al-ma'ad* while traveling on pilgrimage. His work *'Ilam al-muwaqqi'in* is a book on the foundations of jurisprudence. He also wrote on many aspects of earthly life, such as love, and he authored a comprehensive work on the effects of Satan on human affairs (*Ighathat al-lafhan*).
12	**IMAM 'ABD AL-QADIR AL-JILANI (d. AH 561, Baghdad)** Imam 'Abd al-Qadir al-Jilani ('Abd al-Qadir b. Musa b. 'Abd Allah, Abu Muhammad) was one of the great mystics of Islam and the founder of the Qadiri sufi order. He wrote *al-Fath al-Rabbani, Futuh al-ghayb, Fuyudat al-Rabbani*, and *al-Ghunya li-talibi tariq al-haqq*.
13	**IMAM AL-JUWAYNI (d. AH 478, Nishapur)** Imam al-Juwayni was a Shafi'i jurist and theologian; the Nizamiyah school in Nishapur was built for him by Nizam al-Mulk. He wrote *al-Burhan* (lit., the proof) and *al-Waraqat* (lit., paper sheets, a popular manual set to verse that many memorized); extensive commentaries; a work on the principles of Islamic jurisprudence; and many works on theology, among which are *al-Irshad* and *al-Shamil*. Imam al-Ghazzali was among his most famous students.
14	**IMAM AL-MUZNI (d. AH 264, Egypt)** Imam al-Muzni (Ismail b. Yahya b. Ismail, Abu Ibrahim) was a student of Imam Shafi'i, and a Shafi'i scholar in his own right. He was considered a key promoter of al-Shafi'i's school and wrote *al-Mukhtasar*, a summary of the school's rulings.
15	**IMAM AL-NAWAWI (d. AH 676, Nawa)** Imam al-Nawawi (Yahya b. Sharaf Abu Zakariyah Muhyi al-Din) was an imam of the later Shafi'i school, the author of *Riyad al-salihin* and *Minhaj al-talibin*. He wrote but did not complete his commentary on Sahih al-Bukhari; his complete commentary on Muslim's Sahih is considered to be among the best in its class. He authored *al-Arba'in*, or *Forty* [hadiths], and many other works. He was known for his brave political stance and successfully petitioned the Mamluk sultan Rukn al-Din Baybars on behalf of Damascene residents who sought relief from heavy tax burdens during a drought that lasted many years.
16	**IMAM AL-QURTUBI (d. AH 671, Egypt)** Imam al-Qurtubi (Muhammad b. Ahmad b. Abu Bakr, Abu 'Abd Allah al-Ansari) was a scholar of hadith, theology or creed (aqidah), and author of the extensive Qur'anic commentary, *al-Jami' li-ahkam al-Qur'an*. He also wrote on Arabic grammar and the science of Qur'anic recitation.
17	**FAKHR AL-DIN AL-RAZI (d. AH 606, Herat)** Fakhr al-Din al-Razi (Muhammad b. Umar b. Hasan b. al-Husayn, Abu 'Abd Allah) was an encyclopedist; he wrote on theology, philosophy,

Table 2.1 *(cont.)*

	medicine, and a Qur'an exegesis (*Mufatih al-ghayb*), described by scholars as everything but Qur'anic commentary, because he included philosophy, theology, grammar, rhetoric, and more. He was known for his many public debates, which sometimes incited crowds and mobs against him. He was a luminary and a scholar's scholar. He wrote a great work (*al-Mahsul*) on the principles of Islamic jurisprudence; considered a main text of the discipline.
18	**IMAM AL SAKHAWI (d. AH 902, Cairo)** Imam al-Sakhawi (Muhammad b. 'Abd al-Rahman b. Muhammad) was a Shafi'i jurist known for his biographies and histories, including *al-'Alan bi-al-tawbikh li man thamma ahl al-tarikh*, a work on historiography. He was Ibn Hajar al-'Asqalani's neighbor and student; he traveled throughout the Islamic world, to Mecca, Medina, Damascus, and throughout Syria; ultimately he returned to Cairo where he taught hadith.
19	**IMAM AL-SHAFI'I (d. AH 204, Cairo)** Imam al-Shafi'i (Muhammad b. Idris b. al-Abbas, Abu 'Abd Allah al-Qurayshi al-Makki) studied with Imam Malik and Abu Hanifah's students in Baghdad, then moved to Egypt and founded the later Shafi'i school. He authored *al-Umm* and *al-Risalah*, the original work on usul al-fiqh (Islamic jurisprudential principles). He traveled far and wide throughout the Muslim world in search of knowledge and spent time with Bedouins in order to learn classical Arabic before it was corrupted and changed by the growing Muslim world.
20	**IMAM TAJ AL-DIN AL-SUBKI (d. AH 711, Cairo)** Imam Taj al-Din al-Subki ('Abd al-Wahhab b. 'Ali b. 'Abd al-Kafi, Abi Nasr) was a Shafi'i jurist and the author of *Tabaqat al-Shafi'iyah al-kubra*, a comprehensive biography of Shafi'i scholars arranged chronologically, then alphabetically. Al-Subki was from a long line of scholars; his father was Taqi al-Din al-Subki, a contemporary of Ibn Taymiyah with whom he had many public debates.
21	**IMAM JALAL AL-DIN AL-SUYUTI (d. AH 911, Cairo)** Imam Jalal al-Din al-Suyuti ('Abd al-Rahman b. Abu Bakr b. Muhammad, Jalal al-Din) was a polymath: a hadith master, historian, and exegete. He is one of the famed Jalals of the Tafsir al-jalalayn. He grew up an orphan in Cairo; at the age of forty, he gave up successful work teaching and committed himself to writing books; and completed over five hundred books in various disciplines. Al-Suyuti wrote perhaps the most comprehensive manual on Qur'anic sciences, *al-Itqan fi 'ulum al-Qur'an*, which he completely revised upon finding more source material. His autobiography is *Tahadath bi na'mat Allah*; it is unique in Muslim literature.

Table 2.1 (*cont.*)

22	**IMAM ABU JA'FAR AL-TABARI (d. AH 314, Baghdad)** Imam al-Tabari (Muhammad b. Jarir, Abu Ja'far) is most known as a historian, jurisprudent, and Qur'an scholar. He founded his own school of fiqh (al-Jaririyah) and wrote a commentary on the Qur'an, *Jami' al-bayan*, commonly known as *Tafsir al-Tabari*, as well as *Tarikh al-rusul wa muluk*, a multi-volume history.
23	**IMAM ABU JAF'AR AL-TAHAWI (d. AH 321, Cairo)** Imam al-Tahawi (Ahmad b. Muhammad b. Salama, Abu Ja'far) was a Hanafi jurist and a hadith scholar who studied at al-Azhar. He studied with al-Muzni and was a Shafi'i jurist, then with Ahmad b. Imran and followed the Hanafi school. He is known for his work *al-Aqidah al-Tahawiyah*, a concise summary of the essentials of the Islamic creed. He wrote a commentary on the Qur'an and a work on hadith entitled *Mushkil al-Athar*.
24	**QADI AYYAD (d. AH 544, Marrakesh)** Qadi Ayyad was a Maliki scholar of hadith and Arabic, and the author of *al-Shifa'*, a biography of the Prophet Muhammad. He also wrote on hadith, including works on al-Muwtta' and a highly regarded commentary on Sahih Muslim. His works on the hadith sciences continue to be studied by scholars today.
25	**IMAM AHMAD IBN ASHIR (d. AH 1163, Sila)** Imam Ibn Ashir (Ahmad b. Ashir b. 'Abd al-Rahman al-Hafi al-Silawi) wrote a book titled *al-Fahrasta*, biographies of famous scholars of his time; and wrote *Tuhfat al-za'ir*, a biography of Ahmad b. Muhammad b. 'Umar b. Ashir al-Andalusi who died in 764 or 765.
26	**IMAM AHMAD B. HANBAL (d. AH 241, Baghdad)** Ibn Ahmad b. Hanbal (Ahmad b. Muhammad b. Hanbal, Abu 'Abd Allah al-Shaybani) was a scholar of hadith who traveled for sixteen years throughout the Islamic world in an effort to gather hadith. He memorized one million hadith, thirty thousand of which were recorded in his famous work, *al-Musnad*. He survived the trials (al-mihna) over the createdness of the Qur'an, a doctrine advocated by the Mut'azili, who had persuaded the Abbasid caliph to adopt the position and enforce adherence to it.
27	**QADI IBN KHALDUN (d. AH 808, Cairo)** Qadi Ibn Khaldun ('Abd al-Rahman b. Muhammad b. Muhammad b. Muhammad) originally trained as a government employee and served under various rulers; his involvement in many (failed) usurpations led to his retirement from politics. He emigrated to Cairo, but in the course of the journey lost his family and all his property in a shipwreck off the coast of Alexandria, Egypt. In Egypt he was appointed a Maliki judge (and dismissed and reappointed many times); there he wrote his most

Table 2.1 *(cont.)*

	famous work, *al-Muqaddimah*. This book is considered the first work on sociology and historiography, a science that he invented. Ibn Khaldun's history, *Kitab al-'ibar*, is one of the first detailed Berber histories. He was, during his long and eventful life, also ambassador (from Damascus) to Tamerlane.
28	**IMAM MALIK B. ANAS (d. AH 179, Medina)** Imam Malik (Malik b. Anas b. Malik) was a jurist and founder of the school of Islamic law that bears his name; he wrote the famous book of hadith, *al-Muwatta'*, which is known for taking into consideration the practice of the people of Medina. He is also considered part of the golden chain of narration, the most authentic chain to be found in Bukhari and Muslim. Imam al-Shafi'i was one of his most well known students.
29	**RABI'AH AL-'ADAWIYYAH (d. AH 185, Jerusalem)** Rabi'ah al-'Adawiyyah is, in the view of some, the first woman Sufi. Born in Basra to a destitute family, she eventually accepted the mystic path, became an ascetic under the tutelage of Hasan al-Basri, and later introduced her own spiritual insights to the Sufi tradition. In particular, she is the source of the concept of Divine Love (mahabbah), which emphasizes that an ascetic's motivation in worship and the service of God should be love, not hope or fear.
30	**IMAM AHMAD ZARRUQ (d. AH 899, Takrin)** Imam Ahmad Zarruq (Ahmad ibn Ahmad ibn Muhammad ibn 'Isa) was a scholar from Fes, Morocco. He was orphaned of both his mother and father within the first seven days of his birth. His grandmother, an accomplished jurist, raised him and was his first teacher. He later became one of the most prominent and accomplished legal, theoretical, and spiritual scholars in Islamic history, and is considered by some to be a renewer of his time (mujaddid). He was also the first to be given the honorific title "Regulator of the Scholars and Saints" (muhtasib al-'ulama' wa al-awliya').

Source: Zaytuna College (2018b).

describes Ghazali as seeking to emphasise spiritual presence – that is, the state of being wholly present and mentally involved in one's life, to carry out one's religious duties and responsibilities not as a chore or unconscious exercise but as a meaningful activity that demands one's attention and focus, no matter how small the task. Awareness of one's being and deeds is necessary for living a full, pious life. Yusuf states that one should not treat prayer as a rote activity to be completed before moving on to other things, but as an act of worship that requires one's mental involvement, a denial of other things going on around the person to focus on the communication with the spiritual and divine. He talks about the importance of ihsan in Ghazali's message, which Yusuf links to the necessity of moral action outside of oneself. He argues that the essence of ihsan is 'to do something valuable and productive with your life, to leave the world better for having you in it'. This is a continuous goal, and the nature of humanity demands constant reminders that death is near, and moral action cannot be put off to a later date. Yusuf argues that this is the primary message of the *Ihya'*: that living a good life requires knowledge and spiritual awareness, but also constant vigilance against the self and the lesser appetites that distract people from what is good. Yusuf states that Ghazali understood tawhid not as an abstract philosophical concept, but as a necessary focus on God to the exclusion of everything else, including oneself. Yusuf calls Ghazali an iconoclast, who 'wants to tear down the idol of the ego'. The *Ihya'* better than any other work encapsulates this necessary message (Yusuf 2011b).

Yusuf has produced an oral translation and commentary on Ghazali's *Alchemy of Happiness* and the Persian-language abridgement of the *Ihya'*, which he recorded as part of a Rihla session from 2006 (Yusuf 2006a). Similarly, the *Purification of the Heart*, a poem by the Mauritanian Sufi saint and scholar Muhammad al-Mawlud al-Ya'qubi (d. 1905) that Yusuf translated and commented upon, is based largely on the *Ihya'*. Yusuf's commentary focuses on the idea that the weaknesses in society are due to the weaknesses in people's hearts, in their inner purity. Learning and spiritual awareness are the keys to rectifying those weaknesses, and Yusuf makes constant reference to Ghazali in his commentary (Yusuf 2006a).

Other scholars listed in Zaytuna's perennial faculty share a similar emphasis on shari'ah as well as cultivation of inner spirituality. Ahmad Zarruq, the sixteenth-century Moroccan Maliki Sufi jurist, listed in Table 2.1, is also an important member of Zaytuna's perennial faculty to whose writings Hamza Yusuf refers frequently. In his book on Zarruq, Kugle (2006) highlights the important role that Hamza Yusuf has played in introducing Zarruq's work to Muslims in the West; he notes that for Yusuf, Zarruq is an exemplar of inward-directed Sufi spirituality, 'but contained – and constrained – within a framework of mainstream, legalistic piety' (Kugle 2006). Both Ghazali and Zarruq were legalistic Sufis who understood Sufism in terms of inward spirituality that requires a basis in conventional religious learning and should be directed towards moral action. In addition, they both criticised what they saw as morally deficient practices, among both the 'ulama and fellow Sufis, particularly in terms of sectarianism, which they saw as harmful to the community. Yusuf thus draws on medieval scholars who combined Sufi influence with conventional scholarship into a moderate, spiritually focused, piety-minded view of Islam. The same could be said of the Egyptian Shafi'i scholar Jalal al-Din Suyuti (d. 1502), whose works feature in Zaytuna's curriculum and whom Yusuf has cited as an authority. Similarly, Hamza Yusuf likes to quote the work of contemporary scholars who in his view are representative of this approach but are not well known among modern-educated Muslims. Yusuf has been instrumental in making Shaykh Bin Bayyah, a Mauritanian Sufi-jurist, popular among Muslim audiences in the West; he acts as Bin Bayyah's official translator when the latter has to address an English-speaking audience. As Bin Bayyah's website highlights, his goal is to 'revive the tradition of "Islamic humanities" by teaching the comprehensiveness of Islamic theology, the rationalism of Islamic law, and the subtleties of Arabic language and poetry'.

4 ISLAMIC RATIONALISM AND THE MODE OF TEACHING

The preceding sections have explained in detail how the Islamic rationalist movement conceptualises traditional Islam. This section will highlight how this dual emphasis on acquiring legalistic knowledge of shari'ah and purifying one's inner self has implications for the teaching methods that these scholars adopt. Their focus is not solely on communicating to young Muslims the core principles of Islam but equally on helping them to experience the inner mystical dimensions of the faith through participation in retreats, performance of collective rituals, and acting as role models. Thus, in reviving the authentic Islamic tradition these scholars are also re-emphasising the authentic modes of Islamic knowledge transmission. They are thus very clear that without securing an ijazah from a traditionally trained teacher one must not teach. As Winter (2014b) notes in his article on the importance of madhhabs, today the lack of traditional scholars in Islamic law, hadith and tafsir has given rise to an understanding of the religion that is not true. That the Salafis and the modernists attempt to interpret Quran and hadith without engaging with more detailed commentaries or having training in Islamic sciences is a serious concern for these scholars. Apart from the risk that such an approach poses of misinterpretation of the text, in their view it also entirely neglects the focus on personal training and the importance of making the students absorb the Islamic moral and ethical code in their everyday lives.

In the next chapter, we will see that all these scholars consciously chose to study with authorities who were trained through the traditional Islamic scholarly platforms where the teachers claim a continuous chain of transmission from the Prophet and his companions. Their emphasis on showing respect for one's teacher is highlighted in the humility and gratitude that they express towards their teachers in their speeches and writings.

Reviving the Great Books

The other important aspect of the rationalist scholars' teaching method is to focus on teaching a major Islamic text in detail, as was traditionally the case in madrasahs, as opposed to developing a syllabus consisting of a combination of books. In traditional Islamic education platforms, the learning was measured according to which great texts a student had studied in detail with an established scholar; further, the major books were seen as a complete syllabus, whereby each and every part had to be studied in detail. The emphasis that scholars in this network place on reviving the study of major texts is best illustrated by looking at the online courses offered by SeekersHub in the area of fiqh, 'aqidah, tasawwuf, Quranic Studies, and the Arabic language, in addition to a few others. Each course is eight to twelve weeks long and normally focuses on a specific text. For example, its hadith course focuses on the study of major hadith books such as Sahih Bukhari; its fiqh courses aim to cover classical texts from the Malaki, Shafi'i, and Hanafi traditions; and its tasawwuf courses especially draw on works by Imam Ghazali. Yahya Rodhus, who teaches the Ghazali texts on SeekersHub online courses, adopts a similar approach at his newly established al-Maqasid Institute. While a proper Islamic Studies programme is being developed, teaching focused on the study of specific books has already started. The 2016 fall classes focused on *Mafahim Yajib an Tusahhah* (Notions that Must Be Corrected) by Shaykh Muhammad Alawi al-Maliki. The al-Maqasid Institute advertises this book as being a 'masterpiece in which Shaykh Muhammad Alawi al-Maliki offers words of caution against extremism and invites the Muslims to the path of Ahl al-Sunnah wal-Jama'ah, the hallmark of which is tolerance and moderation. Sayyid Muhammad expertly clarifies the correct position relating to numerous "controversial" contemporary topics whilst maintaining strict adherence to the Quran, the Sunnah, and the way of the Salaf' (al-Maqasid 2018).

Similarly, Hamza Yusuf, as noted in the preceding section, has played a key role in reviving classical Islamic texts from earlier generations for his listeners; Kugle (2006) highlights the role played by Hamza Yusuf in reviving Zarruq's work in the West. Scott (2013), citing his interview with Hamza Yusuf, notes how he regards his own role in introducing prominent Islamic scholars from the past to Muslims in the West as one of his main contributions. Re-engaging with books by these great scholars is, in the view of Hamza Yusuf, the key to reversing the disconnection from their real intellectual heritage that many Muslims feel:

> Our real situation is this: we Muslims have lost theologically sound understanding of our teaching. Islam has been hijacked by a discourse of anger and the rhetoric of rage. We have allowed for too long our minbars to become bully pulpits in which people with often recognizable psychopathology use anger – a very powerful emotion – to rile Muslims up, only to leave them feeling bitter and spiteful towards people who in the most part are completely unaware of the conditions in the Muslim world, or the oppressive assaults of some Western countries on Muslim peoples. We have lost our bearings because we have lost our theology. We have almost no theologians in the entire Muslim world. The study of *kalaam*, once the hallmark of our intellectual tradition, has been reduced to memorizing 144 lines of al-Jawhara and a good commentary to study it, at best. (Yusuf 2018a)

Hamza Yusuf's emphasis on reviving the great books is also evident in the curriculum of Zaytuna College, which focuses on the study of major classical texts from the Islamic tradition as well as the Western tradition. Here Hamza Yusuf is also inspired by the 'Great Books' movement, which started in the United States in the 1930s at the University of Chicago, in addition to the traditional Islamic training that he received, especially in Mauritania. This movement focused on what were seen as Great Books that represent the best in their field and must therefore be read. All kinds of books, fiction and non-fiction, could fall into this category, going all the way back to the ancient Greeks. The main objective of this movement was that 'the broad accessibility and reading of great books would result in liberal education for all that would bring about a democratized culture' (Lacy 2013: 6). Hamza Yusuf's father studied one of the Great Books courses at Columbia University, and he was so influenced by it that he named Hamza Yusuf (Mark Hanson) after the teacher who had taught that course, Mark Van Doren. In its description of a Muslim Liberal arts education, Zaytuna College quotes Hutchins (1954) as writing: 'No man was educated unless he was acquainted with the masterpieces of his tradition.' Zaytuna College sees itself as an Islamic extension of the Great Books curriculum:

Many great American scholars and thinkers have lamented the decline of the liberal arts in the West and committed themselves to a revival of liberal education. Their vision endures today in religious and secular institutions such as Thomas Aquinas College, St. John's College, Columbia University, Shimer College, Williams College, and Bard College. Zaytuna is the first Muslim college to join the movement. (Zaytuna College Catalog 2014–2015)

In the 1999 meeting in Leicester, where (as noted in the previous chapter) these scholars had deliberated on a plan to undertake da'wah in the West, it was also agreed that they would help to produce good English translations of key Islamic texts with contemporary commentaries. Thus, helping Muslims to appreciate and re-engage with the classical Islamic scholarly texts in all Islamic sciences is key to the teaching philosophy of these rationalist scholars.

Working on the Self: The Role of Retreats

As discussed in detail in the preceding chapter, these scholars are keen to focus on teaching the Islamic texts, but they are equally concerned with encouraging Muslims to learn to actually imbibe Islamic values in each and every aspect of their lives, hence their focus on ihsan and tasawwuf. For them Islam is a living tradition and it must therefore be taught through example.

The importance of keeping the suhbah of people with good moral character is thus strongly emphasised by these scholars. Their focus on retreats, in my view, is a way of creating that suhbah, even if for a temporary period. Even though these retreats are short, ranging from a few days to a maximum of three weeks in the case of Rihla, for students who attend them the bonding created with the scholars and their fellow participants becomes an important source of mutual reinforcement of religious commitment. Many of my respondents noted how they try to ensure that they attend at least one retreat per year, if not more, as it re-energises the 'iman'. Rosales, which also hosts the al-Ghazali and Zawiyah retreats, is one of the important sites for these retreats. Rihla, however, is the oldest and the most influential of all the retreats run by this network of scholars, as it covers the largest number of subjects, has most of these scholars teach on it, and is spread over three weeks. The Sacred Caravan 'umrah trip also serves as a retreat, where the participants get to perform 'umrah as a group under the guidance of one of the rationalist scholars. SeekersHub, al-Maqasid, and Ta'leef also run short retreats, usually spread over two to three days, up to a maximum of a week.

Irrespective of the specific theme covered in a given retreat, all of these retreats have a shared focus on making the participants withdraw from their everyday realities and reflect on issues of Islamic ethics and morality, in addition to learning about specific texts. Since the scholars teaching on these retreats dine, pray, and accommodate individual meetings with the students even after the seminars, the students get an intensive exposure to ideal Islamic ethics and moral code. Further, the participants form bonds with each other, and some remain connected with each other on return from the retreats.

Avoidance of Religious Titles

Thus far I have been using the word *scholar* to refer to the individuals in question; now it is appropriate to discuss briefly how they and their students use the Islamic titles. All of the Islamic rationalist scholars avoid specialised religious honorifics such as *'ulama* or *mufti*; instead most of their students refer to them as *shaykh*, a more general title of respect. This demonstrates their reservations about claiming formal religious authority; it is, however, also reflective of their overall approach, which emphasises humility and caution in interpreting religious texts. These scholars routinely advise and respond to questions by their students and participants and, as we will see in Chapter 5, they adopt clear positions on issues; but they never claim to issue a *fatwa* (legal ruling). This cautious engagement with Islamic texts in itself is very important in shaping their appeal, as it is consistent with early Islamic scholarly tradition as well as the Western scholarly tradition, both of which require scholars to argue with caution and to qualify claims where necessary, instead of claiming absolute truths.

CONCLUSION

Mathiesen (2013: 193) in his article on traditional Islam notes that the term 'traditional Islam' was coined in the West, and that its Arabic translation, *al-islâm al-taqlîdî*, hardly exists. He notes that this term was initially associated with the work of influential scholar Sayyed Hussein Nasr, who initiated the Perennialist movement, which generally was also labelled as traditionalism. Since 1987, Mathiesen (2013: 194) argues, the term 'traditional Islam' as used in Western scholarship has dropped the perennialist association and instead is being used to refer to mainstream Sunni positions, with a particular focus on reviving 'what is considered authentically rooted in revelation, has crystallised under the banners of scholarly consensus (*ijmāʿ*) and been passed on as Islamic knowledge (*ʿilm naqlī*) in chains of scholarly authority (*isnād*)'. He also contends that the dominant understanding of traditional Islam in the West is being promoted by figures such as Tim Winter and Nuh Keller; he argues that in his own fieldwork with Muslims in the West, he has found this movement to be particularly influential.

In this chapter, I have tried to present what traditional Islam represents, in terms of both its content and the modes of Islamic knowledge transmission that it considers authentic. In developing this understanding, I have also argued why in my view the term 'Islamic rationalism' captures better than 'traditionalism' the appeal of these scholars and the specific contribution that they are making to contemporary understanding of Islam. These scholars' own preference to be labelled as traditionalists is understandable, given that they are trying to establish that the Ashʿari-Maturidi theology that they espouse, their reliance on madhhabs to find answers to contemporary questions that are consistent with Islamic fiqh, and their strong appreciation for tasawwuf form the foundations of classical Islamic scholarship. But, given that all Islamic movements claim to present traditional Islam[19] (even those that adopt very restrictive readings of the text), this chapter has tried to illustrate how the specific contribution and appeal of this movement to its followers is better captured through emphasising its role in reviving Islamic rationalism. The distinctive contribution of these scholars is to demonstrate that Islam always was a religion of reason, but a reason that is not limited to intellect but that also credits inner spiritual experience, thereby being superior to the narrow interpretations of reason and rationalism shaping Western philosophical discourse.

In Part II of this volume, we will see why such a concept of Islam is appealing to young educated Muslims who are well integrated in modern institutions but also feel that the West is lacking in spiritual dimensions. We will see how the rise and spread of this movement also presents an important critique of modernity, which is much in line with concerns raised by some prominent Western intellectuals. Developing this appreciation is also key to understanding why I and other scholars, such as

---

[19] See George Makdisi's (1997) work on Ibn ʿAqil, for instance, which illustrates how it is the Hanbali scholars who have historically asserted the claim to be traditionalists. The proponents of Ashʿari-Maturidi kalam were more often than not presented as the rationalists.

Walbridge (2011), argue that the twenty-first century is seeing the revival of Islamic rationalism, and that this movement is on course to grow stronger with time. In the later chapters of this book, I present the evidence to support this assertion. But, in order to appreciate why these converts have come to play such an important role in reviving Islamic rationalism among educated young Muslims in the West, and why they have also begun to influence their counterparts in Muslim-majority countries, it is important to first understand in which Muslim-majority countries and with which scholars they secured their Islamic knowledge. Equally importantly, we need to understand their socio-economic backgrounds and the factors that shaped their conversions. Only when we properly analyse these two dynamics can we understand why these converts have become influential intermediaries in introducing modern-educated Muslims to the rationalist and philosophical dimensions of their own tradition.

3

Learning from the Old Geographies of Islam

Acquiring Specialist Knowledge

Not all converts to Islam develop an appreciation for the rationalist–mystical balance which, as argued in the previous chapter, represented mainstream Sunni Islamic orthodoxy until the eighteenth century. Many, in fact, join puritanical movements such as Salafism, which became influential in the twentieth century (Bano 2018a); others get drawn to one of the many newly emerging Sufi groups, which pay little attention to the legalistic and ritual aspects of Islam;[1] and a few others gravitate towards militant groups such as ISIS. How did the converts who today are leading the revival of Islamic rationalist scholarship among modern-educated Muslims in the West develop an appreciation for classical Islamic scholarship? Did they acquire their Islamic knowledge in Western universities where they were students at the time of their conversion – or in the mosque and Islamic schooling networks operating in the West? Or did they seek this knowledge in the formal centres of learning in Muslim-majority countries, such as the al-Medina University in Saudi Arabia, which primarily caters to foreign students; the al-Azhar University in Egypt, which is the oldest seat of classical Islamic learning; or the Deoband madrasah network in South Asia, which is particularly influential among Muslims of South Asian origin? The answer is largely in the negative: while pursuing some or all of these options, these scholars

---

[1] Shem Friedlander, a famous American Sufi writer who has written more than nine books on Sufism and shares time between Istanbul, Cairo, and New York, has also expressed concerns about some of the Sufi-inspired groups in the West, where Sufism is presented as a spiritual experience which needs not necessarily to be associated with Islam (lecture attended in Istanbul, April 2017).

secured their real Islamic knowledge, as they have come to practise it, at none of these formal platforms; instead they consciously chose to study with the traditional Islamic scholarly networks that could demonstrate a continuity in their teaching practice from the times of the Prophet and his companions.

Looking at the biographies of the first- and second-generation scholars in this network, it is noticeable that on conversion all of them spent varying lengths of time studying in Muslim-majority countries. During this time, they invested in learning Arabic, conscious of its importance in acquiring Islamic knowledge; they also pursued study of Islamic sciences with traditionally trained scholars. Their decisions to move to Muslim-majority countries to pursue Islamic knowledge was not unusual; even among the second-generation Muslims in the West, those keen on seeking specialist Islamic knowledge opt to travel overseas in pursuit of higher Islamic learning. What, however, is noteworthy about these scholars is the choice of the Islamic education platforms from where they decided to acquire their Islamic knowledge. Most second-generation Muslims who travel overseas to pursue Islamic knowledge choose one of the three formal institutional platforms mentioned above: al-Azhar or al-Medina universities, or one of the larger Deoband madrasahs.[2] The scholars in this network, on the other hand, settled for none of these options, even though they were exposed to them; instead they explored multiple platforms in a number of countries and eventually settled for more informal Islamic scholarly networks[3] led by scholars who claim to have been part of an uninterrupted chain of Islamic knowledge transmission from the time of the Prophet.

The first generation of scholars leading this Islamic rationalist revival movement selected these institutions through trial and error; tracing the educational trajectories that they followed on travelling overseas, it becomes clear that before settling down with the scholars to whom they credit their learning they tried other places. The second-generation

---

[2] Access to Deobandi madrasahs in South Asia has, however, been restricted since September 11, due to their alleged support for the Taliban.

[3] It is worth noting here that some might assume that Deoband madrasahs represent the informal teaching style of the madrasahs in the earlier period of Islam, unlike al-Azhar or al-Medina universities, which are part of the formal state bureaucracy (Bano 2018a). Compared with the traditional Islamic scholarly networks, the Deoband madrasah network is, however, relatively formal, as it adopted a fixed curriculum and a formal examination system, issuing degree certificates to compete with the Western educational institutions introduced in colonial India.

scholars in this network did learn from the experience of those from the first generation. By the third generation, which (as outlined in Chapter 1) consists of second- and third-generation Muslims from within the mainstream Muslim diaspora communities, the learning starts under the tutelage of these first- and second-generation scholars in the institutions that they have established in the West. There is, however, a recognition that these students must also go overseas, both to learn Arabic and then again at an advanced stage of their learning to study more specialised Islamic texts with experts in Muslim countries. The first-generation scholars recognise that building the capacity of the institutions they are establishing in the West will take time; meanwhile, students have to continue to travel to Muslim countries to pursue more advanced studies. In order to appreciate the significance of the choice made by the first-generation scholars to study with informal Islamic scholarly platforms rather than with the more formal institutions, it is important to understand how the formal Islamic education platforms in the Muslim world underwent numerous transformations during the colonial period.

Between the eighteenth and twentieth centuries, Islamic scholarly networks in most Muslim countries saw a major change in the content of their curriculum, as well as in the mode of Islamic teaching. It is important to understand the history of this formalisation of Islamic education under colonial rule and the continuation of this trend under the post-colonial modernising Muslim states in most of the Muslim-majority countries. This will help us to appreciate the importance of the informal platforms where these scholars studied, and to understand why they are playing an important role in reintroducing young Muslims to the rationalist and philosophical dimensions of their religion. This chapter will thus map the institutions and Islamic religious milieu that have influenced these scholars' understanding of Islam; in doing so it will also illustrate why the rationalist sciences witnessed a decline in the mainstream Islamic educational institutions between the eighteenth and twentieth centuries, and why the informal Islamic education platforms remained more effective in preserving the classical Islamic scholarship.

I COLONIAL RULE AND FORMALISATION OF ISLAMIC EDUCATION

It is not in dispute that Islam inspired a rich scholarly tradition that not only enriched the Islamic sciences but also made significant contributions to the fields of science, mathematics, humanities, and the arts; what

Western scholarship is divided upon, however, is when Islamic education acquired the formality associated with the rise of the college and university system in the Western tradition (Makdisi 1981). Even though madrasahs emerged in the early centuries of Islam, complementing the earlier practice of mosque-based halaqahs, the teaching method remained informal and focused on studying a major book in detail, instead of trying to cover a formal curriculum. Similarly, a student's learning progress was not assessed through centrally administered examinations but through the individual assessment of his teachers; an ijazah from the teacher, instead of a degree, marked the completion of one's education (Berkey 2002; 2007; 2014). Thus in building the reputation of a young scholar the names of his teachers were more important than the name of the madrasah in which he might have been enrolled. Over the centuries, many factors contributed to the rise or decline of prominent centres of learning within Islamic societies. The fall of Baghdad to the Mongols in the thirteenth century, which led to the burning down of major libraries of the Islamic world, was for example one of the strongest setbacks to the Islamic scholarly establishments, yet Muslim societies managed to support vibrant scholarly networks whenever a stable Muslim political order was established.[4] What, however, did succeed in dramatically altering both the content and mode of Islamic knowledge transmission in the Muslim world was the spread of Western colonial rule; its impact became particularly noteworthy from the mid-nineteenth century onwards, when Western political authority began to decisively displace Muslim political authority in many contexts.

During the colonial period, the relationship between the Islamic education platforms and the state was totally transformed for a number of reasons: one, Islamic education platforms lost state patronage, and the declining status of Muslim elites also reduced individual sources of patronage (Bano 2017); two, the legal and political framework was transformed, whereby the Western legal and political framework replaced shari'ah,[5] making madrasah education irrelevant for securing employment in modern institutions (Bano 2017); three, colonial rule introduced Western educational institutions, from primary schools all the way to

---

[4] This is visible in the emergence of three vibrant Muslim empires in the later centuries: Ottomans, Mughals, and Safavids (Robinson 1997).

[5] Although Muslim empires did develop specific laws to deal with everyday issues, shari'ah remained the overall guiding framework under these empires, and *qadi*s (the judges) operated under Islamic law (see Bano 2017, chapter 2).

tertiary education, and these became the main providers of education in society (Bano 2017). This dramatically altered political/economic context eroded the prestige traditionally associated with the Islamic scholarly platforms. Many Islamic scholarly establishments did try to compete with these Western educational institutions by giving up the informality of the traditional Islamic learning process and adopting a formal curriculum, holding annual examinations, and shifting to a class-based instruction method, instead of continuing the tutorial-style method whereby teaching was tailored to the level of each individual student.

Some institutions such as Deoband in India led such efforts from within (Metcalf 1982); others, such as the famous al-Azhar mosque and madrasah in Egypt, faced pressures from within as well as from the modernising state to do the same (Zeghal 2007). However, the adoption of modern teaching methods or assessment techniques did not make these institutions more competitive vis à vis their Western educational rivals; the Western educational platforms were too far ahead in scientific knowledge by this point for the Islamic scholars to catch up with them (Bano 2012b; 2017). The scholars in madrasahs also faced a major challenge in gaining access to the latest scientific knowledge, because it required a command of Western languages (Bano 2012b; 2017). Further, the adoption of the language of the colonial power as the official language of the state dramatically reduced the professional usefulness of languages associated with Islamic scholarship (such as Arabic, Persian, and Urdu) and consequently also their status.

In such a context, madrasah education came to focus increasingly on the study of Islamic sciences such as the Quran and hadith; other subjects gradually received declining attention within the madrasah curriculum. Further, even within the Islamic sciences, in most cases it was the more textual approaches, rather than the more reflective and philosophical approaches, that survived best. While this shift is often blamed for the relative rigidity and lack of creativity within contemporary Islamic education, seen from an institutional survival perspective, in a time of scarce resources, this refocusing was the most viable option. It enabled the Islamic scholars to focus on Islamic sciences concerning 'aqidah and 'ibadah (rituals), given that the political elites as well as the wider Muslim community rarely consulted the Islamic scholars on matters of *mu'amalat*s (social transaction), as these were now seen to fall within the domain of the specialists trained in Western educational institutions. Here it is also important to understand an important sociological shift that had occurred in the way in which Muslim elites engaged with Islamic scholarly platforms under such changed circumstances. As the Western educational institutions became the primary routes to acquiring elite status, Muslim elites abandoned madrasah education; in fact, even the families of prominent Islamic scholars, whose members occupied important positions in the princely courts and acted as prominent jurists under Muslim political authority, themselves moved towards modern educational institutions.[6] Consequently, Islamic scholarship over time came to rest in the hands of the economically marginalised sections of Muslim societies. Further, the drying up of the sources of patronage restricted the educational facilities that these Islamic platforms could offer to their students and teachers.

The factors listed above have had a direct bearing on the deterioration of Islamic scholarly standards; the formal madrasah students in the Muslim world today, especially those who train to become future scholars,[7] come predominantly from the poorest and lower-middle-income sections of society, especially from the rural areas.[8] Further, even families that do send their children to madrasahs more often than not send their brighter children to a modern school.[9] This is a pragmatic choice, as the more intelligent child is expected to have better chances of success in a modern school. At the same time, sending the less intelligent (and/or the more problematic) child to madrasah does not create any

---

[6] See Robinson (2001) for insights into the decline of the leading Farangi Mahal madrasah in India; Pierret (2013) for a detailed analysis of how men from petty trading families or migrants from rural areas moved into scholarly professions in Syria in the early twentieth century, as the families of elite 'ulama left in favour of Western educational institutions; and Eickelman (2007) for a similar analysis for Morocco.

[7] Children from affluent families at times also undergo a *hifz* (Quran memorisation) process at a madrasah, but this process lasts for a maximum of two to three years, after which the children return to regular Western-style schools; it is extremely rare for a child from an affluent family to complete a full madrasah education, or to become an Islamic scholar.

[8] Arguably, in Egypt, Saudi Arabia, and Turkey, where the state has tried to formally regulate religious authority by encouraging more university-based Islamic teaching, the scholars are better paid financially than in most informal Islamic scholarly platforms, as the former receive formal state salaries and related benefits. But academic professions in general are not necessarily respected in these countries as they are in the West, due to the poor quality of university education. In most Muslim countries, teachers in Islamic Studies faculties have relatively low social status, and it is often assumed that they work in these faculties because they could not enter more competitive faculties such as medicine, engineering, or economics: an assumption that is often applied also to the students enrolled in the Islamic Studies faculties.

[9] Studies of madrasah enrolment, including my own (Bano 2012b), show that the majority of the parents who do send their children to madrasahs send only one child, while others are sent to regular schools and colleges.

religious dilemma for the parents, as this decision, being an act of religious devotion, makes the actual performance of the child a secondary concern. The following reaction of one of the senior Islamic scholars who runs a large madrasah in Karachi, Pakistan, captures the essence of the challenge faced by Islamic education platforms in most Muslim countries from the start of the colonial period: 'When the society gives us the weakest child, what kind of scholarship does it expect its madrasahs to produce?'[10]

It is also important to note here that in the Middle East the postcolonial period did bring about increased resources for some of the prominent Islamic education platforms.[11] This, however, did not lead to an intellectual revival within these Islamic scholarly platforms; nor did this move succeed in attracting societal elites or individuals from upper-middle-income strata of society back to these Islamic educational platforms. This is because the reinvestment in Islamic education platforms was aimed not at reviving traditional Islamic learning; instead it was aimed at further reforming it to fit the Western modern standards. Thus, al-Azhar mosque lost its independence in 1961 when Gamal Nasser brought it under state control and transformed it into a university. Al-Azhar today offers degrees in modern disciplines, but the quality of its Islamic education has witnessed serious deterioration in standards (Bano 2018a). Elsewhere, the Kemalist regime in Turkey entirely banned madrasahs, instead establishing modern departments of theology that were required to teach Islam from a Western rationalist perspective. The scholarship produced within these departments, however, largely failed to win credibility among devout Muslims, as it was aimed at secularising the religion, rather than promoting serious engagement with it (Bano 2018a). This marginalised status of Islamic education platforms and Islamic knowledge, which has its origin in the encounter with colonialism, has

---

[10] Interview conducted in Karachi in 2008 during fieldwork for *The Rational Believer* (Bano 2012b).

[11] Al-Azhar was nationalised in 1961 under Nasser. Consequently it lost its endowments and its independent status. Some al-Azhari scholars, such as al-Gomma, argue that the resources that became available through the state were greater; Zeghal (2007) also argues that access to state resources helped al-Azhari to expand its educational network. In Turkey, under Atatürk, the madrasahs and *tekke*s (Sufi lodges) were closed, but the state did gradually move towards establishing Departments of Theology, and Diyanet, the Turkish Directorate of Religious Affairs, today has a staff of more than 150,000 as the state takes the responsibility for providing imams in mosques (Agai 2007).

thus not been reversed – even in the Middle East, where some post-colonial states did invest resources in Islamic education institutions.

While the above-outlined shift in Islamic knowledge transmission is a widely shared reality across Muslim societies,[12] in some countries, due either to the limited duration of colonial rule or to lower levels of economic development at the time of colonial encounter, the influence of Western education on changing public sensibilities and routes to economic advancement was less decisive. Here some of the West African countries with a strong Islamic heritage provide important examples. Islamic knowledge platforms in northern Nigeria, a context in which I have done extensive fieldwork with Islamic scholarly platforms over the last ten years, for example, today face very similar challenges to those outlined above (Bano 2008; 2009); yet the '*Ilmi* schooling system, whereby a Muslim of any age can choose to study a book with a respected scholar at a time convenient to both, has survived despite the odds.[13] As we will see, the case of Mauritania, where Hamza Yusuf acquired much of his Islamic training, presents a similar example: Yusuf himself has noted that the country's low level of economic development and limited exposure to the West has in his assessment been key to its preserving the traditional practices of Islamic knowledge transmission. Similarly, in Morocco, although Qarawiyyin, a leading Islamic university until the early twentieth century, underwent major reforms at the behest of the modernising state (Zeghal 2008), thereby losing its prestige as a leading Islamic scholarly platform, the informal Islamic teaching platforms and Sufi networks proved relatively successful in protecting their turf.

Within the Middle East, in Syria, where in the post-colonial context the Baath regime did not try to nationalise or shut down leading Islamic scholarly platforms[14] (unlike the situations in Egypt and Turkey, respectively), the independent Islamic scholarly networks also proved fairly resilient. And while, with the establishment of Saudi Arabia in 1932, the Salafi–Wahhabi understanding of Islam became the official Islam in the

---

[12] As the Turkish case shows, even those Muslim countries that were not directly brought under colonial rule, or were brought under colonial rule for short periods, such as Syria, underwent the same pressures to modernise in accordance with the Western educational and development model (Pierret 2013).

[13] For the overall loss of status of Islamic education vis-à-vis Western education even in this context, see Bano (2008) and Höchner (2010).

[14] As Pierret (2013) illustrates, this neglect was not a sign of benevolence but an expression of a deep-rooted conviction among the senior officials of the Baath regime that religious conviction will erode among the public in response to the spread of modern education.

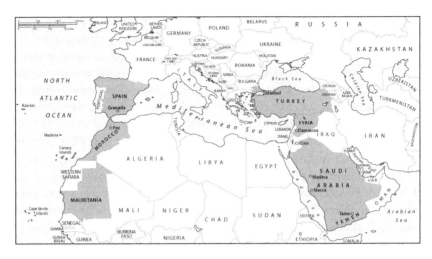

Map 3.1 Key Sites of Traditional Islamic Learning

Saudi Kingdom, Hijaz, the region that encompasses the holy cities of Mecca and Medina and which historically attracted prominent Islamic scholars from all Islamic traditions, to date manages to retain a rich diversity of Islamic scholarly platforms which continue to deploy traditional Islamic teaching methods to transmit Islamic knowledge to the next generation.

It is these informal Islamic scholarly networks that were least touched by the modern state and whose scholars even today gain their legitimacy by establishing their lineage from the Prophet and his companions that, as we will see in this chapter, best preserve the classical Islamic scholarly tradition as outlined in the previous chapter. It is precisely these informal Islamic scholarly networks that appealed to the rationalist scholars under study in this volume. By considering these informal Islamic scholarly networks and understanding the socio-economic profiles of the traditionally trained scholars who lead them, it becomes clear why they are reliant on the Western converts who study with them to introduce them to the educated and well-to-do members of their own tradition.

2 PLACES OF LEARNING

Tracing the places of learning and the influences that the Islamic rationalist scholars absorbed on their conversion shifts our focus decisively towards the Muslim-majority countries; however, there is one location within Europe which, due to its distinct historical association with Islam and an Islamic revival that it witnessed during the 1970s, does merit inclusion in this list. Granada, the last capital of Moorish Spain, came to house a small community of Spanish reverts[15] to Islam, starting in the late 1970s and early 1980s. Since then that community has grown slowly but steadily in and around the Albayzin area[16] of Granada. This is the community in which both Dr Umar and Hamza Yusuf also settled for some time on initially travelling out from the United States in the early 1980s. Abdus Samad, the head of Rosales, also comes from this very community of initial Spanish reverts; and Tim Winter, although he never lived in this community, was connected with it from the very start.[17] It is thus worthwhile to start mapping the influences absorbed by these scholars by looking at the Spanish Muslim community of the 1970s; this period is also important because it is the experience that Dr Umar and Hamza Yusuf had with Shayhk Abdalqadir as-Sufi Murabitun, the English Sufi convert from Norwich who was leading this Spanish community of reverts, that many close to this network of scholars argue played a role in influencing Hamza Yusuf to develop reservations in the long term against the adoption of formal Sufism and its emphasis on bay'ah.

Granada, Spain

The total population of the Spanish Muslim community is today estimated to be anywhere between 20,000 and 30,000;[18] though today spread across Spain, this community has had its traditional base in Granada. The Albayzin area of Granada at the base of the mighty Alhambra and its visible Arab and Islamic remains, further enhanced by a recently constructed mosque, have since the 1970s been an important base for Spanish reverts. Yet Granada was not where the community had

---

[15] They call themselves 'reverts' as opposed to 'converts' because their forefathers were Muslims; in general the word 'revert' is preferred by many converts to Islam, due to Islam's underlying teaching that all children are born innocent.

[16] The Albayzin neighbourhood is situated at the base of Alhambra, constituting the most striking architectural remains from the rule of the Muslim Nazarid dynasty in Andalusia. Though neglected for many centuries, it is today the centre of tourism in Granada and acts as an active reminder of the Muslim presence on the Iberian Peninsula.

[17] Samad mentions knowing Tim Winter from the visits that the latter used to make to the Granada Muslim community in early 1980s.

[18] Including the immigrant Muslim population, the total number of Muslims in Spain is estimated to be close to 200,000.

originally tried to settle. In the late 1970s, there were only a handful of Spanish reverts to Islam and they initially tried settling down in Cordoba, which once housed prominent centres of Islamic learning, before moving to Seville and then finally finding a more permanent home in Granada. From the interviews and fieldwork I have conducted with the first generation of Spanish reverts in Granada, many of whom I have met during my visits to Rosales between 2012 and 2017, and with others who are engaged with the main mosque in Granada in the Albayzin area, it is easy to discern that these reverts to Islam had been primarily attracted to the rationalist and deeply mystical dimensions of Islam. For those familiar with the Andalusian Islamic heritage this will come as no surprise, given that Moorish Spain was home to some of the influential Islamic philosophers and mystics, Ibn Sina and Ibn Rushd included.

The interviews suggest that these reverts were largely from a humanistic orientation, were politically from the left, and were critical of the excessive materialism that had come under attack in the 1970s anti-war and hippie movements; these reverts were in many ways products of those very movements, whose members were experimenting with non-Western ideologies and cultures. In this context, especially given the intellectual and mystically deep orientation of Andalusian Islam, some Westerners were thus drawn towards Islam; it offered an alternative ideology, but one which also provided some historical familiarity, due to Spain's Moorish past. The ultimate conversions within this community of Spanish reverts, however, were based on deeper reflection on the Islamic emphasis on God as one supreme being, compared with the doctrine of the Trinity in Christianity.

As one member of this early Muslim community in Granada explains, he converted to Islam in 1981, when Muslim converts could be counted on one's fingers. For him, as for most of his fellow converts, the appeal of Islam was highly theological. Equally compelling was the committed moral behaviour of the members of this small community of initial converts, and their ability to make Islam appear not as a foreign identity or culture: 'When I saw these initial converts, I had no idea that they were Muslims, as they were like me; they were not trying to dress up in Arab clothes. They explained to me that Islam is not just religion, it is a complete way of life. You are Muslim not just in the mosque, but also when you step out of it, in your relationship with your family, in your business, and so on. For me this feeling of being guided in every aspect of one life was important,' explained this respondent.

Though based in Granada, the community drew converts from all over the country. This particular respondent was from the north of Spain and was exposed to this community when posted to the south under compulsory military service. He initially struggled to understand why people would convert to Islam: 'At that time, we were under Franco; Islam for us was only for Arabs and Moors,' he explains. His curiosity, however, made him ask questions which ultimately led to his conversion; as he notes, 'I took the *shahadah* (conversion to Islam) the day after I left the military service.' This shahadah took place in the house of a fellow revert, as at that time there was no mosque. Facing strong resistance from their own families, these reverts became each other's families. The bonds forged among them, as I have found in my fieldwork, remain very strong even today; they still rely on each other, and their children, some of whom are now in their thirties, have grown up knowing each other more closely than their immediate cousins.

It was amid this small but tightly knit community of Spanish reverts, whose members were very interdependent and were learning Islam from each other as they went along, that both Hamza Yusuf and Dr Umar found themselves, soon after converting to Islam. Hamza Yusuf was at this time a very young man in his early twenties; Dr Umar, who had recently obtained his PhD from the University of Chicago, was in his early thirties. Like other members of this community, both contributed to the building of this community and learned from each other. Given his academic training, Dr Umar began to give formal lessons in Arabic language to other members. Samad, the head of Rosales, also comes from this same community of Spanish reverts. Looking at his profile and examining the factors shaping his conversion will help us to understand the attitudes and propensities of these initial Spanish reverts to Islam; it also helps us to understand why they were attracted to the more rationalist and mystical dimensions of Islam.

Samad, who was a young musician, was exposed to Islam in the late 1970s through neighbours who were part of this newly established Muslim community. Their conduct and manners impressed him and his wife, a fellow revert who undertakes a major share of the everyday running of Rosales.[19] He converted in 1980, but his conversion was not instant. Prior to his conversion he felt he was an atheist, although he always did believe that there was some force in nature. Every summer he was drawn to the natural beauty of the land owned by his family on the outskirts of Granada, where today Rosales is situated. At school he

---

[19] In particular she supervises the kitchen, especially during the retreats, when between 150 and 200 people have to be fed three times a day.

studied classical music, and his hobby was dancing; he was also part of the traditional dance group of the village. It is ironically his interest in music to which he credits his conversion to Islam: 'Classical music made me come to Andalusian music, and this made me realize that Andalusian music was very close to my village music,' he notes.

His rejection of all kinds of violence or excessive use of state authority led him to refuse to take part in the compulsory military subscription prevalent in Spain at that time, prompting him to leave for America at the age of 18. Working his way across the United States, he reached San Francisco, where he was attracted to the politics of the left and became part of the hippie movement. In Los Angeles, his musical talent helped him to secure a job. However, he was forced to return to Spain two years later to meet his compulsory military draft obligation. Samad recalls being with the Spanish special forces in Morocco on 20 November 1975, the day General Franco died, but after that he was soon allowed to leave the military and return to Granada. Once back, he established a recording studio in the Albayzin area, at a location close to where the Granada mosque now stands. It was here that he encountered members of the Spanish Muslim community, some of whom were his neighbours. He found them appealing, as they 'were very faithful people and without any trouble and without bad ideas, and that is why I liked them,' explains Samad.

As their interactions grew, some of them started to ask him to consider converting to Islam. Initially, resenting such suggestions, Samad checked them harshly. They respected his decision but left him a recording of Andalusian music from North Africa. It was through this music that, as Samad notes, 'I discovered Islam; listening to this music, I began to have an image of Islam which was very beautiful.' He recalls: 'On the machine which shows you the waves of the voice, because I knew the music writing, I could see that when you played the Quran, it created perfect lines.' He thought it was impossible for someone in this world to do it; in his words, 'the notes, the signs were perfect'. Joining a group of Spanish Muslims on their way to Morocco enabled him to explore the roots of Andalusian music. Despite this growing affinity with the Quran and mystical music, the years 1978–1980 remained a period of lingering questions for him. He was convinced of the basic theology of Islam, of the concept of creation, and of its basic tenets, as well as its ability to inspire the arts and good moral conduct. He did not drink much alcohol or eat pork, so such prohibitions in Islam were not difficult for him to follow. The most difficult part when thinking of converting to Islam for him was the commitment to perform five daily prayers and get up in the cold for *wudu'* (ablution).

It was finally in the late 1970s, when he was actually in Morocco for a local music festival, that he converted. Involved in the organisation of this festival, he had to travel to Rabat by car with four of his Muslim Moroccan friends and fellow musicians. On Thursday, a week before the festival, his friends stopped for evening prayer at a mosque; he stayed in the car, but as he recalls:

In Morocco there is a tradition that after Maghrib (evening prayer), we just recite, and they put microphone in the old *medina* (city). So, they began to recite Quran. I felt very special while I was listening to this recitation and then I felt something very strange. I began to cry and I could not stop. I felt very happy and I did not know what was happening to me ... I put my face down on dashboard because I did not want people to see me and I kept crying. And I cried till I could not cry more. And it was like that for twenty minutes. I think they were reciting Surah Yasin. At the same time I felt it was for a very, very short time, but at the same time very, very long. Short because I wanted it to continue; long because it was very intense.[20]

He did not say anything to his Moroccan friends when they returned to the car, but he did end up taking the first boat back from Tangier to Spain. On coming back to his home, without saying anything to his wife or family, he took a *ghusl* (bath), changed into clean clothes, and went to the *zawiyah* (study circle), where he took the shahadah just before '*Asr* (afternoon prayer) with Dr Mansur, one of the senior members of the community of Spanish reverts to Islam. As he recalls, 'after two years of knowing me as Antonio, they now knew me as Abdus Samad [his Muslim given name]. And, everyone was very happy.'

My interviews with numerous reverts from this generation show that Samad's profile was fairly typical of the members of this community; the artistic propensity of these early reverts is visible in the activities in which many of them are currently engaged (some are actually calligraphers, potters, or artists), while others who were engaged in other professions also shared these artistic and humanistic leanings. For them the appeal of Islam was the beauty that it inspired, the clear conception of God that it offered, its deep mysticism, and the higher moral and ethical behaviour that it inspired. The artistic, leftist, and humanist tendencies of this community of Spanish reverts are also visible in the important role played by Shaykh Abdalqadir. Although eventually his involvement in this community proved divisive, he was an influential figure among these early

[20] Interview, Rosales, 24 June 2014.

Spanish reverts. Many of them had spent time with him in Norwich, while he also maintained a base in Granada. The profiles of the members of the small community of English converts to Islam who embraced Islam in the 1970s under the influence of Shaykh Abdalqadir show traits very similar to those of Samad: they were prominent photographers, musicians, artists, and the like. As one member of the Norwich Muslim community explained during a talk in London: 'It was a hippie spiritual reading of Islam; Islam was little known and it was more like Buddhism than the Islam that everyone knows after 2001.'[21]

These were thus mainly the artistic, philosophically oriented, and politically left-leaning individuals who in the spirit of experimentation that marked the 1970s encountered Islam and found a strong appeal in its theology and its moral dictates. They became each others' families. It is perhaps due to the deep associations developed within this small but closely knit community that the eventual estrangement of some of the Spanish Muslims from Shaykh Abdalqadir left a particularly bitter taste for both sides.[22] In 1984, half of the community moved away from Shaykh Abdalqadir, while the others remained with him. Dr Umar, Hamza Yusuf, and Abdus Samad became part of the former group, which was led by Dr Mansur; and it is the members of this half of the Spanish community of reverts that we see most notably represented at Rosales today. It is also because of the close association developed during this time with this Spanish Muslim community that Rosales remains for Dr Umar a very important base, and why he makes a deliberate effort to deliver lessons in Spanish during his visits to Rosales.

The split within this Spanish Muslim community over the role of Shaykh Abdalqadir unfortunately continues to divide the Granada Muslim community to date. The mosque in Albayzin remains in the hands of the community led by Shaykh Abdalqadir. It is this Spanish Muslim

---

[21] Speaker at the screening of *The Strangers* at the Rumi Cave, London, 5 October 2014. The movie, directed by Ahmed Peerbux and Sean Hanif Whyte, records the story of conversions within the Muslim community in Norwich. Details available at http://thestrangers.co.uk/, accessed 13 March 2018.

[22] Tensions grew as some started to question Shaykh Abdalqadir's educational credentials and management of community funds, and criticised him for becoming too involved in the personal life decisions of the followers. Hamza Yusuf does not like to talk about his time with Shaykh Abdalqadir; in interviews with me, Dr Umar acknowledged that, due to these tensions, a split did occur within the Granada Muslim community of the early 1980s but did not want to elaborate on this.

community, which was very tightly knit but which eventually became divided into two camps, that was an important early destination for some of the scholars in the rationalist network. It is thus easy to understand why Tim Winter and Dr Umar commit themselves to returning to this community each year to co-lead the al-Ghazali retreat, and also why Dr Umar likes to hold his Zawiyah retreat here in addition to a few other places. Even Rihla was organised at Rosales for three years (2009–2011) before it moved to Turkey.

Informal Study Circles in Mecca and Medina, Saudi Arabia

Saudi Arabia, in particular the holy cities of Mecca and Medina, proved the next important destination for the scholars from the first generation; it was, however, not the official Wahhabi and Salafi readings of Islam that inspired them. Instead, during their time in Saudi Arabia these scholars benefitted from the rich milieu of Islamic scholarly networks, especially those combining Sufi training with study of fiqh. Dr Umar and Abdus Samad in particular spent a very long time in Saudi Arabia, while Tim Winter, who moved there from Egypt, also stayed in Jeddah for a couple of years, working as a translator before returning to the United Kingdom. Finally, though never based in Saudi Arabia for a prolonged period, Hamza Yusuf kept returning to Mecca and Medina for 'umrah and Hajj, thereby staying connected with the other three. Time spent in Saudi Arabia is thus important for mapping the association that developed among these scholars and for appreciating how they ended up following many similar shaykhs as their teachers.

Dr Umar moved to Saudi Arabia in 1984, after he and others had fallen out with Shaykh Abdalqadir. One of the Eritrean Sufi scholars whom he followed was based in Medina and he encouraged him to take up a position at King Abdul Aziz University in Jeddah to teach religious studies. In this capacity Dr Umar taught comparative religion. Although he did not find the students very engaged, he valued his time at the university, as it enabled him to better understand different religions. During this time, he had only three commitments: his family, the teaching and spending time with the shaykhs in Mecca and Medina. He was particularly influenced by a number of Eritrean shaykhs. Shaykh Bashir, his first main shaykh, was from Eritrea and he introduced Dr Umar to another Eritrean shaykh, Shaykh Mohammad Abu Bakr, who remained Dr Umar's shaykh until his death in 2003. Dr Umar credits much of his learning to the time spent with these shaykhs, who inculcated in him an appreciation for balancing his knowledge of the fiqh with greater emphasis on absorbing the Islamic moral code. These shaykhs impressed on him that the real *salaf* (members of the first generation of Muslims) were definitely concerned with the law, but they were also concerned with the heart: with overcoming the ego.

Though staying away from the Wahhabi and Salafi readings of Islam, Dr Umar did learn to appreciate the plurality of Saudi society. The fact that he taught comparative religion enabled him to discuss many different issues with the students. He also did teach Islamic creed, and the book he was required to teach was, he felt, well developed.

Abdus Samad's experience in Saud Arabia was very similar. He had moved to Saudi Arabia at the same time as Dr Umar and studied with many of the same shaykhs. While Dr Umar moved to Saudi Arabia through securing a position at King Abdul Aziz University, Abdus Samad was actually invited by King Fahd. His Moorish origin and his back-ground as a local musician had on conversion won him some attention in Islamic circles, leading to receipt of an invitation from King Fahd to travel to Saudi Arabia for Hajj. During the meeting with the King, Samad expressed his desire to learn Arabic and Islam in Mecca. Two months on, he received an invitation to move to Saudi Arabia to pursue Islamic Studies; he moved there with his family in 1984. In Mecca, he entered a new world. Before converting to Islam, he had a shaykh in Morocco, and the Saudi rigidity in Islam did not appeal to him and his wife. Like Dr Umar, Samad therefore secured most of his Islamic knowledge in the informal study circles led by shaykhs in Mecca and Medina; he followed the same shaykhs as Dr Umar. As he notes, 'in the morning I was with the Salafis and in the afternoon with the shaykhs. In the morning I was in the Umm al-Qura University, in the afternoon I went for *dars* (lessons) to my shaykhs.' From the very beginning of his conversion he had a very clear idea about the importance of tasawwuf, which he notes helped him to maintain a balance between Sufism and Salafism.

Tim Winter similarly spent a few years in Saudi Arabia, learning in private study circles with some of the same shaykhs, although particularly with shaykhs from the Ba'alawi tradition from Yemen, who were based in Jeddah at the time. On conversion Tim Winter had spent some time in Egypt including a year studying at al-Azhar, but later moved to Saudi Arabia, where he worked as a translator while studying with the shaykhs in the evenings (ABC 2004). Like Dr Umar and Abdus Samad, he also found the Wahhabi strands of Islam too restrictive; but like them he also came to appreciate that there is plurality in Islamic understandings within Saudi society – as he elaborated in a radio interview (ABC 2004):

I've lived in Saudi Arabia, I know some of the Wahabi scholars, and there are really two broad tendencies within what's conventionally called Wahabism at the moment. One you might define as the Royal Saudi Wahabies, that is to say the regime loyalists in Saudi Arabia, who certainly speak out very courageously against terrorism; ... but then an uneasy relationship with them, you have the radicals, who you might call the Wahabies of Mass Destruction ... And they exist in very uneasy tension at the moment in Saudi Arabia, each claiming legitimate inheritance of the original Wahabi mantle, that the movement was launched 200 years ago in Central Saudi Arabia.

In presenting these dual categories of Saudi Salafism, Winter was trying to argue that not all Wahhabis should be labelled as radical or extremists, while also highlighting the challenge they face with Saudi Salafi Islam: 'But nonetheless, it's also the case that the great majority of people who do believe in the legitimacy of terrorism to secure purportedly Islamic ends, do tend to subscribe to the rather literalist, dry, intense Wahhabi theology. So there is a problem there, but you certainly shouldn't generalise' (ABC 2004).

Thus, Saudi Arabia did serve as an important site for securing Islamic knowledge for the first generation of scholars leading the Islamic rationalist network. Hamza Yusuf, as noted above, also kept returning to Mecca and Medina, and it was during his Hajj visit in late 1990s that he convinced Dr Umar of the need to return to the United States and work with him and other scholars to undertake da'wah there. Admittedly, the Islam that they learned was not from the formal Wahhabi and Salafi Islamic educational platforms; but the fact that these scholars could access these pluralistic Islamic scholarly networks in Saudi Arabia shows that the religious milieu in Saudi Arabia has been richer than often recognised (Bano 2018a). Not only has a rich network of Islamic scholarly traditions, including the Sufi networks, continued to operate in Hijaz under the Saudi state, but many have followers among the Saudis. Thus, ironically Saudi Arabia, which is normally associated with promoting radical Salafi and Wahhabi strands of Islam that these Islamic rationalist scholars openly criticise, has been an important site for their pursuit of Islamic knowledge.

Damascus, Syria

The other destination through which the first generation of scholars also passed, but one which became more important for some of the scholars from the second generation, is Damascus, in Syria. Jihad Brown and Faraz Rabbani spent a number of years studying with traditionally trained scholars in Syria, in particular in the cities of Damascus and Aleppo, while Yahya Rhodus and Usama Cannon also spent short periods of time there. Syria has historically been a key location for the promotion of Islamic scholarship. Capital of the Umayyads, the first dynasty in Islam, Damascus and other major Syrian cities historically have supported a rich tradition of classical Islamic scholarship. The combining of the Ash'ari-Maturidi theological tradition with rigorous study of Islamic fiqh, while at the same time nurturing strong mystical practices, which (as noted in the previous chapter) is recognised by many as the classical Islamic orthodoxy, is strongly representative of Syrian Islamic scholarship. Traditionally, the Shafi'i madhhab was particularly strong in Syria as well as in Egypt, while under the Ottomans the Hanafi madhhab became equally influential.

Although Syria did not undergo prolonged colonial rule, as it was a French protectorate for only a relatively short period, the societal elites had begun to experience the competition posed by the rise of Western colonial powers from the early nineteenth century, as was the case for the Ottoman Empire. Thus, as in the case of most other Muslim countries, Islamic educational platforms, despite historically being very vibrant in this region, became marginalised during the nineteenth century in favour of newly established Western educational institutions. As Pierret (2013) has mapped in great detail, by the turn of the twentieth century not only the societal elites but also members of the prestigious Islamic scholarly families had deserted Islamic education in favour of Western educational institutions. Consequently, new families of Islamic scholars emerged in the twentieth century from relatively humble backgrounds to fill the resulting vacuum in the sphere of Islamic scholarship. The twentieth century thus became a period of great Islamic revival in Syria, as these new scholars tried to reinstate a vibrant Islamic scholarly network.

The Syrian experience, however, differed from that of Egypt and Turkey, in that the post-colonial Syrian state did not actively try to tame the religious authorities in order to gain popular legitimacy. In particular, members of the Baath Party, which has been in power since the 1970s, were largely of the view that religion faces an inevitable decline in the face of modernisation. Thus, unlike al-Azhar in Egypt, which was nationalised in 1961 and subjected to a major modernisation programme with controversial outcomes,[23] Islamic teaching in Syria remained largely in the hands of the Islamic scholarly families that had emerged during the twentieth century. Continuation of Islamic teaching through these families helped to preserve the traditional modes of Islamic knowledge transmission. Further, the Syrian Islamic scholarly tradition, being historically strong on Ash'ari-Maturidi Islamic theology, combined with the study of fiqh and tasawwuf, also preserved the classical Sunni orthodoxy; Ibn Arabi is actually buried in Damascus.

It is thus not surprising that from the 1990s,[24] the country had become a popular destination for the pursuit of Islamic learning among many Muslims from the West and from other Muslim countries (Böttcher 2002). Even before that, Western converts were attracted to it. Nuh Keller, for example, moved to Syria in the 1970s to obtain Islamic education with traditionally trained shaykhs. It is also worth noting that, in addition to these informal Islamic scholarly networks, from the 1960s onwards a few Islamic education foundations also became quite important platforms for promoting Islamic learning. Two of these in particular became very influential: the Abu Nour Foundation and Mahad al-Fatih. The former, which adopted a more Sufi approach, received active support from the Baath regime; its head, Shaykh Ahmed Kuftaro, who led a Sufi tariqah, held the post of the Grand Mufti of Syria for two decades (Böttcher 2002; Pierret 2013). His highly tolerant readings of Islam and support for inter-faith dialogue suited the secular sensibilities of the Baath regime.

This active co-operation with the state enabled Shaykh Kuftaro to expand his mosque and foundation-based educational network, so that at the time of his death in 2001 the Abu Nour Foundation was the most visible Islamic scholarly establishment in Syria, hosting many foreign students. Imam Zaid Shakir, one of the co-founders of Zaytuna College, spent many years learning at the Abu Nour Foundation in Damascus. Active collaboration with the state did, however, compromise Shaykh Kuftaro's legitimacy in the eyes of many fellow scholars. Mahad al-Fatih, the other foundation that became influential during this period, was established by a relatively more conservative scholar, Shaykh Falfour,

---

[23] Al-Azhar was turned into a university, and its teaching mandate was expanded to include faculties in modern sciences, such as medicine. In addition, teaching methods were changed. These reforms have led to a deterioration in teaching standards, and reliance on the state has compromised its moral authority (Bano 2018a).

[24] In 2011 the protests inspired by the Arab Spring spread also to Syria; the resulting civil war has made Syria inaccessible for the pursuit of Islamic learning. Many Syrian scholars have, however, relocated to Istanbul, where they offer private lessons (Bano 2018a).

who chose to keep a greater distance from the state. At the time of my fieldwork in Syria in 2010, however, the dynamics were changing: the son of Shaykh Falfour, now leading the al-Fatih Institute, was actually proving more effective in winning support from the state, while Shaykh Kuftaro's son, who now led the Abu Nour Foundation, was falling out of favour, due to his allegedly erratic behaviour. Until 2011, however, both the Abu Nour Foundation and Mahad al-Fatih remained popular destinations for converts and Muslim students from overseas to pursue Arabic and Islamic Studies.

While education in these two foundations was more formalised than studying with individual shaykhs, because they were independent they still preserved the traditional teaching methods and curriculum more effectively than was possible at al-Azhar, which since 1961 has had to operate as a formal state university. More importantly, neither of these two foundations became so influential as to crowd out the independent networks of scholars and Sufis who continued to have their own individual followings (Böttcher 2002). Further, from the 1990s onwards, the Ministry of Awqaf began to offer Islamic courses for both men and women in the mosques, enabling many of these independent scholars to teach on those courses. The relatively more effective survival of traditional networks of Islamic knowledge transmission in Syria during the twentieth century made the cities of Damascus and Aleppo in particular popular destinations for overseas students to pursue Arabic and Islamic Studies. The Islamic rationalist scholars under study, especially those from the second generation, thus also benefitted from these opportunities.

Faraz Rabbani travelled to Damascus in 1997 with his wife, Shireen Ahmed, who herself teaches at SeekersHub and undertakes a heavy administrative load. Both studied in Syria for many years before moving to Amman; they returned to Canada only in 2007. Yahya Rhodus also spent a short period of time in Syria studying Arabic and Islamic sciences before moving to Yemen. Although the conflict in Syria that started in 2011 has made the country inaccessible for members of the third generation of scholars being trained within the rationalist network, many are still in the tutelage of Syrian scholars who have relocated to Istanbul and other parts of Turkey since the conflict. Further, some Syrian scholars, like Shaykh Yaqubi, a very prominent and outspoken Syrian scholar who comes from a respected family of Islamic scholars, has since the 2010 revolution relocated to the United States and actively speaks on many of the platforms associated with this network of Islamic rationalist scholars.

Fez, Morocco, and Tarim, Yemen

Morocco, in particular Fez, has been another important location which attracted scholars from within the rationalist network. Historically, Morocco has been an important base of maghrabi Islam, with its strong focus on the study of Malaki fiqh, rationalist theology, and tasawwuf. This strong traditional emphasis on promoting both Islamic fiqh and tasawwuf makes the Moroccan Islamic tradition historically very rich and closely associated with the Andalusian Islamic scholarly tradition. Many of the prominent early Islamic scholars from Morocco thus fit the category of Sufi-jurists, namely scholars who are known for their erudite knowledge and application of Islamic law, while also nurturing deep mysticism. The profile of Ahmad Zarruq, a sixteenth-century Moroccan Sufi-jurist who is listed in the perennial faculty of Zaytuna College (see previous chapter) and whose writings have been widely popularised by Hamza Yusuf, is a classic representative of the appeal of Moroccan Islam to the rationalist scholars.

In understanding the importance of Morocco it is also important to understand that, as in other Muslim countries, the Islamic education network there suffered from similar challenges in the colonial and post-colonial periods and faced similar challenges and marginalisation. Yet, as in Syria, the traditional Islamic scholarly networks were preserved somewhat better in Morocco than in other places, including Egypt and Turkey. As Zeghal (2008: 13) notes, state-led reforms 'involved rationalizing and modernizing the methods and contents of teaching: opening the curriculum to scientific subjects and foreign languages, imposing standardized tests, and turning teachers into civil servants'; yet, due to the more complex nature of the Moroccan state, where a royal family claiming lineage from the Prophet himself was in power, the reforms were promoted in a more subtle manner (Zeghal 2008). Thus, although the royal family itself helped to erode the authority of Qarawiyyin, a leading centre of Islamic learning, especially from the 1930s onwards, as it wanted to reassert its identity as a central site of Islamic authority, it allowed the pressure on Qarawiyyin to build through secular critics, rather than directly pushing a major reform agenda (Zeghal 2008).

In this more cautious balancing act by the royal family in power in Morocco, as opposed to the dramatic reforms to Islamic education platforms pushed by secular states in Egypt and Turkey, the traditional networks of scholars were preserved better. Thus, Qarawiyyin eventually did lose much of its prestige as a leading centre of learning in the Islamic world, but these independent networks of scholars and Sufi tariqahs remain very strong in Morocco and thus continue to act as important venues for teaching and learning the Arabic language, Maliki fiqh, and tasawwuf. The Darqawiyya, or Darqawa Sufi order, which is a revivalist branch of the Shadhiliyah brotherhood, is one of the orders which influenced some of these scholars. It exalts poverty and asceticism. It gained widespread support among rural communities and the urban lower classes. Its popularity was increased by its use of musical instruments in its rituals. But this is just one example; many other similar Sufi networks continue to thrive in Morocco and continue to host and receive students from within the third generation of the Islamic rationalist network.

Like Morocco, Yemen has been another important location for some within this network of Islamic rationalist scholars, and again it is one where the traditional method of transmission of Islamic knowledge has been better preserved, although it has its own distinct history and character. A particularly important site for traditional Islamic learning in Yemen is Tarim, a historic town in Hadhramaut, in South Yemen. Yemen has a large population of Sayyids,[25] so that many scholars in Tarim claim linage from the Prophet himself or his companions. Imam al-Haddad, who wrote some very influential books on theology, law, and tasawwuf, is one of the most prominent scholars from Tarim. The Hadhramauti community is also credited with helping the early spread of Islam to East Asia. Starting from the eleventh century, traders from Tarim and other parts of Hadhramaut took Islam to Indonesia, Malaysia, and southern India. The 'nine saints' venerated in Indonesia are all known to have come from Tarim (Worth 2009).

Tarim, and the Hadhramaut valley in general, is economically not well developed, and this fact has arguably helped to preserve the traditional structure of the society, the higher status of the Sayyids, and the importance attached to investing in Islamic education and preserving the classical Islamic teaching practices. During the socialist revolution of 1979–1990, the Islamic scholars were subjected to much state oppression, which forced many to leave the country. However, after the toppling of the socialist government, Islamic scholarly platforms underwent a revival. One important platform that was established in the 1990s was Dar al Mustafa, which became the primary base for learning Islamic sciences for Yahya Rhodus. Dar al-Mustafa claims to be the true representative of the

---

[25] Sayyids are the direct descendants of the Prophet Muhammad.

Ba'alawi scholarly tradition. The two prominent scholars leading this institution today are Shaykh Habib Umar bin Hafiz and Habib Ali al-Jifri. Habib Umar claims to be a descendant of the Prophet through his grandson Imam Hussain. Born in Tarim, Habib Umar received his early Islamic training from his father, who was also a prominent Islamic scholar. Taught by traditional methods, Habib Umar memorised the Quran and core texts in key Islamic sciences, especially fiqh and hadith. Later he studied with scholars in many locations, including Hijaz. He returned to Tarim in 1985 and established Dar al-Mustafa, with a focus on offering traditional Islamic teaching. Habib al-Jifri is the other influential scholar at Dar al-Mustafa. He is leading the institute named Kalam in the United Arab Emirates. The activities of Kalam are focused on reviving the Islamic rationalist sciences.

It is, however, important to note that both Habib Umar and Habib al-Jifri have in recent years become controversial for adopting what many Sunni Muslims believe are positions that are promoting factionalism within Islam. Like Shaykh Al-Goma in Egypt, who took an extreme position against the Muslim Brotherhood, even justifying the killing of its members (Bano 2018a), these two scholars are seen to promote active hostility against political Islam and Salafism. Habib al-Jifri in particular came under heavy pressure when he was credited with leading a conference in Russia where Sunni Islam was defined as being necessarily Ash'ari and Maturidi, leading to the exclusion of other mainstream Islamic movements, whether Salafism, Wahhabism, or others. As will be discussed in detail in Chapter 7, such a position has stirred unease about these scholars, even among followers of the Islamic rationalist network.

In the case of Rhodus, this close bond is understandable, given that they are his main scholars. He came to Yemen after he had studied with visiting Mauritanian scholars in California, and after he had travelled to Mauritania to study with prominent shaykhs, including Murabit al-Hajj, Hamza Yusuf's main teacher (see next section). After that he moved to Damascus, where he spent some time studying the Arabic language, grammar, and Quranic recitation, before moving on to Tarim in 2000. In Tarim, with Habib al-Jifri and Habib Umar, Rhodus studied core Islamic sciences including hadith, tafsir, 'aqidah, fiqh, sirah, and Arabic poetry. He also acts as an official translator for both Habib al-Jifri and Habib Umar. But this strong association with these scholars, and those of their mindset, in my view potentially poses the strongest risk to the long-term credibility of the Islamic rationalist network. This is an issue that is thus addressed in some detail in Chapter 7.

Mauritania

Last but not least, one of the most important sites for Islamic learning for Hamza Yusuf himself has been Mauritania. Yusuf credits his learning in most detail to Murabit al-Hajj, a Mauritanian shaykh living in the middle of the Sahara desert with whom he trained for more than three years. From among the contemporary scholars whose work he most frequently quotes to answer contemporary fiqhi questions, Shaykh Bin Bayyah, again a Mauritanian Sufi-jurist, is most noticeable. In terms of its history and economic development, Mauritania is different from most other Muslim contexts mapped above; in the basic simplicity of life there and the lack of intrusion of foreign values and goods, it would come closest to Tarim. Close to 90 per cent of Mauritanian land lies in the Sahara. The underdeveloped nature of this society has played a role in helping to preserve the traditional forms of Islamic learning. It is worth briefly tracing Hamza Yusuf's educational trajectory on travelling overseas after his conversion, in order to understand what he found compelling about the Mauritanian experience.

Hamza Yusuf has elaborated on many occasions how he spent many years in the United Arab Emirates, where the teaching methods did not impress him; teachers in the formal institutions were insulting towards the students and taught poorly, prompting him gradually to seek out networks of shaykhs teaching in private circles. It was in the United Arab Emirates that he started to study with one Mauritanian scholar who was also a judge in the Shari'ah court; Yusuf was greatly impressed with his high moral character and depth of knowledge and subsequently was introduced to other Mauritanian shaykhs. Studying with them in particular impressed on him the importance of memorisation, noting that his teachers told him that Mauritanians 'distinguish between daylight scholars and nighttime scholars. A daytime scholar needs light to read books to access knowledge, but a nighttime scholar can access that knowledge when the lights are out, through the strength of his memory and the retention of knowledge,' (Yusuf 2013n). Noting that he had by this point studied many of the main texts but did not remember them, he further adds, 'Shaykh Hamid procured a slate for me and began teaching me the basics again, but with rote memorization. It was humbling, but edifying, to see how this tradition has been carried on throughout the ages with these time-tested models,' (Yusuf 2013n).

It was during his stay in the United Arab Emirates that one night he dreamed about meeting Murabit al-Hajj, who was eventually to become his primary teacher. He left the United Arab Emirates in 1984, arriving in Mauritania a year later, travelling via Algeria. Yusuf has shared quite extensively the details of his experiences in Mauritania with al-Hajj, but also his impressions of the country and its premodern character: '(A) lot of people (there) didn't know about America; Just that there was a country called America. I actually met people in the Saharan desert that did not know America as a place. It was very amazing to see people that weren't just pre-modern, but they were pre-modern people that had no interaction with the modern world,' (Yusuf 2013o). He further notes, 'When I got to the Sahara, I was just so overwhelmed by a people that basically had no Ministry of Education so to speak. They had no school system, they had no salaried teachers, and they had no budgets for books, nothing. Yet these extraordinary schools exist out there,' (Yusuf 2013p). Ultimately, reaching Murabit al-Hajj, who was settled in the middle of the Sahara desert in Tuwamirat, a place that Yusuf notes completely overwhelmed him with its ethereal quality and a place that time seemed to have forgotten about, Hamza was instantly struck by his noble character. Al-Hajj in turn asked him, '"Is it like the dream?",' (Yusuf 2013q) which made Yusuf burst into tears, because in his dream their encounter had been very similar. For several years Yusuf stayed with al-Hajj, who insisted on his sharing his tent. Hamza has often spoken very highly of al-Hajj's wife, Maryam, referring to her as 'one of the most selfless people I have ever met,' (Yusuf 2013q).

In al-Hajj, Hamza found the model of ultimate devotion to God and pure humility that he had been searching for. He has often talked in his lectures about al-Hajj's daily routine to emphasise the rigorous effort required to reach the state of ihsan (that purity of faith achieved when one prays as if one can see Allah). As Hamza Yusuf recounts, al-Hajj would get up every night at 2:30 or 3:00 and begin the tahajjud prayer. He would often recite for a few hours, repeating the verses and weeping. A little before dawn he would start to recite the Quran, then make call for prayer, pray his *nafl* (optional prayer) and then take his place to lead the prayer. After sunrise he would pray the *Ishraq nafl*, after which he would return to his tent and have some fresh milk. Then he would start to teach his students until about 1:00 pm, at which point he would measure his shadow to determine the time for his midday prayer, before making the call for prayer. After leading the congregational prayer he would again return to the tent and resume his teaching until the afternoon. He would usually eat a small amount of rice and drink yogurt, as is common in West Africa, and return for the afternoon call and prayer. After this he would again resume his teaching and sometimes listen to the recitation of the Quran. During moments of quietness in his teaching, one could hear him saying with almost every breath, *La ilaha illa Allah* or reciting the Quran. After sunset he would give the call for the evening prayer and after leading the actual prayer would again carry on with dhikr and listening to or reciting the Quran. After the night prayer, he would repeatedly recite the lines from Imam Shafi'i's *Diwan* that remind oneself of death and constantly ask for forgiveness. As Hamza Yusuf notes:

I have never seen anyone like him before him or after him, and I don't think that I ever will. May Allah reward him for his service to this deen and his love and concern for the Muslims. He was never known to speak ill of anyone. . . .

Shaykh Murabit al-Hajj is a master of the sciences of Islam, but perhaps more wondrous than that, he has mastered his own soul. His discipline is almost angelic, and his presence is so majestic and ethereal that the one in it experiences a palpable stillness in the soul . . . I was told by many people from his family that had I seen him in his youth, I would have been even more astonished at his devotional practices.

He is recognized in Mauritania as being one of the last great scholars, and his fatwa is highly respected among the people of West Africa who know of him, and they are many. (Yusuf 2013r)

Capturing these details about Murabit al-Hajj gives us a valuable insight into why the Islamic rationalist scholars place so much emphasis on focusing on perfecting one's soul. They themselves have actively sought out scholars who could demonstrate high levels of inner piety and devotion to God. It is because of this need to constantly work on cleansing one's inner self if one is to actually worship God as he should be worshipped that these scholars place so much emphasis on tasawwuf.

In addition to crediting much of his learning to Shaykh Murabit, Hamza Yusuf also actively draws on the scholarship of Shaykh Abdullah Bin Bayyah, another leading Mauritanian shaykh, who is also Professor of Islamic Studies at the King Abdul Aziz University in Jeddah. Bin Bayyah specialises in the study of four Sunni madhhabs with a particular focus on Malikism, but he equally promotes tasawwuf. He defends many Sufi practices, such as dhikr or visiting the graves of the saints, as being integral to Islamic tradition. However, at the same time he emphasises that true Sufism can only follow after observing the basic ritual practices and Islamic legal dictates; like the Islamic rationalist scholars, Bin Bayyah keeps asserting that ihsan, the ultimate stage of piety mentioned in Hadith Jibril, and one that the Sufis strive to achieve, can only be reached once one has mastered the first two levels of faith, Islam and iman (Bin Bayyah 2018).

Fluent in Arabic and French, Bin Bayyah emphasises the importance of tasawwuf in these words:

That space of overflowing love, light, passion, insight, transparency, transcendence, and spirituality must have some container and some action to exist within and by. Actually, it is the inseparability and interdependence of the body and the soul. There must be a discipline with its own rules and terminology to represent such perfection aspired to by the highly-determined. That discipline took various names such as 'sermons', as used by Al-Bukhari, and 'asceticism', as in early Sunnah. Eventually, it was agreed to be named 'Sufism', just as the discipline of Shar'iah rulings was called Fiqh. (Bin Bayyah 2018)

Bin Bayyah either leads or is a member of many global Islamic platforms, such as the Forum for Promoting Peace in Muslim Societies, the Islamic Fiqh Council, the International Union of Muslim Scholars (from which he resigned in 2014), and the European Council for Fatwa and Research, a council of Muslim clerics which aims to explain Islamic law in a way that is sensitive to the realities of European Muslims.

CONCLUSION

These networks of traditionally trained Islamic scholars, which have been harboured in some Muslim-majority countries more effectively than others, thus have been the primary source of Islamic knowledge for the Islamic rationalist scholars who today are spreading the same teachings to their modern-educated followers in the West and also increasingly in Muslim-majority countries. In addition to the above-mapped sites, Turkey has had a vibrant Islamic scholarly revival under the AKP (Justice and Development Party), and is currently an important site for Islamic learning for students of some of the Islamic rationalist scholars. Rihla was hosted in Turkey between 2012 and 2016. Similarly, scholars in this Islamic rationalist network are hosting joint teaching programmes with institutions or scholars in Turkey.[26] In addition, Amman in Jordan by virtue of hosting Nuh Keller's Al-Qibla Institute also draws students from this network, especially those interested in pursuing an intensive Arabic-language programme. Finally, while al-Azhar, with its reformed university-style education, has not been the primary educational site for

---

[26] One important collaborator with this rationalist network in Turkey is Professor Recep Şentürk. He did his PhD at Columbia and is a prolific writer (Bano 2018a). He is Professor of Sociology at Fatih University in Istanbul and the Director of the Alliance of Civilizations Institute.

any of these scholars, many of the al-Azhari scholars are highly respected among them and are invited to their retreats.

Further, even after returning to the West, these scholars remain deeply connected to their teachers in the Muslim world and also invite them to address their own students. While confident in their ability to develop strong Islamic institutions in the West, the Islamic rationalist scholars recognise that the process will take time, and that there will always be a need for collaboration and learning from scholars based in the Muslim-majority countries.

A closer examination of the platforms where these scholars have studied has also shown how the Islamic scholarly platforms that have better preserved the traditional mode of Islamic teaching are the ones that were less exposed to colonial influence and least exposed to state-led reforms. Hamza Yusuf has himself often reflected on this issue:

> I was very affected by these people [Mauritian scholars]. They affected me because I hadn't seen people like them. Now the secret of these people is simply one thing and one thing only, and I'm convinced of this now, after thinking about it for a long time. These are people that the colonials never got to, because they were in the middle of the Sahara desert. And Europeans tend to not like to be in conditions where they don't have all the perks that go with staying there. And Mauritania is an extremely difficult environment to stay in. (Yusuf 2013m)

But, as is evident in the example of Mauritania, the platforms that have better preserved the traditional Islamic scholarly networks due to being less exposed to modern Western institutions are also often unable to fully relate to contemporary challenges. This, as we will see in the next chapter, is precisely why these converts have come to play such an important role as mediators between the traditionally trained scholars and the young modern-educated Muslims of today. After all, why could these tradition-ally trained scholars from whom these converts learned not reach out to these Muslims themselves? The answer resides in recognising the tacit knowledge of Western reality that these converts bring to Islamic schol-arship. To fully appreciate the importance of this argument, we need to consider the socio-economic profile and educational background of these converts. Such an analysis will help us also to understand why they were attracted to traditional Islamic scholarly networks espousing a rationalist-mystical balance in the first place, and why they are better able to connect to the modern-educated Muslim youth than are the traditionally trained Islamic scholars from whom they themselves learned.

4

Teaching in the New Geographies of Islam

Having Tacit Knowledge of Reality

White converts to Islam are often featured in the Western media, but – as is the case with the media coverage of Islam in general – mainly for the subjects' radical propensities. Such coverage often fuels assumptions that the white coverts normally come from among the marginalised and reactionary youth who convert to Islam in response to life's frustrations and personal failures, rather than due to any inner reflection or contemplation. Also, it is true that many converts, with the typical zeal of newcomers, are genuinely attracted to more textual Islamic traditions such as Salafism; the al-Medina University thus attracts many white converts, although when interpreting this choice it must also be acknowledged that Salafism does not equate with Islamic militancy. The converts leading the Islamic rationalist revival, however, did not follow this path; instead, despite being exposed to the more literalist movements, they settled on traditional Islamic scholarly platforms that promoted rational theology, classical legal scholarship, and deep mysticism. These scholars' conversion to Islam followed periods of thoughtful reflection and contemplation, and their socio-economic profiles defy the media image of reactionary white converts to Islam. This chapter explores the socio-economic and educational backgrounds of these scholars and their motives for conversion, in order to understand why they gravitated towards the more rationalist and deeply mystical yet legalistic readings of Islam. The resulting analysis demonstrates that, rather than coming from marginalised segments of society, these converts largely came from relatively privileged backgrounds, and their conversion was not a result of hostility towards their own societies but an outcome of deeper soul searching. In Islam they found answers which they could not find in their own tradition. Islam appealed to them mainly because it acknowledged the Christian tradition and built on it – not because it offered a complete departure from it.

The profiles of the rationalist scholars, especially those in the first generation of converts, show that they come primarily from white, upper-middle-income families. From an early age these individuals became interested in questions of theology and human existence. They received education in good schools (and in some cases in elite private schools) and prestigious Western universities. Further, as was the case with the Spanish reverts of the 1970s, they were in general of a humanistic disposition, in that most were students of literature, languages, or music. These individuals converted to Islam after much soul searching and reflection on questions linked to Christian theology. It is thus very important to understand that in converting to Islam these individuals were not entirely rejecting their own societies, and nor do they support such positions now. Islam appealed to them because it builds on what they valued about their own societies and religion, and in doing so it could fill some of the gaps that they found in their own tradition. In fact, to date these scholars are protective simultaneously of their Islamic identity and of their Western heritage. They are not rebelling against the West, although they are critical of some of the outcomes of Western modernity, especially excessive materialism; rather, as we will see in the next chapter, in their view Islamic morality and ethics are very much in tune with true Western values.

This chapter will demonstrate how these converts' socio-economic and educational backgrounds are key to understanding their ability to influence young, modern-educated Muslims. Their backgrounds give them tacit knowledge of the reality experienced by such Muslims living in the West and their counterparts in the more affluent and urban centres of Muslim-majority countries. As discussed in Chapter 1, the concept of tacit knowledge highlights the importance of experiential knowledge that we acquire through exposure to everyday reality. The socio-economic and educational background of these scholars is markedly different from that of a typical Islamic teacher in the mosques in Muslim countries, as well as those in the West; these scholars' tacit knowledge of everyday reality is thus very different from that of the mosque-based scholars. Instead, the profiles and everyday experiences of the Islamic rationalist scholars are very much in line with those of the young, modern-educated Muslims whom they are trying to influence.

In the subsequent chapters, we shall see how this shared knowledge of the everyday realities of modern society is key to explaining the constantly expanding network of followers of the rationalist scholars in the West, as well as among the members of upper-income groups in Muslim-majority countries. It is precisely this tacit knowledge of the realities of modern Muslim youth that has created an important role for these converts to act as mediators between the traditionally trained scholars from whom they themselves learned and the Muslim youth whom they are trying to influence. The traditionally trained scholars, for reasons discussed in the previous chapter, even if they belong to the rationalist Islamic tradition, lack the command of Western languages and the knowledge of modern life that would enable them to relate Islamic dictates to the changing times in a meaningful way, or impress the modern-educated Muslim youth with their understanding of Islam.

I MIDDLE-INCOME AND UNIVERSITY-EDUCATED

In the first generation of rationalist Islamic scholars, all three key figures leading this network – Hamza Yusuf, Tim Winter, and Dr Umar Faruq Abd-Allah – are from well-to-do, white, middle-class families. Tim Winter's father was a respected English architect. As a child Winter was educated at the elite Westminster School. He graduated from the University of Cambridge with a double first in Arabic in 1983 (*Independent* 2010). Hamza Yusuf's parents were also professionals and they placed a high premium on education; as Yusuf himself notes, he went 'to extremely good schools in the United States' (Yusuf 2013k). In his words, 'I went to a private Jesuit school, . . . So, I was used to a very high standard of education in the West' (Yusuf 2013k). Dr Umar's father was similarly very well educated and was a scientist; at the time of his conversion, Dr Umar himself was studying on a master's course at Cornell University. After his conversion, he did a PhD in Islamic Studies at Chicago University under the supervision of the famous Islamic reformist scholar Fazlur Rahman.

Among the second generation of scholars, the family profiles are slightly more diverse, but, nonetheless, overall many traits are shared. Yahya Rodhus, who comes from a well-to-do middle-class American family from Kansas City, Missouri, holds a BA in Near Eastern Studies from the University of California, Berkeley, and an MA in Islamic Studies from the Graduate Theological Union, and is currently doing research for a PhD in Theology and Religious Studies at the University of Cambridge with Tim Winter, while undertaking active teaching himself. When he first enrolled as an undergraduate student in UC Berkeley,[1] his parents were in a position to pay off his entire tuition fee. Jihad Brown, who (as noted in Chapter 1) has as yet not initiated an institution of his own but is an active member of this network of scholars and delivers lectures and gives seminars at events linked to this network, also comes from a white middle-class family. He had received degrees in Psychology and Near East Studies from Rutgers University before embarking on a rigorous study of classical Islamic Sciences with scholars in the Middle East (Lamppost 2018).

Compared with Yahya Rhodus and Jihad Brown, the co-founders of Ta'leef, Usama Canon and Mustafa Davis, have more mixed family backgrounds; they consequently also had slightly different initial motives for conversion. Raised in Fontana, California, Canon notes that his friends knew him in his youth as the light-skinned black nationalist; in his talks he highlights his mixed ancestry by acknowledging the following influences among his ancestors: 'Baptist, black, Mormon, white, Italian, Irish, Oklahoma and Andrew Jackson' (Islamic Monthly 2012). He acknowledges that as he grew up he thus grappled with questions of race and identity, particularly because he notes that he himself was of lighter complexion than many of his family members. He has often talked about how his white family was very white and his black family very black, and how he was exposed to both of these aspects of his heritage. As a high school student in the 1990s, Canon was influenced by the Black Consciousness Movement and took part in demonstrations and protests led by black and Hispanic students (Islamic Monthly 2012). Mustafa Davis, a fellow convert and co-founder of Ta'leef, has a similarly mixed racial background. Their initial conversions to Islam, as we will see later in this chapter, were thus triggered by developments within the Black Consciousness Movement.

Within the second generation of scholars in the Islamic rationalist network there is Faraz Rabbani, who, unlike the others, was born into a Muslim family and thereby inherited the Islamic tradition. As noted in Chapter 1 of this volume, in the third generation of scholars being trained in the network the majority are born Muslims, but in the second generation, Faraz Rabbani is the only born Muslim to have become very visible in this network. In terms of his socio-economic profile, however, he has much in common with these converts, as he comes from a well-to-do

---

[1] On first being admitted to this programme, he dropped out within the first week. He, however, later re-enrolled and completed the degree.

middle-class immigrant family in Canada. Growing up, he moved with his parents between Canada, England, Egypt, and Spain, before returning to Canada to complete his high school and university education. He thus refers to himself as a 'global nomad' (Rabbani 2018). Like others, he received a good education and did his undergraduate degree in economics and commerce from the University of Toronto (Rabbani 2018).

Thus, these scholars overwhelmingly come from either middle-income or slightly upper-middle-income family backgrounds in the West, and most were privileged to have had access to good schools and were able to pursue higher education in leading Western universities. Further, not only did they mostly come from middle-income families who placed a high premium on education, but according to their own accounts their families were also relatively tolerant of religious and cultural plurality and nurtured relatively liberal (or at least tolerant) values. Hamza Yusuf has revealed the most detailed information in public about his parents. He has always talked very highly about his mother's liberal political orientation and ethical behaviour; his deep respect for her moral outlook was captured best in the tribute that he wrote in her memory on her death in 2016:

She lived through the Great Depression, World War II, the Vietnam War, and the Civil Rights Movement, which she was actively involved in long before many others joined. My mother spent her life serving others. She never complained and was the most ethical person I have ever known. She hated bigotry, prejudice, and any form of discrimination. She spent her life fighting against injustice. Some of my earliest memories involve civil rights marches, on which she always brought along her children. She marched with Dr. King and Cesar Chavez, and even in her late eighties she marched in San Francisco against the war in Iraq. All her life, she volunteered in various organizations and served for years on the Homeless Committee in Marin County. (Yusuf 2016b)

He further added:

While baptized a Greek Orthodox due to her father's heritage, she was raised a devout Catholic. She had a long interest in Sufism and loved the poet Rumi long before he was popular in the West. She was a member of the Buddhist Songhai for much of her later years and practised Tibetan Buddhism. In 2010, in Fez, Morocco, she took the Shahadah with Sidi Ismail Filali Baba. Yet many years ago, just after I had first embraced Islam, I was telling her about the faith when she said to me, 'I knew the Prophet Muhammad was a prophet long before you were born, dear.' She had also taken me to a mosque when I was twelve to pray the Friday prayer in order to expose me to an important world religion. She lived in my home for the last two years of her life and always prayed with us, even going into prostration despite the difficulty. (Yusuf 2016b)

He has similarly often talked about the intellectual bent of his father, David Hanson, who died in 2016 at the age of 89. Again the tribute that Yusuf (2016a) wrote in memory of his father captures his politically liberal outlook:

He was a good father, and the single most well-read person in the Western canon I have ever met. The Huntington Library gave him a small cubicle, where he carried on his work on Elizabethan manuscripts. My last conversations with him were about the Liberal Arts, of which he was a life-long student. He lived with me on and off for the last few years and remained independent until the last few weeks of his life.

Referring to his ultimate conversion to Islam, Yusuf noted, 'During his stay with us, he always joined in prayer with my family. A few weeks ago, he said the shahadah with his physician, Dr. Asad Tarsin, and requested that he be buried as a Muslim. I washed his body with my son and two close friends yesterday. We will bury him this morning' (Yusuf 2016a). In another place, he has noted how his father defended his son's new faith to the critics. Talking about how people had a very negative image of Islam at the time of his conversion, he has mentioned: 'One of my father's friends, who was a lawyer… they were just in conversation, and he mentioned that Islam is just an idiot's religion. And my father said, "Well, my son is a Muslim actually, and I don't think he's an idiot"' (Yusuf 2013h).

Dr Umar's parents, who were from western Nebraska, though from a somewhat more conservative background than those of Hamza Yusuf and Tim Winter, similarly seemed to have a relatively tolerant approach. His mother and father were also very supportive and did not object to him becoming a Muslim.

2 INTEREST IN THE HUMANITIES AND ARTS

In addition to coming from educated, middle-class, largely tolerant families, the Islamic rationalist converts shared another trait, in that in general they were attracted to the arts and humanities. Tim Winter has talked on many occasions about how, along with his dissatisfaction with the Christian concept of the Trinity, Islamic arts, the Arabic language, and the riches of Islamic civilisation had attracted him. As he explained in a radio interview: 'We [Muslims] have great traditions of singing the praises of God and of the blessed prophet, in an almost infinite variety of modes. The African Islamic sound is very different from the Bosnian Islamic sound, the Turkish Islamic sound, the Uzbeks, the Malays. Islam is not just one civilisation, but a huge range of civilisations, which all have their own particular way of being Muslim, as it were metaphorically facing the same direction of prayer in Mecca, but from often quite different directions. It's a diverse world.' (ABC 2004). Elaborating further on how the beauty of the arts and architecture associated with Muslim civilisation inspires faith, he added:

Well, Islam is not just a great enterprise of faith and works, but it's produced some of the world's great civilisations. You think visually of the great world that stretches from the Taj Mahal to the Alhambra, some of the world's great architecture. It also has wonderful sounds as well, and the key to Islamic tonality and melody is actually the formal recitation of the Holy Qu'ran. I used to walk down a little street when I was living in Cairo in the early morning when the shopkeepers were putting out their wares, and I counted 38 shopkeepers who actually were listening to the 24-hour a day, wall-to-wall Qu'ran radio station, which sort of invested the mundanity of their lives with the fragrance of the absolute. That's certainly my favourite sound, it was one of the things that magnetised me and brought me towards Islam, and it is the greatest of the Islamic art, the naked, unadorned, projection of the human voice into some great dome of a sacred space; that still moves me more than any other sound. (ABC 2004)

Hamza Yusuf is similarly known for his extensive reading of literature and philosophy from within the tradition. In addition to his knowledge of the Islamic texts, he is also known for placing a strong emphasis on aesthetics and beauty in Islam, as is also emphasised (and appreciated by his followers) in his own style of dress. During my interview with Faraz Rabbani, noting how Yusuf is known as an avid reader, he mentioned with some amusement how some of his followers try to figure out which book Hamza Yusuf is currently reading, on the basis of the speeches that he gives at any given point. His mother captured his interest in reading literature from a very early age in these terms (Yusuf 2013g): 'One of the things that really stood out in my mind, and I've never really gotten over it, was when he was about 11 or 12, he was an avid reader and he told me he had read *War and Peace*, and so I assumed he had read a comic book story of *War and Peace* ... It's a long book. But the movie came out, the Russian film, and it was 3.5 hours (long). So, I took him to see it, and during the intermission, he was discussing the difference between the book and the film. So I was convinced he had read it.'

Dr Umar was also a student of literature and history. It was these interests, and in particular his exposure to black literature, that initially attracted him to Islam. When he was a master's level student, his wife at the time, who was German, bought for him the book *Black Ice*, in which there were references to Malcolm X. He decided to take the course on Black Literature in the next term and began to read ahead of the start of the term. The African American literature greatly impressed him, but the autobiography of Malcolm X proved the ultimate draw. He recalls reading it all night. One of the things in Malcolm X's writing that most impressed him about Islam was the presentation of Islam as a religion that abolishes fear.

These ideas particularly resonated with Dr Umar, given the liberal atmosphere of the 1960s and 1970s and the growing visibility of the civil-rights movements. Further, like Abdus Samad, Dr Umar was strongly opposed to war and to being drafted into military service. As a master's student at Cornell University in late 1960s, he was at risk of being drafted to serve in the war in Vietnam, although he was very against the war and had been active in the anti-war movement himself. He had decided that, if pushed, he would move to Canada or work in the army as a translator. This strong internal resistance to being forced to take part in a war that he did not believe in, while at the same time being exposed to Islam through Black American literature and in particular the biography of Malcolm X, seemed to have accelerated the intensity of his internal self-reflection. Under the law he had the right to resist the draft on the basis of conscientious objection – a plea which he did successfully defend on his ultimate conversion to Islam. His conversion, however, resulted in the break-up of his first marriage, as his wife could not feel the same way about Islam.

A similar humanist orientation is evident in the profiles of Yayha Rhodus, Jihad Brown, Usama Canon, Mustafa Davis, and Faraz Rabbani. Mustafa is even today primarily a photographer and filmmaker and he lives in the San Francisco Bay Area. Noting his first meeting with Usama Canon, when both were college students, Mustafa Davis (2011) describes his own profile in these terms: 'I was sporting dread locks, wearing a Haile Selassie shirt, baggy jeans, suede Pumas, sunglasses and a Sessions snowboarder jacket. I was the quintessential hard to label California Bay Area pseudo hip hop hippie skater.' He and Canon took the same Spanish classes, and both were musicians and artists. Canon had the code to the piano room in the music hall, and both of them would sneak into the room, sit and play music for hours, and talk about spirituality. They did this for an entire semester. Faraz Rabbani similarly was an avid reader; he acknowledges that he also loves classical Islamic poetry and singing, though at the same time cautioning against prohibited forms of music or indulging too much even in approved forms of music.

The academic trajectories of Yahya Rhodus and Jihad Brown in Western institutions, in addition to the classical Islamic training that they chose to pursue in Tarim and Damascus respectively, similarly establish their interest in the humanities and philosophical sciences.

3 INTEREST IN THEOLOGY

For all these scholars, especially those from the first generation, ultimately, however, their conversions were due to their reflection on existential concerns and the fact that they had experienced a certain discomfort with Christian theology. In particular, their core concerns stemmed from the doctrine of the Trinity. Talking about his conversion, Tim Winter has explained that he went into religion through a dry and bookish route. He recalled making a conscious effort to compare various philosophies and theologies and also acknowledges that interactions with Muslims had nothing to do with it, as he had never really met a proper Muslim before converting. For him, he notes, 'it was very much principles first and then the realities of the community after'(ABC 2004). As he has explained in a number of media interviews, he comes from a family of Norfolk nonconformists, some of whom were Congregationalist ministers, mostly in small chapels. In an interview with ABC Radio, he noted that among the non-conformists there were certain hesitations about the doctrine of the Trinity: 'Perhaps a certain Anglo Saxon pragmatism could never quite get its mind around the intricacies of at least the classical definitions of three in one. Many people in the seventeenth and nineteenth century had reservations about the authenticity of the later doctrine of the Trinity, and whether it actually made sense to solid, no-nonsense, English pragmatists. So I come very much out of that tradition,' (ABC 2004).

Talking about his actual conversion, Winter explains how he had reflected seriously on the meaning of life, 'and trying to figure out where I was, what I was heading for'. As noted in the case of Abdus Samad, he also credits the overall mood of the 1970s, 'the tail end of the sort of hippy trail to India', when people were experimenting with all 'sorts of oriental, exotic alternatives to solid, middle-class, tedious, worthy, Christendom' (ABC 2004). Instead of being attracted to totally different philosophies such as Buddhism, Winter became attracted to the Middle East. As he noted in the interview, going beyond Christianity to a more exotic culture 'would have represented too much of a tearing, too much of a ripping out of my soul, of some of the stories that were there from my childhood, and were really part of who I was' (ABC 2004). He explained that he did not really want to be anything strange or exotic: 'I wasn't looking for an alternative identity, but rather for a way of continuing in some way with what I already knew, and the person of Jesus was very much central to that, sort of unbesmirchable, great hero of the West's religious history. But at the same time, squaring my conscience with the core doctrines, and it came to a point where I really could no longer recite the Creed in church and accept the doctrines of incarnation, atonement, and Trinity' (ABC 2004).

Winter has spoken in detail about the challenges presented to him by Christian dogma. The doctrines of the incarnation, atonement, and the Trinity failed to convince him, and in his understanding they did not reflect what historians in the 1970s were discovering about the original teachings and lifestyle of Jesus. He has talked about the major crisis in New Testament scholarship concerning the question of whether the 'Christ of faith is actually the same person as the Jesus of history, the great resurrected Christ that you see in the cupolas of misty Byzantine domes, staring down from on high; is that actually the same person as that amazing wandering rabbi of first century Palestine with his extraordinary message of reconciliation?'(ABC 2004.)

Similarly, Winter has spoken about the incarnation as being a necessarily unconvincing concept. As he has argued: 'The Jesus that appeals to me is the Jesus of, say, the parables, particularly the Prodigal Son, who is ultimately a Jewish teacher, that the great message of the Hebrew Bible is that human beings can be reconciled to God through God's infinite power to forgive, that the prodigal returns to the father, and there's no sign of a vicarious atonement, or the father suffering on the son's behalf. He just forgives him and embraces him. I think that's the highest form of monotheism for me, and I find that enshrined in Islam actually rather more accurately than at least in the developed forms of Christianity that I was brought up with' (ABC 2004).

Thus, the simple definition of one God in Islam appealed to him: 'One of the great mysteries of God is that the nature of God is pure compassion, and the God of compassion which is to be known by human beings, and has created the world as a diverse range of signposts, beautiful signposts pointing back to him. So wherever I look, whether it's the beauties of the Australian outback, or the English countryside, or the deserts of the Middle East, I see the beauty of God, and that arouses in my heart a desire to return to God, to love that God' (ABC 2004). In his interviews he has talked about the importance of God's eminence in Islam that appeals to him. He has emphasised how the Quranic image of God is of one who is utterly unlike ourselves, yet in the Quranic understanding he is closer to humans than their jugular vein; he is with them wherever they may turn. As Winter notes: 'And whatever we see in terms of beauty in the world, in people's faces, in humans, mutual compassion and love, there we discern that basic thirst that human beings have for the source of nourishment and richness and fullness that is in God. So it's a kind of nostalgia. Religion is about awakening a nostalgia that we have for the place where we were before we were born, and the place that we hope we'll return to after our death' (ABC 2004).

He has also noted the appeal of the shared core rulings of Islam, arguing that one of the riches of Islam for him is that 'the core liturgy, the core practices of worship and of fasting and of charity, are the same everywhere, and have never changed. No well-meaning, liberal, woolly-minded reformers have said "Let's do mosque worship in a slightly different way"' (ABC 2004). He adds, 'I go into a mosque and I know exactly what I'm going to get, a beautiful, unchanged, perfect ritual from a great age of faith, and I find that to be a unique privilege, one of the great things of being a Muslim for me, is that our core practices don't change, and I think probably never will change' (ABC 2004). Equally and importantly, he has emphasised Islam's appeal as an integral element of the Abrahamic tradition. For him this ensures that, as an Englishman, he does not experience the religion as something foreign. Islam might appear different, but in reality, he notes, it is part of the Judaeo-Christian scriptural, Middle Eastern family of faiths. In his words: 'I still love Jesus and Abraham, Moses, Jacob, Isaac, Ishmael, they're all revered in the Qur'an, they're the great figures of my early childhood, and I still revere them to this day. So I don't feel it's an alienation' (ABC 2004).

At the time of his conversion, Dr Umar was largely secular. His parents belonged to two different Christian traditions. During his teenage years, his family attended a Lutheran church. He had been confirmed in that Lutheran church and used to be involved in the church activities; he would, for example, help the pastor by lighting the candles in the church. However, he distinctly remembers the moment when doubts began to take root in his mind about Christian theology. After he had been confirmed, one day when they were walking out of the church, his father asked him in a reflective mood if he really believed in the Trinity. This question startled him, as he looked upon his father as a very authoritative figure. His self-reflections led him to approach the pastor with his doubts about the doctrine of the Trinity. Finding his questions problematic, the pastor tried to frighten him into believing. This generated even more severe doubts about religion in his mind. His self-reflections, however, ultimately convinced him of the importance of religion, but now with a focus on one God – and it was this that made Islam very appealing.

Hamza Yusuf's journey to Islam presents a very similar narrative. He was propelled into deep thinking about life and its purpose after a car accident in which he narrowly escaped death. That was in 1977, when he was barely nineteen years old, about to start Junior College at Ventura. The experience led him to reflect very deeply on the subject of life and death and the meaning and purpose of life. This self-reflection resulted in his conversion to Islam a year later. As he has noted, 'the idea of mortality is something that hit me very early on in life' (Yusuf 2013e). His Catholic school education had, as he has noted, exposed him to religion. He now became particularly interested in reading about what happens after death and began to read across different traditions. He found Islam to have made the most substantial contributions to after-death literature and understandings.

Like Tim Winter and Dr Umar, Yusuf has also acknowledged the prevailing spirit of the 1970s as being conducive to explorations of other traditions, particularly other religious traditions. However, like Winter, he has also noted that for most this exploration was normally focused on exploring the exotic. Talking about the time of his conversion, he has noted, 'This is 1977, probably '76, '77, prior to the Iranian Revolution and what was happening then. Islam is the last place that people look in the United States, traditionally. You'd look at Buddhism, Hinduism, probably Shintoism or Daoism, before someone would think about looking at Islam' (Yusuf 2013h). His continued reading ultimately convinced him of the truth of Islam, although he notes that initially this was not what he had hoped to do: 'Well, I bumped into the truth a few times, and I had a choice to brush myself off and get on with it, or to become Muslim, and Alhamdulillah, by the Fadl of Allah, I chose to become Muslim' (Yusuf 2013h). Like Winter, Yusuf has also emphasised how it was not interaction with Muslims that led to his conversion, but the conviction that he developed in Islam through his readings and certain signs that he saw: 'I didn't bump into a Muslim; I bumped into a Qur'an, a translation of the Qur'an; that was the beginning. I didn't read that much (of the Qur'an) before I became a Muslim. I read, in fact, a few chapters. I just had some strong indications' (Yusuf 2013i).

Within the second generation of Islamic rationalist scholars, actual theological concerns again played a key role in attracting most of the converts to Islam – as they continue to do in the third generation of converts being trained under these scholars.[2] Yahya Rhodus has recalled growing up in a religious household, an experience which led him to explore the potential for spiritual fulfilment beyond an exclusive emphasis on the Christian tradition in which he was born. He started to reflect on the purpose and meaning of life at a young age. As he has noted, growing up he felt that life was simultaneously crammed and empty: 'crammed, ironically, with empty values and empty of meaning' (*Islamic Monthly* 2012). The typical stresses faced by an average middle-class American family left him questioning the real purpose of life. Religion and spirituality made life much more meaningful than the pressures and stresses of the material world. From early on he developed an interest in people from different backgrounds and cultures, with the result that at high school he had friends from different ethnic backgrounds. This interest in different cultures and civilisations is one of the key factors that Yahya Rhodus has explained as being the foundation of the strong friendship that flourished between him, Usama Canon, and Mustafa Davis – all three of whom first met in 1996 in Berkeley, California.

Given these dispositions, Rhodus began to read extensively about other cultures. One of the books he notes as having had a particular influence on him was *Mutant Message Down Under* by Marlo Morgan, a fictional account of the experiences of an American woman during the time that she spent with a nomadic Aboriginal tribe in Australia. The Aborigines burn all her belongings – clothing, jewellery and credit cards – and teach her to live in their rustic world of simplicity. This experience has a major influence on her, making her 'return to the basics of life, reconnect with nature and replace her materialistic values with "Divine Oneness"' (*Islamic Monthly* 2012). Rhodus says that his journey into embracing Islam in 1996 was similar. By the time he was nineteen and living in Santa Clara, California, a chance encounter with a visiting Mauritanian scholar so moved him that he decided to follow the scholar to the mostly desert country of Mauritania the next summer (*Islamic Monthly* 2012). Although enrolled at the University of California, Berkeley, Rhodus dropped out after only one week of classes (*Islamic Monthly* 2012). The journey changed his life. He set out to replace his materialistic values with spirituality and began pursuing a formal education in Islamic studies with Mauritanian scholars. With no running water

---

[2] While majority of the students in the third generation are born Muslims, there are also some converts.

or electricity, he was forced to return to the basics of life and rely on nature for subsistence, while learning to connect to the natural world. On a daily basis, he spent his time engaging with scholars who helped him to reconnect to his natural spiritual state (*Islamic Monthly* 2012). Thus, much like Hamza Yusuf's experience in Mauritania (documented in the preceding chapter), it was the appeal of humans in a natural setting, devoid of the material compulsions of the modern age, that attracted Rhodus to Islam.

Usama Canon's conversion to Islam took a slightly different route, but ultimately the deepening of his conviction in Islam occurred for very similar reasons. Unlike Rhodus, at the time of his conversion Canon was attracted to Islam as a form of social resistance: he had become associated with the Black Muslim movement, and Islam provided answers to his questions about his own identity. As noted in the preceding section, identity politics had been very important to Canon, who comes from a mixed-race family. Thus he acknowledges how, as a teenager, he embraced a Muslim identity as a form of popular resistance before formally embracing the religion itself. He was first exposed to Islam through his older brother, who become a member of the Nation of Islam. This, as Canon notes, inevitably became a point of contention in their mixed-race home (*Islamic Monthly* 2012). His brother later converted to orthodox Islam, thus influencing Canon to become likewise interested in Islam (*Islamic Monthly* 2012), although he ended up pursuing a very different understanding of Islam through the networks that he entered through the Zaytuna Institute.

It was his personal experience of conversion that in turn shaped the work that Usama Canon is doing at the Ta'leef Collective, which is focused on supporting Muslims from all different backgrounds, especially new converts. Although Canon loved his new community of Muslims, he struggled to connect with the brothers from whom he was learning (*Islamic Monthly* 2012). Gradually, he encountered classically trained Islamic scholars and moved towards the Zaytuna Institute; in particular, he became close to Hamza Yusuf. His own experience made him recognise the gap between what he was learning and the inability of more orthodox scholars to reconcile that learning with his own realities. Ta'leef Collective thus has come to focus on filling that gap. His different background and different route into Islam have meant that Canon has developed a very important and distinctive role within the Islamic rationalist network. Of all the scholars profiled here, he is seen as less of a scholar and more of a dynamic Muslim speaker who can relate to Muslims of all orientations, especially the fresh converts and those who come from different backgrounds. He is regarded as a particularly effective speaker and motivator among those young people who struggle with identity issues, as he himself did when growing up.

The conversion to Islam of Ta'leef's co-founder, Mustafa Davis, was closely related to the experiences of Canon. Feeling burnt out by life in downtown San Jose, working nights waiting tables and going to school during the day, he talked to Canon about his need for a fresh start and considered a return to Catholicism to get his life in order (Davis 2011). Canon, who had been exposed to Islam by then, encouraged him to think about Islam. Later, when he visited a bookstore with a view to buying a copy of the Bible, he was attracted by the Quran and also by Martin Lings's book on Muhammad. As he explains,

I opened it [the Quran] to a random page which just happened to be the very first page of Chapter Maryam. I read it from beginning to end and remember getting chills in my body as it explained in great detail the miraculous birth of Prophet Jesus (peace be upon Him). I had no idea that Muslims also believed in the miraculous birth of Jesus nor that they did not believe He was God's son. As Christian it never made sense to me that God would have a son.

Without understanding why, I found myself weeping in the bookstore holding on to a copy of a translation of the Qu'ran. I decided to buy it so I could read more about what Muslims believed. In my emotional state I completely forgot to buy a Bible and left the bookstore. (Davis 2011)

While for the key scholars in this network it was an increased conviction in the validity of Islamic reasoning that led to conversion, for Faraz Rabbani, a born Muslim, it was this sense of constantly changing national identity, due to living in different countries, that on reflection made him appreciate that ultimately his most important identity was that of being a Muslim. 'Having come from so many places, when he began to reflect on who he was, he discovered the only clear answer was "a Muslim"' (Rabbani 2018). At university, he became active with the Muslim Students Association (MSA) at a local and national level. He helped to develop the National MSA Starter's Guide and founded and ran the *Muslim Voice*, the magazine produced by the University of Toronto MSA. He did his Bachelor degree in Economics and Commerce at the University of Toronto, but gradually became more interested in the serious study of Islam.

CONCLUSION

By tracing the family backgrounds, the educational experiences, and the personal characteristics of the scholars within the Islamic rationalist network, this chapter has illustrated how these scholars converted to Islam in response to deep personal reflection and soul searching. They came to Islam not as a reaction against the West, but as a result of active contemplation on questions about the purpose and meaning of life, which were important to them. These were individuals educated in respected Western educational institutions who explored questions of theology and human existence and found Islam to provide the most convincing answers. Some among them, such as Usama Canon and Mustafa Davis, were initially attracted to Islam as a form of political resistance, but on conversion they too soon gravitated towards the more spiritual dimensions of the faith. While feeling a deep sense of connection with the Western tradition, these individuals were troubled by the growing materialism of the West, which they saw as a by-product of modernity and secularism. The profiles of these scholars lend support to a growing perception that the disciplines that one studies might have an influence on how one engages with religious texts.

In *Engineers of Jihad*, Gambetta and Hertog (2016) examine profiles of leading Islamic militants of the past few decades and conclude that the majority of them had a background in engineering. A popular line of reasoning in literature concerning the profiles of prominent Islamic militants today thus speculates that, because many of them come from a scientific background, they have a propensity to interpret the religious texts literally. Humanities students, on the other hand, are argued to adopt a more pluralistic reading of religious texts, in line with the critical thinking encouraged in fields such as arts and literature. Such assertions and supporting evidence need to be treated with caution, given that they can lead to the unfair profiling of Muslims with scientific educational backgrounds. The findings reported in this chapter by no means contribute to such an assertion; they do, however, show that an orientation towards humanities is conducive to making a scholar gravitate towards what in this book has been defined as Islamic rationalism.

Further, by establishing that these scholars come from well-to-do, professional, middle-class families and that they were educated in respected Western institutions, this chapter has presented evidence as to how the tacit knowledge these scholars have of the everyday reality is very shared with that of the young university-educated Muslim youth whom they are able to attract. These scholars and the young Muslims whom they are influencing thus have common experiences of everyday reality, unlike the imams or scholars staffing the regular mosques or Islamic teaching networks. As we will see in the subsequent chapters of this book, this shared tacit knowledge of everyday reality is key to understanding the popularity of the rationalist scholars among young Muslim university students, especially those who come from relatively well-to-do and culturally progressive Muslim families. It is this shared tacit knowledge of contemporary life that enables these scholars to relate Islamic teachings to the everyday realities of the modern world in a way that makes sense to their young followers.

Ultimately, however, the core message of this chapter is that the appeal of the Islamic theology, its 'aqidah with a focus on only one God (as compared with the Christian doctrine of the Trinity), has been key to the conversion of the scholars leading the rationalist network. Their movement towards Islam, however, was not a complete rejection of Christianity; rather, Islam's appeal rested on its claim to be a continuation of the Judeo-Christian tradition. The profile of Jesus was and still remains very important to these scholars, and the fact that this is so even within Islamic tradition is important to them. Similarly, the chapter has illustrated that the sense of certainty conferred by the definitive text of the Quran within the Muslim tradition also had its appeal. These comparative religious accounts, when presented to the young educated Muslims by converts, become particularly effective in convincing them of the superiority of the Islamic tradition. It is this that makes these converts so important to the Islamic revival among the modern-educated and affluent Muslim classes in the twenty-first century.

5

Mixing Dispersed Knowledge

Real-Life Implications

In the preceding chapters, we have seen how the Islamic rationalist scholars under consideration in this book have both specialist knowledge of traditional Islamic scholarship and tacit knowledge of the realities experienced by young modern-educated Muslims; but what does the mixing of these two forms of knowledge result in? What are the real-life implications for Muslims' understanding of their faith and the everyday choices that they have to make as members of Western societies governed under secular law when they mix these two forms of knowledge? Due to their tacit knowledge of Western realities, do the Islamic rationalist scholars argue for blending in with the dominant culture, or do they argue for respecting secular norms while still making choices distinct from those made by other members of their host societies? This chapter will address these questions by looking at how these scholars approach contemporary issues of significance to young Muslims who want to be true to their faith yet be integrated into modern institutions. In doing so, the chapter will demonstrate how these scholars, while arguing on the basis of the traditional sources, do provide different responses from those typically offered to these young Muslims by their mosque imams. Further, their approach is also different from those of other reformist Islamic scholars introduced in Chapter 1. Unlike the others, these Islamic rationalist scholars do not talk about the need to 'reform' Islamic law: instead they argue for reviving the traditional method of Islamic reasoning to relate Islamic law, morality, and ethics to the needs of the time.

Islamic law, in the view of these scholars, does not need to undergo reform, because the traditional methods underpinning Islamic legal theory are inherently able to adapt to changing contexts – an issue discussed in detail in Chapter 2. The widely covered 2014 debate between Hamza Yusuf and Tariq Ramadan at Oxford University's Oxford Union helps to bring this difference into sharp relief.[1] In this debate, Yusuf expressed his reservations about the use of the term 'reform', on the grounds that it implies a need for total restructuring; instead, he argued that the basic foundations of Islam are solid and remain relevant today: all they need is some renovation. Such an outlook, he argued, is closer to the actual idea of *tajdid* that has been central to Islam and the growth of Muslim societies over time. Such an approach also emphasises that the Islamic tradition must be embraced in its entirety, because its followers cannot pick and choose. In many of his talks, Yusuf has emphasised this point and warned about the risk of falling into religious error because of piecemeal engagement with Islam (Yusuf 2013a). The emphasis on engaging with the entirety of Islamic tradition is also reflected in Zaytuna's curriculum; the college brochure states: 'Students will find the Zaytuna curriculum to be holistic, with its emphasis on universal principles and themes, rather than fragmented into isolated subjects and disciplines' (Zaytuna College 2014: 7).

However, as noted by Shaykh Abdullah ibn Hamid Ali – a full-time faculty member at Zaytuna who specialises in Islamic Law and self-identifies as a neo-traditionalist (Ali 2012) – following the tradition in its entirety does not mean blindly enforcing the consensus of the legal scholars from earlier generations, as what they deemed appropriate for that time might need to be adapted to take account of contemporary changes. He elaborates on his argument by giving specific examples: the impracticality of demanding that monetary transactions in the United Kingdom or the United States be conducted according to the procedures expected in the classical Islamic schools of law; and efforts by Western Muslims to enforce the consensus of the Maliki jurists that *jum'ah* (Friday prayer) be conducted in one central mosque (Ali 2012). Thus, the Islamic rationalist scholars are defending the traditional method of Islamic reasoning, and challenging assertions that basic principles or methodological tools of Islamic reasoning are in need of reform; but equally they are arguing for using the provision available within the traditional methods of Islamic reasoning to adapt to the changing times if followers are to stay true to the underlying principles of Islam. To advance such

---

[1] Oxford Union. 2012. 'Tariq Ramadan and Humza Yusuf Debate: Rethinking Islamic Reform.' [Video] YouTube. [Available Online: www.youtube.com/watch?v=rBXMGgR7XU; Accessed 1 May 2018].

positions, these Islamic rationalist scholars draw on the scholarship of Islamic jurists and Sufi scholars such as Bin Bayyah, who, like Yusuf al-Qaradawi, has written extensively on the importance of *fiqh al-waqi'* (jurisprudence of the time) as well as on *fiqh al-aqalliyat* (jurisprudence of minorities).

Waqi' literally means 'reality', and in terms of Islamic legal theory it refers to the lived realities of Muslims at a given time. The concept of waqi' requires an appreciation of how the modern context differs from that in which Islam was revealed (Bano 2018a). It allows for the development of new hermeneutical categories and approaches which enable reform in Islamic law. The concept of waqi' has also been very influential in the development of a new genre of fiqh labelled fiqh al-aqalliyat, which has allowed for the adaptation of many Islamic principles to Western secular law to make it easier for Western Muslims to cope with the particularities of their immediate context. Al-Qaradawi, a prominent Islamic jurist, maintains that there is a broad range of issues that affect waqi'; he argues for acknowledging that exceptional circumstances (*darurat*) occur in people's lives, that religious rulings change according to time and place, and that religious laws should be implemented gradually (Razavian 2018a). Bin Bayyah similarly argues for *tahqiq-al-manat* (refinement of the cause) to closely analyse the text in order to understand the reason why a ruling was decreed, in order to apply that reason to the new context of today (Razavian 2018a). Supporting similar reasoning, Ali Gomaa, a prominent scholar from Egypt,[2] argues that we understand Islamic law through the traditional literature, namely the Quran and Sunnah, but the process of deriving a ruling (*ifta'*) requires an additional step, namely developing a proper understanding of the realities of the time (waqi') (Razavian 2018a).

The contributions of these three scholars are important, because they are arguing for the adoption of a more expansive notion of ijtihad whereby its tools are used not just to find answers to questions where there were no earlier rulings in Islamic law, but also to change rulings that already exist. These scholars' justification of the fiqh al-waqi' approach rests in the Islamic concept of *maslahah* (the common good), which requires that – unlike the ritual practices (ibadah) – transactions (mu'amalat) such as marriage, leasing, and sales are intended to serve

---

[2] Though highly respected for his writings, he became controversial after taking very extreme positions against the Muslim Brotherhood after the Morsi government was toppled by General al-Sisi (Bano 2018a).

the utility and common interest of the Muslim community and thus are more amenable to change based on circumstances (Razavian 2018a). Together the concepts of waqi' and maslahah enable these scholars to remain committed to the textual sources while simultaneously arguing for reform.

Refraining from making any direct contributions to these deeper Islamic legal debates, the Islamic rationalist scholars refer their students to the works of senior scholars who are highly respected for their training in classical Islamic Sciences while themselves staying focused on deploying the reasoning offered by these senior scholars to develop appropriate responses to contemporary questions. Given their tacit knowledge of the realities of modern life that they share with university-educated Muslim youth in the West and their counterparts in the urban centres of Muslim-majority countries, the Islamic rationalist scholars do what the traditionally trained scholars are less able to do: provide practical responses from within the Islamic tradition which enable these young Muslims to engage confidently with modern realities. In the subsequent sections of this chapter we shall thus see what actual life choices emerge for young Muslims when the Islamic rationalist scholars try to apply Islamic reasoning to contemporary everyday realities.

I RECONCILING MUSLIM AND WESTERN IDENTITIES

A good point from which to start examining the implications of the teachings of the Islamic rationalist scholars for young Muslims is the advice that they offer to their followers on any tensions the latter might feel between their religious and national identities. For young Western Muslims who adhere to traditional Islamic teaching from more conservative platforms, such as the Deobandi madrasahs or Salafi preachers, Islamic teachings can easily end up creating an irreconcilable difference between their identity as Muslims and that of their nationality. Here the reference is not to the militant form of Islam, which is a distinct phenomenon that affects only a small segment of Muslim youth, but the everyday frictions that young Muslims feel between the Islamic moral and legal dictates and the everyday choices that they face as members of Western societies. One outcome of such readings of Islam is the closed Muslim enclaves that persist in many Western countries, where a parallel reality to that of the dominant culture is created by transplanting institutions and values from the Muslim-majority countries; another consequence of such teachings is the internal dilemma or guilt that young Muslims might feel when they do immerse themselves in Western institutions. Against such readings of Islam, which isolate young Muslims from the broader society, the Islamic rationalist scholars provide an entirely different frame of reference. Rather than presenting Islamic and Western values in opposition to each other, or going to the other extreme and arguing for accepting the dominant culture and compromising on core Muslim values, these scholars are keen to demonstrate a natural harmony between Islam and core Western values.

The scholars in this network are keen to assert that Islam has historically proved very effective in adapting to different contexts while preserving its core values, and for the young Western Muslims there is an obligation to develop an Islamic tradition that is organic to their context. Hamza Yusuf (2011d) has argued for developing a language of Islam that is focused on the local realities, as have Dr Umar and Tim Winter. These scholars are very clear that such blending is mutually beneficial, and that Islam historically flourished due to its ability to embed itself in local contexts. Talking about this idea, Yusuf has argued that, just as different vessels give the water different colours while the water itself remains the same, the same is true of Islam's inherent ability to adapt to different cultures and contexts (Yusuf 2011d). Promoting this synergy between the two value systems is central to the very philosophy of the institutions that they have established.

Zaytuna College officially acknowledges its key goal as developing an understanding of Islam that is relevant for the American context. It recruits its teachers from among American Muslims who might have trained in the classical tradition in the Muslim world but who have grown up mainly in the West, especially in the United States, and thus understand the local values; its student body to date is mainly American. The college also organises events and fundraisers focused on highlighting Muslims' loyalty to the United States. Virginia Gray Henry, a Muslim convert who is a descendant of Revolutionary War hero Patrick Henry, was invited to speak at Zaytuna College's first convocation ceremony. After her speech, Yusuf drew a connection between the American Revolution and Zaytuna, noting that the latter was an example of that revolution's drive for liberty (Scott 2013). Similarly, at the Cambridge Muslim College in the United Kingdom, the primary focus of its original one-year degree course is to help traditionally trained Dar al-'ulum graduates relate to British realities; its four-year Islamic Studies degree, which will focus on the Islamic Sciences, was launched only recently, in 2017.

The rationalist scholars are keen to inculcate in young Muslims a sense of belonging to their home countries, and to make them appreciate that the Western countries do uphold the protection of basic liberties for all, irrespective of race and religion, which must be appreciated. Hamza Yusuf has noted how it is easier to be Muslim in America than in many Muslim countries, due to the oppressive nature of regimes in many Muslim countries (O'Sullivan 2001). He has also openly talked about how, having been taught in good schools in America, he was shocked to see the education system in the United Arab Emirates, where students were cursed and punished by their teachers. These scholars are thus keen to make young Muslims appreciate the tolerant values inherent in Western societies: values which, these scholars maintain, are consistent with Islamic moral dictates. The increasing opportunities open to Muslims in the West to pursue higher education and acquire material prosperity has also been noted by these scholars as positive aspects of Western societies (O'Sullivan 2001). Appreciating this openness, however, does not make these scholars argue for renouncing Islamic values or compromising on Islamic legal dictates if they do end up clashing with Western values. For example, based on his own experience of learning in the Middle East, Yusuf places a strong emphasis on the importance of memorisation, along with reflective reasoning, in his teaching at Zaytuna College. This he does even though Western education institutions refuse to acknowledge the value of memorisation. Similarly, as we will see in subsequent sections, on all issues where there is a basic difference of understanding between Islamic legal or moral dictates and Western liberal norms, be it in relation to gender, homosexuality, approaches to science, or economics, the rationalist scholars are keen to acknowledge those differences and defend them – while also demonstrating that the two value systems do not have to be in complete opposition to each other.

Rather, these scholars argue that it is this difference between Islamic positions and those stemming from a liberal framework that makes Islam particularly well equipped to make a positive contribution to Western societies. These scholars are thus keen to act as spokespersons for Islam in the West, not only to defend Muslims against certain criticisms but also to argue confidently that Islam has many good things to offer. Talking about the similarity between Islamic values and real British values, Winter has noted that, despite the stereotyping of Islam as clashing with Western civilisation, 'I more authentically inhabit my old identity now that I operate within Islamic boundaries than I did when I was part of a teenage generation growing up in the '70s who were told there shouldn't be any boundaries' (*Independent* 2010). Winter thus actively addresses the issue of British Muslim identity. He has argued that the moral and religious temper of the British best matches Islam: Islam 'is the most suitable faith for the British' (*Independent* 2010). Referring to Islam's historic ability to spread across different cultures and contexts, Winter has argued that Islam is particularly suitable for Western societies which have to accommodate a diverse set of populations today: 'Islam, as a universal religion, in fact as the only legitimately universal religion, also makes room for the particularities of the peoples who come into it' (Winter 2014a). Dr Umar and Tim Winter in particular have both drawn on the example of Islam in China to illustrate how many of the leading mandarins of the Ming dynasty were Muslim, and how Chinese mosque architecture was adapted to the traditional Buddhist temples and in the process ended up creating a beautiful new architectural design for the mosques, while retaining the core dimensions of the mosque design.[3] The Cambridge Muslim mosque project, of which Winter is one of the key trustees, reflects this very adaptive spirit: the architecture of this grand mosque, still under construction, draws on British architectural style to enable the mosque to blend in with the existing landscape.

In Winter's view, as a universal religion with its respect for diversity, coupled with appreciation of pragmatic and practical moral norms, Islam 'is the most suitable faith for the British. Its values are our values' (Winter 2014a). This overlap between Islam and British values is summarised by Winter as follows: 'Its moderate, undemonstrative style of piety, still waters running deep; its insistence on modesty and a certain reserve, and its insistence on common sense and on pragmatism, combine to furnish the most natural and easy religious option for our people' (Winter 2014a). Winter, however, has argued that the challenge for young Muslims growing up in Britain today is that the culture that they see around themselves is that of 'extreme spectacles of binge drinking on Saturday nights, scratchcards, and other forms of addiction apparently rampant, credit card debt crushing lives, collapsing relationships and mushrooming proportions of single lives, a drug epidemic' (*Independent* 2010). He notes how these values are not the traditional British or Christian values that he experienced when growing up, and explains why young Muslims today find it hard to respect what they see of Western

---

[3] Such as the need for the minbar, direction of prayer towards Ka'bah, etc.

society. He therefore argues that Muslims can contribute to European societies if 'we become the great harbingers of ethics and compassion and neighborliness, in an increasingly atomized and self-oriented, materialistic Europe, then I think we'll have justified our presence here' (*Independent* 2010). Noting how Islam is very effective in addressing many of the social problems faced in British society, he has commented: 'It [Islam] is the ultimate cold turkey. You don't drink at all. You don't sleep around. You don't do scratchcards. Or whether there is a kind of increasing polarisation, whereby Muslims look at the degenerating society around them and decide "You can keep it"' (*Independent* 2010).

He has urged British Muslims to keep alive a positive attitude towards diversity:

Islam is, and will continue to be, even amid the miserable globalisation of modern culture, a faith that celebrates diversity. Our thinking about our own position as British Muslims should focus on that fact, and quietly but firmly ignore the protests both of the totalitarian fringe, and of the importers of other regional cultures, such as that of Pakistan, which they regard as the only legitimate Islamic ideal. (Winter 2014a)

Dr Umar also has noted that because the United States immigration process selected Muslims from professional backgrounds, American Muslims tend to have good financial resources and are highly talented. This, he maintains, makes them well placed to contribute both to American society and to Islam.

2 IN DEFENCE OF THE SECULAR STATE AND RETICENCE ABOUT POLITICAL ISLAM

Another challenge for Muslims wanting to live by Islamic dictates in the West is how to live under secular law, especially if there is a tension between the law and Islamic dictates. Should young Muslims follow the law when it clashes with Islam's legal or moral framework, or should they argue for the state's recognition of shari'ah courts, as has been successfully done in the United Kingdom, stay disengaged (as some Deobandi scholars do by refusing to vote), or go all the way to extremes, as does Hizb ur Tahrir, a movement popular in UK universities, which once argued for the establishment of *khilafah* (Muslim rule) even in the United Kingdom. The position of the Islamic rationalist scholars on respect for the law of the secular state is again illustrative of the balanced approach that these scholars advocate, whereby they advise young Muslims to integrate with local institutions yet not comprise on any core Islamic legal or moral dictates. Thus, these scholars are clear about the need to respect a secular state and its laws, but they argue against accepting secularisation as a process that erodes space for religious truth. Drawing on the work of Syed Naquib al-Attas, a Malaysian scholar to whose writing Yusuf often refers, Yusuf draws a distinction between 'secularisation' and the 'secular' state. He states that it is possible for a secular state to uphold religion, while secularisation tries to overthrow all that is religious. Yusuf's main critique of secularism rests in its promotion of a mindset that is excessively materialistic and in which there is no space for God or spirituality. This materialism, he has noted, has led Western civilisation down the route of existentialism and nihilism to a point where the focus on the core purpose of life has been lost. Elaborating on this point in one of his lectures, Yusuf notes:

Unfortunately, there are, for the first time in human history, civilizations that do not have any answer to this question [the purpose of human existence]. This is actually unique in human history. Because human beings have always had some reason for existence. Whereas the current dominant model in Western civilization is really untenable, metaphysically. Because the argument you will find amongst Western people is essentially what they would call, in their terms, an existentialist problem. In other words each person would have to work out what the meaning of his life is for him or herself. That nobody is going to tell you what your life means. You simply have to work it out yourself. And this is why suicide is a serious option in that culture. (Yusuf 2014a: 03:24–04:18)

Attributing such an outlook to nihilism, Yusuf notes: 'The dominant philosophy that is in many parts of the world is actually a philosophy of Nihilism. It is a philosophy of what the Arabs would term *adamiyyah*. That there really is no purpose to existence' (Yusuf 2014a: 04:55–05:11). Yusuf is critical of the 'secular mindset' and attributes many contemporary challenges to it. Devoid of any moral purpose, individuals pursue base instincts which result in meaninglessness: the absence of a higher purpose in politics, business, the military, science, even modern philosophy (Yusuf 2013c). Yusuf thus fears that people are becoming like 'jellyfish' – brainless, spineless beings that eat and reproduce and do nothing meaningful. Just as the pollution of the oceans has, he maintains, created an environment in which only the jellyfish thrives, modern society, with its focus on secularisation, is particularly good at promoting mindless consumption.

Yet, while being critical of secularism as a process that has led to the erosion of religion as an integral part of human existence, Yusuf has no qualms about living under a secular state. He has argued that a secular state does not always have to be in conflict with religion. Drawing on the writings of al-Attas (al-Attas 1995: 29), Yusuf has noted that the secular state does not necessarily have to deny religious values and virtues in politics and human affairs. Instead, Yusuf maintains that the secular state can operate in ways that uphold many of the core principles of Islam, as long as it is focused on establishing social justice. He has cited Finland and Sweden as states that have such a high degree of social justice that Muslims should consider them exemplary. These secular states, he maintains, compare more favourably to the time of the legendary Salahuddin than does contemporary Egypt, which might claim Islam as its guiding principle but is ruled by an oppressive dictatorship (Yusuf 2011f). Thus, his contention is that good governance does not rely on religion, but on a commitment to social justice within a government; religion mixed with politics is, in fact, in the view of the Islamic rationalist scholars, not necessarily a good thing, as it can result in distorting religion for political ends (Yusuf 2013b).

Yusuf and other rationalist scholars stand firmly against the use of Islam by political movements or its abuse as a political ideology, in particular Islamism, noting that political Islamist movements do not necessarily promote religious virtues in society. Yusuf has talked about how turning a religion into political ideology, whether it be Zionism or Islamism, is problematic because it argues for imposing religion from the top: 'An Islamic state is the idea that you can force people to be good Muslims, which is a completely insane idea. It has never existed and it will never exist. If you think religion can be legislated by a government, you are completely deluded' (Yusuf 2018b). Arguing instead for focusing on inculcating religious morality among the people, Yusuf has noted:

Islam is not an ideology, political or otherwise. It is a revelation from God that explains and reminds people of their duties toward their Creator in honoring and worshipping God with gratitude for the gift of life and all the concomitants of that gift, and of their duties toward their fellow creatures as unique and protected creations of God ... Politics involves making sure the mail gets out, allotting appropriate monies for public works, and ensuring the security of a people from internal or external threats; all of these can be done without recourse to any specific religious tradition. (Yusuf 2011f)

Even during the Arab Spring, Yusuf argued for keeping the revolution separate from political Islamist movements:

The lack of an ideology, for me, is the most refreshing aspect of this uprising. The stale rhetoric of 'Islam is the solution' that has marked countless demonstrations for decades is absent. The pathetic socialist slogans of the Libyan revolution as well as the Syrian and Iraqi Arab nationalist slogans are all conspicuously absent. Islam is not a political ideology and hence does not offer a political solution per se; basic morality in politics is the solution. (Yusuf 2011f)

In one of his lectures emphasising the importance of ihsan and its neglect by political Islam movements, Yusuf (2011a) advised the audience to read *The Failure of Political Islam*, written by the French academic Olivier Roy. He has talked about his concern that the failure of the ideologies of Marxism and socialism, which many post-colonial Muslim elites held on to, led to a search for another ideology, and Islamism was that. This ideology came to focus on making demands for social justice but did not address other important aspects of Islam; in particular, the dimension of ihsan, working on purifying the inner self, is in his view most obviously neglected by the Islamists. Drawing on al-Attas, Yusuf has placed heavy emphasis on the need for Muslims to focus on developing individual adab, which he describes as consisting of a complex set of meanings that includes decency, comportment, decorum, etiquette, manners, morals, propriety, and humaneness (Zaytuna College 2018a). He juxtaposes this emphasis on inculcating good adab against the Islamists' focus on bringing about political change by drawing on al-Attas (1978: 114):

The identification of cause with the corruption of knowledge as here suggested, and not with that of leadership as they suggest, significantly shifts the ground wherein lies the root of the problem to that of knowledge, and knowledge is inherent in man as individual, and not in society and state and ummah. So, as a matter of correct strategy in our times and under the present circumstances, it is important to stress the individual in seeking a just solution to our problem rather than the society and the state.

This open critique of political Islam by Hamza Yusuf, as we will see in the final chapter, has become a source of concern to some of his otherwise ardent students. These concerns were reinforced in particular after Humza Yusuf, but also some other scholars in this network, failed to express support for the Muslim Brotherhood in Egypt when it was crushed by al-Sisi and instead subtly endorsed other Egyptian scholars who had sided with al-Sisi's government. These scholars' aversion to political Islam thus makes their critics argue that they are making Muslims look inwards and are encouraging them to disengage from global Muslim concerns. Many of these scholars speak openly about the need for Muslims to focus on their more immediate concerns, such as the challenges of poverty among the Black Muslim population in America, rather than trying to resolve problems in Muslim-majority countries. In my own assessment, their focus on getting Muslim communities to disengage from political causes in Muslim-majority countries and urging them to look inwards instead, their critique of political Islam, and the subtle support they have given to those al-Azhari scholars that endorsed al-Sisi's suppression of the Muslim Brotherhood constitute the strongest threat to the long-term credibility of the rationalist scholars and the spread of the Islamic rationalist revival movement that they have initiated. I argued in Chapter 2 that it is the fine balance between fiqh, rational theology, and tasawwuf that helps to explain the appeal of this movement. As we will see in Chapters 6 and 7, these scholars, especially Hamza Yusuf, are at risk of appearing to lose that balance in eyes of some of their own students.

3 STRONG DEFENCE OF PLURALITY, AND PROBLEMS WITH
SALAFISM AS WELL AS JIHAD

In addition to the rationalist scholars' critique of political Islam, they are also openly critical of Salafism and of militant Islam. Their problems with Salafism stem from its practice of discrediting classical scholarship and encouraging young Muslims to engage directly with the Quran and hadith – an approach which, as was discussed in detail in Chapter 2, clashes with the basic methodological principles of traditional Islamic scholarship and the understanding of the Islamic rationalist scholars. This discrediting of the authority of the traditionally trained scholars to interpret the text is, in the view of these scholars, what makes Salafism at times support militant ideologies. Again the writings of al-Attas have been influential among the rationalist scholars, by highlighting the problem with Salafi approaches which negate the intellectual authority of scholars trained in Islamic sciences. As he has argued:

The chief characteristic symptom of loss of *adab* within the Community is the process of levelling that is cultivated from time to time in the Muslim mind and practiced in his society. By 'levelling' I mean the *levelling* of everyone, in the mind and the attitude, to the same level of the leveller. This mental and attitudinal process, which impinges upon action, is perpetrated through the encouragement of false leaders who wish to demolish legitimate authority and valid hierarchy so that they and their like might thrive, and who demonstrate by example by levelling the great to the level of the less great, and then to that of the still lesser. This Jāhilī streak of individualism, of immanent arrogance and obstinacy and the tendency to challenge and belittle legitimate authority, seems to have perpetrated itself – albeit only among extremists of many sorts – in all periods of Muslim history. (al-Attas 1978: 114)

He goes on to criticise modernists, stating that they barely reach the level of knowledge attained by the great scholars of the past: 'Not a single one of the so-called Modernists and Reformers of our times, including those who masquerade as 'ulama, barely reaches the lowest level of the great 'ulama of the past and men of spiritual discernment who contributed so much to the knowledge of Islam and the Islamic world view, whether in terms of intelligence, virtue and spiritual knowledge, or in terms of volume in original, individual analyses, interpretations, commentaries and other written efforts' (al-Attas 1978: 112).

Sharing similar views to these expressed by al-Attas, the rationalist scholars have thus openly talked about how the adoption of Salafi methods of reasoning can enable some to justify jihad and violence in the name of Islam. Hamza Yusuf in particular speaks very openly against militant Islam. He has condemned the 9/11 terrorist attacks in New York, Islamists' violent attacks on a school in Russia in 2004, the Beslan school hostage crisis, and other atrocities (Yusuf 2007). Along with Shaykh Abdallah Bin Bayyah, Yusuf has called for a peace initiative (Nasir 2014). And, repeatedly, he has argued that following one of the four madhhabs is the best protection against radicalisation. In a radio interview that he gave in Malaysia, he urged Malaysians to stay committed to the Shafi'i madhhab (the dominant madhhab in Malaysia) and warned against the Salafi way of reasoning:

Well, the first thing to remember is a lot of groups claim to be *ahl-sunnah wa'l-jama'ah*. You know, they claim to be. And we should be wary, like I said, of claims. But we should be able to say that we know for certain who was *ahl-sunnah wa'l-jama'ah* in the past. And we should try to be as close to them, and *ahl-sunnah* of the past, for over a thousand years followed one of the four *madhhabs*. (Yusuf 2014c)

Yusuf further warned Malaysians about the sectarianism caused by Salafi thought:

Malaysia has, you have the blessing of uniformity of faith. I just came from Turkey. It's one of the few countries where you go into masjids and they pray the same way. It's a great blessing to have uniformity of faith. This is the way that they used to be in North African countries when I first went thirty years ago, people prayed the same way. Now they, everybody prays different ways. Because all these different factions and ideologies have come in. And people read the *hadith*s directly and they think they can derive the *hadith*s just by "Oh I follow Quran and Sunnah brother." As if Imam Shafi'i didn't follow the Quran and

Sunnah. Did you go and study 17 years? Did you go and study 17 years, the Arabic language to follow the Quran and Sunnah like Imam Shafi'i? Imam Shafi'i went 17 years. He was amassing, he was one of the greatest scholars of the Arabic language. That's why he was able to write his great book in *usul al-fiqh*. Because *usul al-fiqh* is based on language. It's based on understanding the nuances of language. (Yusuf 2014c)

He later went on to give a much starker warning:

And so I'm warning you as people. I'm warning you. I am a warner, and I'm telling you because the Prophet is *bashîr* and *nadhîr*. And his people should be people of *bishara* and people of *nadhara*. They should give good news, but they should also warn people. If you allow these seditious teachings into this country, you will see factionalism, you will see sectarianism, you will see your houses divided. You will see religion become a source of *fitna* and tribulation. You are Shafi'i, this is your tradition. Your *aqidah* is a sound *aqidah*, and you believe in *tazkiyah*, this is your tradition. Hold to your tradition and don't let people pervert your tradition. (Yusuf 2014c)

While in their defence the Salafis present their own reasoning for returning to the original texts (Qadhi 2018), in the view of the Islamic rationalist scholars in reality it results in the destruction of Islam, which is an intellectual project that has been developing for thousands of years. In the view of these scholars, it would be foolish to dismiss classical Islamic scholarship in favour of unscholarly conclusions. Yet it is important to note that, while being openly critical of the Salafi methodology, these scholars are also very keen to build bridges with Salafi-oriented Muslim scholars where possible. Thus, they do engage with Yasir Qadhi, a Salafi preacher in the United States who has gradually come to adopt a more moderate tone (Razavian 2018c). Dr Umar has also stressed the importance of working with Muslim groups from all orientations. Committed to engaging with a diverse set of Muslim communities in Chicago, his home base, Dr Umar was working with one of the local masjids at the time of my fieldwork, despite its very different orientation and even though he did not agree with policies followed by its management committee. He emphasised the need to start a dialogue with anyone who is willing to be open to the truth.

GENDER AND HOMOSEXUALITY

When examining the rationalist scholars' views on gender or homosexuality, we find similar attempts to adopt a balanced approach that will enable young Muslims to relate to their surroundings yet not compromise on core Islamic legal and moral dictates. The Islamic rationalist scholars are thus equally critical of many aspects of Western feminism, which in their view promote antagonism between men and women, as well as of the gender dynamics prevalent in many Muslim countries, which they argue to be too oppressive. They argue for drawing on examples from earlier periods of Islam to understand how Islamic gender norms can give women a proper place in modern society. In defending Islamic gender norms, these scholars in particular draw on scientific evidence. In line with popular understanding within Islamic tradition, they contend that in Islam the two sexes are equal when it comes to acquiring spiritual merit, and that the prescribed differences in their roles reflect their inherent biological differences. These scholars regard Western feminism as having gone too far in denying the basic differences between men and women; they thus draw on scientific evidence to illustrate biological, emotional, and cognitive differences between men and women to build their case. At the same time these scholars do not shy away from criticising the heavy restrictions imposed on women in many Muslim countries, and they are keen to establish that these are products of culture rather than religion.

Hamza Yusuf refers to the *yin* and *yang* nature of the two sexes, drawing on the work of Murata Sachiko (2012), who uses these terms to refer to the emphasis placed on spiritual equality between men and women in Islam, while acknowledging that there are real physical differences between the two: 'The whole point of Sachiko Murata's book was to indicate that really the cosmology of Islam is more akin to the idea of yin and yang. That these are complementary opposites, they are not antagonistic opposites' (Yusuf 2011g). To further defend the Islamic conception of difference in gender needs, Yusuf draws on the work of Anne Moir and David Jessel (1989), who in their book *Brainsex* argue that male and female brains work differently. They define 'brainsex' as the 'distinctive gender-based circuitry that determines how, and explains why, men and women respond so differently to the same emotional and situational triggers'. Yusuf argues that to ignore these scientifically established differences would lead to a society built on lies, which can only prove ineffective in the long term.

At the same time he acknowledges that the status of women in many Muslim countries needs attention, although he is equally keen to establish that the marginalisation of women observed in many Muslim contexts cannot be attributed to Islamic teachings: 'There's no doubt that women have been abused and oppressed in many many cultures, and certainly Islam has not been exempt from that in any way. And we've seen it.

My own experience in the Muslim world I've seen these things' (Yusuf 2011g). However, he credits this to cultural practices rather than to Islam: Muslims 'are dealing with a lot of *jahiliyyah* (ignorance) within the Muslim communities and cultures' (Yusuf 2011g)· Similarly, he is keen to show how some of the more contentious hadiths, which appear to be derogatory towards women, can be recast in a new light (Yusuf 2009). He at times denies the probative force of narrations, or contests the received meaning of these hadiths (Yusuf 2011g). Referring to a hadith that argues that the majority of people in hell are women, for instance, he denies that the narration has any probative force. He argues that it is a singular narration and that it is not possible to use a singular narration for matters of creed ('aqidah) (Yusuf 2011g).

Similarly he is very critical of those interpretations of Verse 34 from *Surah al-Nisa,* which are viewed as subtly endorsing domestic violence. The verse reads: 'If you fear high-handedness from your wives, remind them [of the teachings of God], then ignore them when you go to bed, then hit them.' Arguing that verses cannot be taken literally and that interpreting them requires specialist expertise, Yusuf contends: 'First of all, before you can even understand the Quran you have to give 20 years of your life to study. Twenty years of your life to study. I'm not making this up. You read the condition of *tafsir.* There are 12 knowledges you have to master before you can comment on the Quran.' Yusuf argues that this verse is trying to outline an action plan for marital disputes, and that there are different stages that the couple must go through. He maintains that this verse 'was actually designed to eliminate domestic violence. And that is why the great irony is it's used to justify domestic violence' (Yusuf 2009). Instead, he argues that we need to learn from the strong emphasis that Islam places on promoting mutual respect between the sexes. He makes frequent references to how the Prophet treated his wives with love and respect (Yusuf 2011g). In his speeches touching on gender issues, he often notes how the Prophet consulted his wives on important decisions (Yusuf 2011g). He adds that the concept of women being evil is a Greek and Hellenistic Christian concept, and that the Prophet negated any suggestions that women are evil (Yusuf 2011g).

In terms of the practical implications of Yusuf's teachings, women are encouraged to wear the hijab. However, he attributes the need for this to men's failing: 'It is men's weakness that hijab was given. It is men's weakness. That is from our own spiritual short coming' (Yusuf 2012). This emphasis on conservative dressing is also visible in the Zaytuna College's student guide:

Men and women should always maintain a well-groomed appearance. Hairstyles should be clean and neat, avoiding extreme styles or colors. Shoes must be worn in all public campus areas. Clothing is inappropriate when it is sleeveless, revealing, or form fitting. Men may not wear shorts on campus. If they wear shorts when off campus, they must be knee length or longer. Women's dresses, skirts, and trousers must be full length. Students should not wear leggings, sweats, t-shirts, pajamas, baseball caps, or torn, tight, or ragged clothing in classrooms, meeting spaces, or offices, or at college events. Students may not wear clothing emblazoned with corporate logos. Allegations of violations of this policy should be reported to one of the student affairs deans. (Zaytuna College 2014: 48)

Yet while endorsing the requirement for women to hear hijab, Yusuf does argue that society should not judge harshly those women who choose not to wear it (Yusuf 2010). In doing so, he is trying to advance an approach which in his assessment respects tradition but at the same time does not lead more liberal Muslim youth to abandon Islam: 'We are going to lose our women to the forces out there that are telling them they are oppressed. That are making them feel oppressed. Only their idea of oppression is not the same as our idea. They think it's oppression to wear hijab. And we think it's oppression to be presented in a world in which men have passions which they are less capable of controlling than women' (Yusuf 2012). The Zaytuna brochure also outlines a 'Gender Relations Policy' which instructs students that '[o]utside class hours, students should study and socialize with members of their own gender' (Zaytuna College 2014: 49) and that '[d]ating, sexual activity, or romantic relationships among unmarried Muslim students are not allowed either on campus or off campus' (Zaytuna College 2014: 49).

Tim Winter has advanced very similar arguments in defence of Islamic concepts of gender norms in his paper, 'Boys Will Be Boys' (Winter 2018); Yusuf has in fact often referenced this very paper in his own speeches. In 'Boys Will Be Boys', Winter (2018) draws on recent scholarship in the field of Western feminism and science to argue that Western concepts of gender quality have become increasingly problematic. In particular he focuses on how the sexual liberty that has accompanied feminist resistance has harmed both men and women. He cites three examples from the work of Germaine Greer in defence of his argument. In her book, *The Whole Woman*, Greer (2000) contends that sexual liberty has resulted in increased sexual promiscuity, infidelity, and pornography. He draws on scientific evidence, including evolutionary biology, to prove the physical weakness of women compared with men, and the differences in the psychological traits of the two sexes. In defence of his argument against denying the existence of physical differences between the two sexes,

Winter discusses the deployment of female recruits in the UK military. Explaining that in 1998 the British military adopted 'gender-free' selection procedures to ensure that men and women had identical tasks, Winter notes how as a result women were required to perform more strenuous physical activities, which caused physical harm to some of them. Winter cites Ian Gemmell's (2002) study which showed that, while 1.5 per cent of male recruits had stress fractures, for women the ratio was between 4.6 per cent and 11.1 per cent. The same study also demonstrated that because of their different physical builds, military exercises imposed 33–39 per cent more stress on the female skeleton. Winter (2018) concludes that 'although social changes have eroded the traditional moral reasons for barring women from active combat roles, the medical evidence alone compels the British army to bar women from the infantry and the Royal Armoured Corps'.

Similarly, in his paper, Winter draws on studies that show that the nature of male and female intelligence is different. For instance, he refers to Janet Lever's (1976) research on sex-based differences in the games children play, which shows that girls play games that are collaborative, whereas boys play games that are more rule-based. Lever shows that 65 per cent of boys' games are rule-based, compared with 35 per cent of games played by girls. Winter thus argues that boys are more rule-oriented. Similarly, drawing on evidence from evolutionary biology, Winter (2018) argues that men also take high risks, for reasons of biological survival: in order to attract and keep mates, pre-modern men had to take risks. This is why, today, more men than women participate in high-risk sports. He therefore argues that women are better suited to performing chores at home, because male biology seeks out novelty, with a dislike for repetitive tasks. Winter also relies on the works of psychologist Carol Gilligan (1993), who has argued that men and women have different moral voices and approach moral problems from different angles. Winter uses Gilligan's work to argue that women define themselves in terms of relationships because in the pre-modern world women were primarily involved in the care of family members (Winter 2018).

Winter argues that the shariʿah and this new science which supports calls for 'difference feminism' vindicate each other: 'Equality is no more envisaged by nature than it is by the law of God; indeed, the law of God, for us, is commensurate with natural law' (Winter 2018). Both the shariʿah and the science of difference feminism contend that the concept of equality as sameness is not an effective approach to gender-related questions. They are also in agreement that it is better to approach the issue in terms of opportunity and respect: 'We insist, therefore, that our revealed law, confirmed so magnificently in its assumptions by the new science, upholds the dignity and the worth of women more reliably than secularity ever can' (Winter 2018).

Winter is thus keen to show 'that an opposition to the Shari'ah is an opposition to science' (Winter 2018). He also maintains that by virtue of living and teaching in the West he is 'more in touch with contemporary trends in science and social theory' (Winter 2018) compared with thinkers in Muslim-majority countries, and that this makes it possible for him to show how Islamic concepts of gender norms can be backed by science, and that Muslim scholars need not be apologetic about them. In terms of actual practice, all the rationalist scholars encourage women to wear hijab but allow space for individual choice, advising Muslims not to judge women who might choose not to do so. In terms of gender mixing, as seen in the case of rules followed at Zaytuna College, these scholars find it occasionally appropriate for men and women to mix, such as by attending lectures and discussions together in the same room, because restricting such interactions are seen as counterproductive in a society where all spaces are open to both men and women. Yet, they do actively encourage the exercise of constraint in the level of social interactions developed between the two sexes, and they place great emphasis on the need for both men and women to dress modestly. The line is clearly drawn on sexual promiscuity: for both men and women, sex outside marriage is prohibited. Thus, their teaching aims to enable young, modern-educated Muslim men and women to appreciate the logic of Islamic gender norms but also to have the confidence to engage with the opposite sex and be comfortable in mixed-sex settings, while recognising that any attempt to develop sexual intimacy outside marriage is completely off limits. Such an approach thus differs from the one advocated by very conservative Islamic movements, such as Deoband, who argue against any mixing of the sexes; it is also distinct from the dominant gender norms in the West, where sexual liberty is today seen as an essential part of individual freedom and well-being.

Just as the Islamic rationalist scholars are confident in their ability to defend different concepts of gender equality that do not have to conform with the demands of liberal theory, they are also very resilient in resisting calls to accept homosexuality. After the Orlando shooting on a gay night club by a young Muslim man, the US media was again abuzz with discussion about Islam and intolerance, in this case of homosexuals. Appearing on a US TV show, Hamza Yusuf again presented a balanced argument. He argued for everyone to respect individual freedom of choice, emphasising the need for tolerance by drawing on the Quranic verse that affirms that there is 'absolutely no compulsion in religion' (ERIN 2016). At the same time, he did not hesitate to state his opinion that, on the basis of his own study of Islamic tradition, the vast majority of Muslims would never accept homosexuality as lawful. He went on to emphasise how the Quran is explicit in its condemnation of the act, and a long tradition of Islamic jurisprudence defines homosexuality as unlawful. He noted that Islamic scholarship makes provisions for dealing with such sexual urges: for example, fatwas were issued which permitted people with such urges to relieve themselves in order not to indulge them. He further stated that he recognises that homosexual attraction is a real human urge and he certainly feels sympathy for people who are struggling with it, but he is clear that such an action cannot be endorsed: 'But I'm not sure they want our sympathies; they want full recognition of their lifestyle, and my religion tells me that I can't accept that. But I can't – and won't – impose my beliefs on others, either verbally or otherwise. I'm not going to judge people' (ERIN 2016). Asked what advice he gives to young Muslims who might be struggling with such urges and seek his counsel, he answered: 'I say that I'm not going to deny your experience but my recommendation is not to actively engage in behavior outside of what is permitted in the religion. I know that people can live celibate lives, I did it myself for many years' (ERIN 2016). These scholars have expressed very clearly that one cannot change the basic principles of Islamic law and morality in response to pressure to be 'politically correct'.

4 APPROACH TO SCIENCE AND ECONOMICS

The approach of the Islamic rationalist scholars to scientific progress and economic development is related to their critique of heavy material consumption. They do not address these issues as frequently or in as much detail as the subjects discussed above; their writings and speeches, however, do suggest that in the assessments of these scholars, the developments in these two fields have contributed to the processes of secularisation: public confidence in scientific and related technological innovation is believed to have contributed to the displacement of religion and nurtured the culture of extreme consumerism whereby an obsession with the acquisition of material possessions has undermined the human need to search for the purpose of life. These scholars claim to respect scientific truths and even use relevant evidence to advance their own arguments, as was illustrated above in the case of their reasoning on gender differences. For them there is no difference between Islamic and scientific knowledge, as Islam draws no such distinction between different forms of knowledge. But these scholars question the use of scientific evidence or progress when it starts to push the boundaries of Islamic moral and legal dictates. They are thus appreciative of scientific contributions in the fields of bio-ethics, medicine, engineering, astronomy, and other scientific fields that improve human well-being; however, they are critical of scientific reasoning when it is used to discredit spiritual truths, or to over-exploit natural resources, thereby endangering the planet, or to promote genetically modified food production and extreme consumerism. Scholars within this network routinely refer to such concerns in their speeches.

While Winter makes use of evidence from evolutionary biology in defence of his argument for the existence of biological differences between the sexes, he is opposed to the theory that humans evolved from pre-historic apes, even though he agrees with the concept of micro-evolution. Thus, in his view, animals can evolve to acquire certain traits, but they cannot evolve from one type of species into another. Winter touches on this topic in passing, while discussing the biological differences between men and women. In critiquing such positions, he tries to find evidence from within Western scholarship, rather than relying solely on a religious argument. Thus, when critiquing the theory of human evolution, he claims that it has come under attack from philosophers and physicists alike: 'Darwinism and neo-Darwinism are of course under attack now, particularly by philosophers and physicists, rather more seriously than at any other time over the past hundred years' (Winter 2018). Further, referring to an article by Nuh Keller (2006), he concludes that thorough-going commitment to the theory of evolution is incompatible with the Quranic account of the origins of humanity (Winter 2018). Following Keller, Winter (2018) accepts micro-evolution, or the 'perpetuation and reinforcement over time of genetically successful strategies for survival'. In his article, 'Islam and Evolution', Keller (2006) analyses claims about evolution using a philosophy-of-science approach drawing on work of a number of Western scholars, including Charles Darwin, Charles Peirce, and Jürgen Habermas. Keller's conclusion is that the claim 'that man has evolved from a non-human species ... is unbelief (*kufr*)'.

Similarly, as discussed in the section on secularism, Yusuf has argued actively against the intense materialism of the modern age. He uses the metaphor of jellyfish to capture his concerns about the state of modern human existence:

The jellyfish are now taking over the oceans. Jellyfish are spineless, mindless – they have no brain, and they have no spinal cords – and they're consumers. They just eat plankton. They're taking over the ocean. Because this in the ocean is metaphysically representative of human consciousness. And this is what is happening to human beings. We have become spineless mindless consumers. Like jellyfish. We're like jellyfish. And just as the jellyfish are taking over the oceans, the spineless mindless consumption is taking over the oceans of consciousness. (Yusuf 2014a)

In this speech, given in Malaysia, Yusuf goes on to warn his audience that the same thing will happen to their society, if they are not careful:

And you're going to get the same diseases in this country. You will get the same thing if you allow these things in, without thinking about what you have. Your families will break down. You'll start building old folks' homes instead of taking care of your parents, you'll just put them in – to let a caretaker take care of them. This is already happening in some Muslim countries. This is what happens, because the Western civilization is a packaged deal. Don't think you could just take a part of it. Arnold Toynbee [a famous historian] said it doesn't work like that. You get the whole thing. (Yusuf 2014a)

Yusuf, in his talks, also links the rampant consumer culture to the climate-change crisis. In one of his talks organised by Reviving the Islamic Spirit, Yusuf dedicated his entire speech to the climate crisis. Speaking about a variety of environmental disasters, such as endangered species, over-fishing, and pollution, he pinpointed consumerism as one of the key contributing factors (Yusuf 2011a).

Similarly, Dr Umar routinely talks about the importance of preserving the natural environment and moving away from a culture of extreme consumerism. During the retreats at Rosales, he always emphasises the beauty of its natural surroundings and how being close to nature helps to nurture the human soul and the spirit. He also encourages people to try to eat organic food; he warns against genetic engineering which manipulates seeds in order to increase the size of fruits and vegetables. This critique of the extreme consumerism of the modern world, and the use of scientific technology to create genetically modified sources of food, encapsulates the rationalist scholars' emphasis on simple living. This in turn has implications for all aspects of life. These scholars would argue that good health does not require us to eat chicken every day; it is better to eat organically raised and halal chicken occasionally, rather than eating modified and unhealthy chicken on a daily basis. Similarly, their teachings help young Muslims to appreciate the importance of securing a good education and a professional career in order to be able to afford the basic comforts of life, but they simultaneously discourage Muslim youth from becoming obsessed with material possessions such as the latest gadgets. These scholars actively argue that an obsession with material prosperity leads one away from exploring the real meaning of life, while also contributing to the unchecked exploitation of natural resources. Thus, in terms of practical everyday living, the teachings of these scholars come very close to the vision of the modern environmental movements that argue for the ethical use of environmental resources and encourage simple living so as not to overburden the planet.

5 ARTS AND AESTHETICS

One other major challenge for modern-educated Muslims is how to enjoy life on an everyday basis within a very strict Islamic moral framework. If listening to music, watching TV, going to a cinema to watch a movie, or having a meeting with a friend over a drink are all forbidden, how is one to make life relaxing or enjoyable? It is in resolving this tension that the teachings of these scholars are particularly helpful when compared with those of very conservative Islamic scholars. Because of their human- ist background, the rationalist scholars are very focused on making young Muslims appreciate the beauty that Islam can inspire. One of their responses to limited entertainment options available to Muslims is to promote poetry. Yusuf has talked about the Prophet's appreciation of poetry, and its place in the very beginnings of Islam (Yusuf 2011e). Similarly, he points out that the prophetic companions appreciated and wrote poetry. Referring to them as 'poet warriors', he notes how they recognised the broader importance of poetry in life (Yusuf 2014b). He argues that God gave man words so that man can express what is in his heart, noting this as the main reason why Arabs valued poetic language and its ability to speak the truth (Yusuf 2011e).

Yusuf argues that speaking the truth of one's heart is the inherent purpose of poetry and is a practice that Muslims must nurture. Poetry, in his view, is a much more meaningful mode of human expression than the TV shows which have become such an integral part of modern culture. Yusuf actively discourages Muslims from watching TV. Writing poetry that is true, and appreciating poetry from the past, in Yusuf's view, helps to resist the corrupting influence of things like advertising, wherein, he argues, poetic language is used to spread lies rather than the truth (Yusuf 2011e). Yusuf encourages Muslims to read the work of famous Muslim poets and he has translated several works of Sufi poetry into English. He does this with a view to spreading the moral and spiritual message incorporated in those poems. Yusuf's appreciation for poetry is, however, not limited to Muslim poets; his speeches feature Shakespeare, Homer, and in particular Romantic poets, whose focus on culture and the inner human spirit overlaps significantly with Yusuf's goal of encouraging inner morality and wisdom. In general he encourages Muslims to read literature, noting that the great books 'encourage introspection and inspire positive change' (Yusuf 2013a; Sandala 2018).

Similarly, the rationalist scholars encourage Muslims to travel to beautiful Islamic architectural sites. They hold retreats at sites which are of Islamic historic significance, aiming to help the participants to develop an appreciation of Islamic arts and aesthetics. These scholars also promote active participation in Islamic art forms, especially calligraphy and paintings. In 2017 Zaytuna College launched a one-year master's degree in Islamic Arts; this will be Zaytuna's first master's degree and thereby reflects the importance that Yusuf accords to the promotion of Islamic arts. Thus, as we have seen in the analysis presented of all the other themes, these scholars do not fail to appreciate the challenge that a young Muslim might feel when trying to live by Islamic norms in a Western cultural context; but instead of justifying complete submergence in the culture of the host society, they argue for finding alternative options. Thus, unlike the strict Salafis or Deobandis, the rationalist scholars do not deny the need for beauty in life, for having opportunities for relaxation, for seeking small everyday pleasures. But, in response, instead of defending going to the cinema or listening to music or watching TV, they encourage people to develop what might be considered higher tastes and modes of relaxation: poetry; listening to spiritually oriented Sufi music; reading classics; cultivating hobbies such as painting, calligraphy, and poetry; and travelling to sites of Islamic historical and architectural significance. Also, these scholars encourage young Muslims to dress well, and they model it through their own careful dressing. Yusuf in particular blends eastern-style robes and caps very gracefully into his everyday western dressing – a fact widely admired by his students. Thus, investing one's spare time in taking care of one's appearance and developing a pleasant demeanour is also encouraged.

CONCLUSION

A review of the position that the Islamic rationalist scholars adopt on key issues that influence everyday decisions confronting young Muslims living in the West (or those living in urban centres of Muslim-majority countries) shows how these scholars are indeed able to use their specialist knowledge of Islam and their tacit knowledge of the everyday reality faced by young modern-educated Muslims to offer everyday life options which respect the core Islamic principles yet allow Muslims to integrate into modern society. The analysis presented in this chapter has illustrated how these scholars stand firm on core Islamic rulings, such as the prohibition on homosexuality, resisting pressure to be 'politically correct', yet present their justification in a way that does not force them into confrontation with their host society. Thus, while they refuse to endorse homosexuality from an Islamic perspective, they argue against judging those Muslims who might live by that option. By advocating this moderate course, these Islamic rationalist scholars help modern-educated Muslims to appreciate how they can be confident Muslims and yet be proud Americans, Brits, or Europeans; how they can respect the laws of the secular state and yet not violate the dictates of Islam; and how they can enjoy life by exploring other art forms, rather than submerging themselves in the dominant entertainment culture shaped by cable TV, movie theatres, clubs, and bars.

The rationalist scholars thus are indeed providing young Muslims with alternatives to the choices offered by a typical mosque-based imam. They are encouraging young Muslims to view Islam as capable of doing more than merely co-existing with Western modernity: that in fact it can enrich the latter by restoring the spiritual dimensions of life. By recognising where Islamic dictates differ from modern Western reality – be it in terms of gender roles, science, excessive consumerism, or exploitation of natural resources – these scholars maintain that Muslims can play a role in convincing their host societies of the importance of preserving the spiritual and moral dimensions of life. Their confidence in standing firm on the core principles of Islam has been critical to making them popular in the Muslim diaspora, as well as among the social elites in the urban centres of Muslim-majority countries. These scholars are also increasingly taking on a more active role as spokesmen of Islam. In its 2017 annual report, Zaytuna College highlighted increased engagement in public dialogue as key to its future mission (Zaytuna College 2017: 7).

The actual attitudinal impact that the Islamic rationalist scholars have on young modern-educated Muslims is to make them more confident of their Muslim identity, while simultaneously encouraging them to respect diversity within Islam, as well as in the broader society. They encourage these young Muslims to appreciate Islam as a complex tradition which allows for adaptation to different contexts and needs of the changing times, while keeping the core unchanged. Drawing on the Sufi tradition and the dictates of ihsan, these scholars also place heavy emphasis on promoting human kindness, and they advise against judging others. Further, their critique of the excessive consumerism and lack of spirituality of the modern age is shared by Western philosophers and thinkers, such as Charles Taylor (2007), who have voiced similar reservations about the extreme materialism of contemporary life, the loss of purpose due to a denial of spiritual truths, and the increased individualism and related isolation of the human experience (Euben 1999).

The only area where we have, however, seen serious tensions emerge from their work is in their approach to political Islam. In particular, Humza Yusuf's decision to publicly associate with Islamic scholars who sided with General al-Sisi and endorsed the oppression of the Muslim Brotherhood (which involved massive human-rights violations) has raised concerns among some of these scholars' students; the balanced approach otherwise associated with these scholars seems to have been compromised. The evidence of growing concern about this issue among their students is to be shared in the next chapter, while the final chapter of this volume will address the implications of these concerns for the future of this Islamic revival movement. For now, this chapter has, however, helped to illustrate how the key to their appeal is their offer of a moderate path to young educated Muslims – which enables them to integrate and prosper within modern society yet be proud of their Islamic identity and heritage, while also being confident of their ability as Muslims to check the excesses of the modern age.

PART II

AFFLUENCE AND CREATIVITY

6

Material Conditions and Attitudes Towards the Texts

Islam of the Prosperous Muslim Youth

It is a Saturday morning in early October, and I am at one of Ta'leef Collective's events in Chicago; more than 150 attendees, mostly young Muslim university students from well-to-do families, are in the audience. It is a mixed-sex gathering, and there are no dress-code restrictions; unspoken rules, however, dictate that men and women sit at opposite ends of the hall. On this particular morning, Dr Umar is to give a lecture on 'aqidah. Why do these young Muslim men and women, already under the pressure of term-time course work, turn up to these lectures, for which a one-way commute to the venue could easily take an hour? This chapter will present evidence to support the core contention of this volume: young modern-educated Muslims, especially those from well-to-do families, are drawn to Islamic rationalist scholars by the scholars' ability to present a form of Islam that supports critical inquiry and logical thinking, while simultaneously promoting deep mysticism. These scholars present to these young Muslims an Islam that stands up to critical reasoning and is consistent with what modern-educated Muslims expect from any field of knowledge. These young Muslims also appreciate the practical guidance that the rationalist scholars are able to offer on how to live as a Muslim and be a confident member of modern society. During my fieldwork, I have had opportunities to interview many young Muslims attending the events and retreats led by these scholars; I have also conducted detailed interviews with many of their more serious students, who are themselves to become future scholars. The interviews reveal great similarities in the socio-economic and educational profiles of the Muslim youth gravitating towards these scholars; they also identify shared reasons these scholars appeal to these young Muslims. But, equally importantly, the interviews reveal fascinating insights into why some young Muslims, especially from the second and third generations, continue to retain their faith in Islam while living in a Western secular society. As a testimony to the richness of the experiences of these young Muslims whom I have interviewed, this chapter presents profiles of a number of them in detail.

Such detailed profiles help to demonstrate what young educated Muslims find appealing about the Islamic rationalist scholars; equally, they illustrate certain shared characteristics: the students come from well-to-do families, are educated in leading Western universities, demonstrate critical modes of thinking, and belong to the societal elites in the Muslim diaspora as well as in Muslim-majority countries. The students of these scholars are thus in a position to influence trends within their communities and beyond. The profiles of the more serious students of the Islamic rationalist scholars – who are to become the third generation of scholars within this network – similarly help to demonstrate how these scholars have been successful in reversing the negative impact of colonial rule on Islamic knowledge transmission, namely the exit of Muslim elites from Islamic knowledge-transmission platforms. The third generation of scholars being trained within the Islamic rationalist network are from affluent Muslim families, as opposed to being from the marginalised segments of society, unlike the majority of the madrasah students and teachers in the Muslim-majority countries. This movement which is leading to a revival of Islamic rationalism is thus a product of the improved material prosperity enjoyed by segments of the Muslim diaspora in the West.

This chapter also reinforces how the rationalist scholars' ability to combine specialist knowledge of Islamic sciences and tacit knowledge of contemporary Western realities is core to their appeal. Those who follow these scholars are impressed by their command of the Arabic language and their study of the Islamic texts; they are, however, equally impressed by their ability to engage critically with Western intellectual and philosophical thought. The way these scholars relate Islam to everyday questions, as outlined in the previous chapter, appeals to the young Muslims who gather around them: the answers that the scholars provide are seen to respect core Islamic principles, while also enabling their followers to be productive members of Western society. The emphasis placed by these scholars on Islam's ability to inspire beauty in all manifestations, as historically associated with the rise of Islamic civilisation itself, also appeals to their listeners. The fact that the scholars are part of Western civilisation (given their European or North American origins) and are educated to high Western standards makes their critique of Western modernity and their appreciation of Islam all the more convincing. Especially for those Western-educated young Muslims who are enamoured by Western civilisation and feel disillusioned with the militant image of Islam that dominates the public discourse, it is particularly reaffirming to have Western converts from well-to-do families, trained in leading Western institutions, tell them about the superiority of their own religion. The real strength of this movement for the revival of Islamic rationalism thus rests in its power to retain within Islam (and create an appreciation for it) the young modern-educated and socially progressive Muslim youth who otherwise might be swayed to adopt the Western secular outlook, while also encouraging the already devout to take a more intellectually engaging and spiritual approach to their religion.

Finally, given that critical thinking and reasoning is one of the core characteristics of the profile of the young Muslims drawn to the Islamic rationalist scholars, it is thus not surprising that their more advanced students and ardent followers observe the scholars' actions very closely and voice their concerns, though with due respect. This critical reflection on the actions of the scholars, rather than blind obedience to them, is arguably very much in the spirit of the original Islamic scholarly tradition, wherein the right to disagree in matters of interpretation was to be respected as long as the right methods of reasoning (as represented by one of the four madhhabs) were followed. This freedom to question the teacher, even when done with due respect, can be seen as a potential risk to the authority of the rationalist scholars. The next chapter will contend that this display of independent thinking and respect for critical reasoning by the students of the Islamic rationalist scholars is actually what will help to sustain and expand the influence of this movement in the long term.

This chapter is divided into two main parts. The first presents the profiles of a number of young Muslims who follow the rationalist scholars and shows how they largely come from an affluent background and gravitate towards these scholars for the reasons explained above. The second part presents detailed profiles of their more dedicated students who show the potential to become the third generation of teachers within the network under study. Together these two sections present evidence in defence of the arguments advanced in this section. Barring one or two exceptions, the chapter mainly draws on the experiences of Muslim university students born and raised in the West; the success that the Islamic rationalist scholars are having in inspiring modern-educated Muslims from affluent families to engage in Islamic knowledge transmission in Muslim-majority countries will be addressed in the next chapter. It is worth noting that the interviews with the young people also reconfirm another starting contention of this volume: that Hamza Yusuf has been central to the rise of this network. The chapter helps to illustrate how today young Muslims are exposed to this network of scholars through any one of the multiple platforms linked to it (Ta'leef Collective, Rosales, SeekersHub, etc.). However, as will become clear through the course of this chapter, many of their ardent students, who today are training to become the third generation of scholars within this network, were initially mainly inspired by Hamza Yusuf; he seems to have had a powerful influence on Muslim teenagers in the late 1990s and early 2000s, when he burst on the scene with his very passionate speeches and became known to Muslim audiences in the West as well as in the Arab world through a show that he hosted on MBC TV.

I GENERAL FOLLOWERS

Interviews with the followers of the Islamic rationalist scholars, and members of their audience, reveal a shared appreciation of three core characteristics of the scholars: one, their sound command of the Arabic language and their study of Islamic sciences under the tutelage of traditional scholars in Muslim-majority countries; two, their emphasis on the use of reason, but a reason that allows for recognition of spiritual experiences; and three, their ability to relate the Islamic legal and moral code to the realities of everyday life. In addition, just as with any other religious or social movement, the ability to connect with like-minded individuals also helps to draw young Muslims to platforms established by the Islamic rationalist scholars. Below I present representatives of four sub-groups within the audience of these scholars, who in my assessment constitute their core audience: university students; recent university graduates; young couples and their children; and young European and North American converts. Obtaining a detailed insight into the factors that attracted members of these sub-groups to these scholars should help the reader to appreciate their real impact.

A Recent Engineering Graduate from Chicago; South Asian Origin; Male

The first profile that I would like to share is that of a recent graduate from a prominent university in Chicago who was about to join a consultancy firm. During one of my summer visits to Rosales, I had found him acting as an assistant to Dr Umar. He had just finished his undergraduate studies in industrial engineering at Northwestern University, Chicago, and on his return was due to join a consultancy company. Explaining his motives for accompanying Dr Umar to Rosales, he explained how, having recently finished school and being due to start work in September, he wanted to make productive use of the summer months that he still had free. Weighing up his options, which involved travelling across Europe, he decided that accompanying Dr Umar to Rosales would be the best option: 'I decided it is a remote location that will help me reflect before I go into the consultancy world.' He had known Dr Umar since he was a child, as his mother used to take him along to his lectures; he remembered praying next to him when he was five. He later lost contact with Dr Umar, but the connection was re-established when the latter began to speak at Ta'leef Collective events in Chicago – a platform with which this respondent was actively associated and which in his assessment helped the converts, but also young secular-oriented born Muslims, to navigate their way through Islam.

However, he explained that his involvement with these organisations had not necessarily been very consistent, noting that he had his own 'religious development issues'. He remembered being relatively uninterested in religious issues during his school years, but it was during his university years that he came to 'really internalize Islam'. He credited a meeting with Imam Suhaib Webb (a popular Islamic scholar in the United States) as convincing him that there was a place for him in Islam. His faith, however, remained shaky until the deaths of two cousins and a close friend made him re-evaluate the purpose of life, which led him to radical self-transformation. From being very hyper-social in his initial years at university, he became quite inwardly focused; gradually, however, he began to engage with a number of Islamic platforms. A personal discussion with Usama Canon on one of his visits to Chicago helped to answer many of the questions with which he was struggling. He went on to attend the Rihla programme, which proved a powerful experience for him: 'That was when I was convinced that I wanted Islam in my life.' Rihla, in his view, proved so important because it focused on teaching the complexity of Islamic sciences but equally on establishing the importance of being in good company. Stating that the content of the teaching was 'great', he pointed out how the courses covered taught about the basics of the heart, the fiqh (one could choose the madhhab that one wanted to study), and the tafsir of key Quranic surahs (especially *Surah*

Waqi'ah). But equally he noted that the companionship was 'great'. He pointed out how people from Australia, England, and other places were there. Above all, the experience was powerful for him as he could sit and get to know each one of the teachers: 'That was fantastic. Just because I was there, I know Imam Zaid, Faraz Rabbani, Yayha Rhodus; I saw him [Rhodus] at a marriage recently and he hugged me.' The capacity of these scholars to develop a bond with those who seek their guidance is something that he found particularly impressive: 'It is miraculous that they have the ability to do so, that is relate to those who seek their guidance and develop one-to-one connections. How do you manage it when so many people love you? But they are amazing people. They do remember your face.'

His family background was important, in his assessment, in eventually making him actively commit to Islam. His parents were very integrated in American society but wanted to ensure that they also preserved their Pakistani culture, so they encouraged their children to maintain a healthy outlook towards Islam as well as towards American society. Noting the challenge of growing up in the West, he admitted that the pleasures of the modern society are very appealing in early youth, but that gradually one finds that 'the life of drinks and sex is not very fulfilling'. He felt he was lucky that he could see that there was something more important, and that with God's blessing he was guided in the right direction. As he said, 'I could have gone the other way, but my family was so strong that this was not possible.' He noted how many scholars routinely talk about the high numbers of young Muslims who are moving away from their religion. He commented that one of the prominent scholars with whom he studied says that scheduling an Islamic class on a Thursday is better than on Friday, because on Friday people go to clubs and other social activities. It is in this context, where many Muslims are becoming disengaged from religion, that he appreciated the real contribution of this network of rationalist scholars, as they are able to make Islam socially relevant for young Muslims like him.

He was particularly appreciative of the Mu'aliff Mentorship programme run by Ta'leef Collective, which addresses the everyday issues faced by young Muslims. In this programme, Ta'leef leaders draw on stories and practical scenarios to elaborate on these issues. There are no inhibitions or hesitations in discussing any issue that a young person might face: 'You might have a Muslim who drinks or whose body is all covered with tattoo[s] but they are not to be judged.' In his experience, converts are very committed, as they choose to follow the faith. However, he was also of the view that everyone, whether born Muslim or not, has to consciously convert to it: 'You have to say that Islam is real. Some have it from the childhood. Others do it at the age of 40–50. It is your choice, it means something to you. Everyone I know converted between high school or college.' Talking about the scholars leading this Islamic rationalist network, he was of the view that these converts can strike the middle ground easily because they come from the West and thus understand the local context very well, while Muslim immigrants try to apply the Islam that they had experienced in Muslim-majority contexts.

This young man, noting the contributions of Hamza Yusuf, emphasised the analytical abilities of the latter, and his thorough knowledge of both the West and the Muslim world, due to his years of study there. He also emphasised other aspects of Yusuf's personality that have won him a devoted following. He noted that he is very good looking and dresses very elegantly, in 'a cool mix of western and eastern elegance'. This, he noted, has played a very important role in impressing young Muslim students from well-to-do families who see in him a role model who can act from within an Islamic framework yet command respect in the West. He commented on how the 'whole Zaytuna look is very cool'. Finally, he also noted the racial dynamics, whereby a European or North American convert from a well-educated background can prove particularly influential; impressed by Western progress, many young university-educated and socially progressive Muslims find their faith rejuvenated when they see converts such as Hamza Yusuf, Tim Winter, or Dr Umar, well trained in the Western scholarly tradition and personally highly attractive, defend their religion.

A Woman in Her Late Thirties and her Teenage Daughter; Naperville (Chicago); South Asian Origin

A woman from Chicago, who was a very enthusiastic participant in the activities organised by this network and also engaged her children actively in them, shared very similar explanations about the appeal of the Islamic rationalist scholars. In her assessment, the psychology of immigrants is different from that of the second- or third-generation Muslims born and raised in the West. She explained how her parents, like most other parents from South Asian Muslim communities, were keen to ensure that their children remained connected to their roots; yet she and her friends from similar backgrounds found it difficult to fully commit to the culture of traditional Islam, as they felt they were American: 'Yes, we are Muslim but we are Americans too. We are proud to be Americans.' In such a context, she noted, there is a tendency among young people to become rebellious, and that is when some of them gravitate towards Salafi networks, whose teachings of Islam are less intertwined with cultural influences. In her view, the Salafi approach gains popularity in Muslim student networks on university campuses because it encourages direct engagement with the text and individual reasoning, which is consistent with the training given in Western academic institutions. It also, she noted, dispenses with reliance on mosque imams, who often fail to win over young Muslims, due to their limited knowledge of the everyday choices that face them and due also to the fact that many of the imams are unable to communicate effectively in English.

Recalling her own experience, she noted how the imam in the mosque attended by her parents was more comfortable teaching in Urdu, which made the minds of the younger audience, who were more fluent in English, automatically switch off. However, in her experience, the Salafi approach, though normally quite effective in attracting young Muslims when they join universities and are receptive to joining networks that offer good companionship, is inherently limited because it leads to 'the blind leading the blind'. On joining a Salafi student network in the university, she found herself teaching other girls who were three to four years junior to her, which led her to realise soon enough that her own knowledge was too limited. That is why she was impressed when she heard Hamza Yusuf speak about the importance of sitting in the suhbah of scholars and saints to learn real knowledge. Today, she is one of those who are fully convinced of the importance of seeking long-term spiritual training in the constant company of scholars who have sat in the presence of great scholars from the previous generation, who in turn have done the same, so that the chain of transmission (*silsilah*) goes all the way back to the Prophet's time. As she noted, 'One has to do that to develop the correct understanding of Islam.' The emphasis placed by the Islamic rationalist scholars on the use of reason, not in a narrow literalist sense but in a way that recognises the importance of spiritual truths, is, in her view, essential to their appeal: 'When you talk to them, you can see they use reason while also recognising the importance of spiritual experiences. This appeals to us who are trained in the Western education system and have developed critical thinking and reasoning abilities but also have religious faith.'

Having married young, this respondent, who was in her late thirties, had involved all her children in the activities of the rationalist network.

Her eldest daughter, who was in the eleventh grade at the time of the interview, was already an active participant. However, while the daughter was impressed by these scholars, her relationship with her Islamic identity was undergoing the same ups and downs as noted for the young engineering graduate. As a high school student, and a practising Muslim, she felt that Islam influenced many of her everyday actions and the choices that she has to make. Explaining that her mother was only 22 when she had her, the daughter described how, when growing up, she had spent a lot of time at her grandparents' house, where performing the *namaz* (the five daily prayers) was an integral part of the daily routine. This is the setting in which she became exposed to Islam; further knowledge came through attending the Islamic school on Sundays and accompanying her mother to numerous Islamic events, especially those organised by the Islamic rationalist scholars. In her assessment, this early exposure to multiple Islamic networks helped her to appreciate the religion but also to recognise that people can have different understandings of Islam. She then had an opportunity to go for Hajj and saw people from different backgrounds and races come together: 'All of them, if asked to define Islam, would express it in different ways, but they were all bowing down to the same Ka'bah and saying the same shahadah.' She explained how her attempts to live by the Islamic code have not always been without their challenges. At one point she wore hijab, but then took it off. She noted how being religious in a secular context continues to raise numerous questions in her mind, answers to which are not easy. 'If everything that one does should be done for Allah, then why attend the school, for example?,' she pondered. She emphasised how in resolving these kinds of dilemma the teachings of the Islamic rationalist scholars really help. Her mother's focus on the metaphysical dimensions of the religion, and her active participation in Sufi teachings, have, she felt, helped her to develop her inner conviction in Islam.

Two Young Female Students at SeekersHub, Mississauga, Canada; Arab Origins

Two of the female students at SeekersHub, whose profiles are reasonably representative of the young Muslims influenced by the Islamic rationalist scholars, identified reasons for gravitating towards these scholars similar to those recorded above. These two cases are interesting because they show how young educated Muslims from families following different Islamic scholarly and mystical traditions gravitate to these scholars for quite similar reasons. The first student described being gradually drawn to the scholars in this network. Having grown up with a very strict version of Islam, she noted how there was always much discussion in her household of halal and *haram* (religiously forbidden). She became involved with SeekersHub, and gradually through that with the entire network of Islamic rationalist scholars; in 2012 she had attended a retreat organised by Revival of the Islamic Spirit, where many of the scholars from this network, including Yahya Rhodus, spoke. At this retreat and on subsequent occasions offering an opportunity to listen to these scholars, she was impressed by the depth with which they approached the subject. During the same period, at the University of Toronto's Mississauga campus, the Muslim chaplaincy had begun hosting short retreats, and through these she became more directly involved with SeekersHub. Her family, who are more Salafi in orientation, discouraged her from joining SeekersHub; this did put pressure on her, but eventually they could not dissuade her. The course on purification of the heart in particular had a special impact on her. Attending these courses made her appreciate that, despite growing up in a devout Muslim family, she had never studied the 'aqidah in depth: 'I had no idea what I believed about God. I realised that instead of just fearing God, seeking God out of love is a very different approach.' It was at SeekersHub that she was also exposed to the performance of *nashid*s (recitations of religious poems common in Sufi tariqahs), which she found very appealing.

Her insistence on joining these activities did provoke occasional arguments within the family. Although gradually her parents became more accepting of her choices, even now she avoids informing her father if she attends a *mawlud* (Prophet Muhammad's birthday), so as not to upset him. At the time of the interview she was volunteering at SeekersHub and helping to write quizzes for some of the courses. Growing up, she had studied in Islamic schools until grade 9 and after that joined a Catholic school. When she entered the university, she found that the Muslim Students' Association (MSA) was a big presence, as, 11 per cent of the population of Mississauga is Muslim. Internally, however, she felt an identity crisis and a spiritual crisis; she did not know what she believed about God. Before joining the MSA in 2012, she had felt somewhat disconnected from the broader Islamic community. Having been with the SeekersHub for over four years now, she was now very convinced of the appeal of traditional Islam. The way the Islamic rationalist scholars explain faith makes sense to her: 'Even if you want to take it from an intellectual point of view, we have such a strong intellectual tradition.

Even on the question of evil, and you come to these scholars and they give you such clear answers.' For her the key appeal of the teachings of the Islamic rationalist scholars is that they emphasise beauty and creativity within Islam. After being told for so long about all the many things she cannot do (watch TV, listen to music, attend a particular school event, etc.), she now understands that Islam does not have to mean excluding all joy from one's life: 'Now I understand how the purpose of the sunnah is to make religion social; art is also encouraged, there is space for arts, singing, all of it is here. They are all part of a whole.'

The other female student from SeekersHub came from a slightly different cultural and religious family background, but her reasons for being attracted to the rationalist scholars were quite similar. She had joined SeekersHub two years ago, when her mother (a convert) started attending their courses. For the daughter the strongest appeal was being part of the community that had evolved around SeekersHub. She and her siblings were home-schooled, so she found this social space particularly appealing. In her experience the people at SeekersHub were not very judgemental, unlike what she found in regular mosque and Islamic settings. Learning under Shaykh Faraz had been very enriching for her, as she found him to be very knowledgeable. She noted that her father, who is of Syrian origin, also greatly respected him. Her mother had been very influenced by Hamza Yusuf and was an American convert.

At the time of the interview, she was volunteering at SeekersHub and helping to organise events there, in addition to attending foundation courses in fiqh. She explained how she had started these courses with a view to covering *fard al-'ayn* (the obligatory knowledge that all Muslims should have) but, once involved, became motived to keep going. Talking about the appeal of the rationalist scholars, she noted that young Muslims feel confused between what they are taught about Islam and the choices that they see around them, and they need explanations; it is, she commented, a 'generation of "why?"'. She explained that although family still remains a major influence in shaping one's religious understanding, there comes an age when one wants to start making one's own choices. She mentioned that in addition to SeekersHub, she attends events organised by other Islamic platforms, including *Risalah* Foundation (a Sufi network in Toronto) and Revival of the Islamic Spirit. She felt that one of the reasons she likes all these platforms was that they provide a comfort zone; at these events she can meet the Arab members of her family whom she might not get to meet much otherwise. In her assessment, Hamza Yusuf was very special for her mother and still remains very influential among her own generation, although the connection is not the same. To her, his appeal is that he took reality and 'smashed it in our face; he does not try to sugar coat'. People tend to be attracted when they are shocked in this way, she argued. She felt that he is extremely knowledgeable and had made a huge difference to young Muslims like her.

A Western Convert and One of the First Graduates of Zaytuna College

Among the avid followers of the Islamic rationalist scholars are also some young Western coverts, and not surprisingly their profiles and motives for conversion are fairly similar to those of the scholars themselves. Now in his mid-thirties, this respondent was among the first graduates of Zaytuna College. At the time of the interview in 2016, he was back at the drawing board, thinking about what to do next, having recently quit his job in the information technology sector. He was at Zaytuna between 2010 and 2014 and on graduation had taught in a few Islamic schools, but none of the positions proved particularly interesting. He described some of the challenges of working with Muslim non-profit organisations that arise from the fact that often they do not operate very professionally. Before joining Zaytuna College, he had already completed his first bachelor's degree and a master's degree in political science in Florida. Thus, like the rationalist scholars, he came from a well-do-to middle-class family and had access to good education. He converted to Islam in 2003 between his junior and senior years and subsequently became involved in the Muslim community in Miami, at the mosque, and in the MSA. Initially, Islam seemed very simple and black and white to him, but as he met more Muslims from different backgrounds and religious affiliations he realised that there are many grey areas. The Muslim community valued his presence, because they found that he, as a Western convert, could more effectively represent them to the broader society. He then travelled with a friend to Tarim in Yemen to learn Arabic, but after a month there they left for Cairo, where they spent 10 months learning Arabic at private institutes. After Cairo, he spent another seven months learning Arabic in Riyadh. In 2010 his application to study at Zaytuna was accepted.

His conversion was supported 'first by the text, then a friend, and then going into the community, where I was received with very open arms'. Islam's appeal to him was quite straightforward: 'It was its theological appeal. I went in without too much baggage. I did not have any life problems; I did not have much ideological baggage either. I had never really for the most part been too rooted in any political group or ideological group.' At Zaytuna he appreciated the more holistic approach to understanding Islam: 'I did not take advantage of it as much as I could as I had already been through college and was a little bit older, but it was a well-rounded education. There was a lot of care for my education at the end of the day. I do feel I learned a lot and saw a lot.' Talking about postgraduation opportunities for Zaytuna students, he mentioned Chicago Theological Seminary, Hartford Seminary, and the Graduate Theological Seminary as possible avenues for pursuing higher education. In line with the efforts of Ta'leef Collective and based on his own experience, he described how nurturing faith in the long term remains an ongoing struggle, and having a supportive community really helps: 'If you come to God a hand's length, he comes to you with the arm's length. In the beginning, it is the honeymoon period, but in the long term it is the effort that matters.'

2 CORE STUDENTS: THE THIRD-GENERATION SCHOLARS

Thus far we have looked at the profiles of some of the regular followers of the rationalist scholars. This section presents profiles of some of their more ardent students, who do not merely attend a lecture or an event with their teachers but are actually pursuing serious scholarship and will become the third-generation scholars within the Islamic rationalist network. The reasons these more committed students are attracted to these scholars are not very different from those shared by the regular followers; but due to their more serious engagement with the Islamic texts, the respondents within this pool were more able to share their assessments of how these scholars compare with other Islamic scholars. Precisely because of this deeper engagement with the Islamic texts, these respondents were also more reflective about the actions and statements of the scholars. Thus, some of the core concerns about the positions taken by Humza Yusuf vis-à-vis the Muslim Brotherhood (noted in the previous chapter) have come from among some of these very students. While public expression of these concerns by some of their own students could at one level undermine the credibility of these scholars, in my assessment the real strength of this movement rests in its ability to attract such reflective minds from within the younger generation of Muslims. It is the critical reasoning and reflective ability among the young people who are attracted by the rationalist scholars to study Islam that make the future of this movement promising – an issue that will be addressed in detail in the next chapter. Mapping the profiles of these students and the factors that drew them to the rationalist scholars helps to illustrate how these future scholars come from socio-economic and educational backgrounds much more privileged than those of their counterparts in Muslim-majority countries, where, as discussed in Chapter 3, responsibility for Islamic education has since the colonial period been mainly in the hands of socially and economically disenfranchised segments of society.

A Former Student of Zaytuna Institute Pursuing a PhD Programme in New York; South Asian Origin

It was quite by chance that I came across one of the first graduates from Zaytuna Institute, who is now pursuing a PhD in the Islam track in the Department of Religion at Columbia University: in a random search on Google I had found his blog about a Turkish scholar on whom I was writing a paper. His profile is typical of the reflective minds being trained by the Islamic rationalist scholars: students who have the confidence to question the decisions of their own teachers, while taking care to observe the respect due to a teacher in the Islamic tradition. It was in 2003 and through a local Muslim Student Association that this respondent heard recordings of Hamza Yusuf and Imam Zaid Shakir. He went on to listen regularly to Hamza Yusuf's lectures online and eventually got to hear Yusuf in person at a fundraising event in New York. As a young Muslim in New York, shocked by the events of September 11, he was keen to understand Islam better but the relative failure of the local imams to provide 'relevant' answers to his struggles as a young Muslim in Manhattan made him question if madrasah education could be meaningful. In this context, the speeches of Hamza Yusuf and Imam Zaid Shakir really appealed to him, inspiring him to apply for a place at Zaytuna Institute. He was among the first three students admitted. Interviewed by me, he recalled Imam Zaid Shakir being the backbone of the institute in terms of actual teaching, as Hamza Yusuf was often away. Yahya Rhodus joined the faculty in the second year and in this respondent's experience was very thoughtful. He recalled Rhodus having a huge library, and on return from Tarim being very cognisant of the need to take time to readjust to Western realities, in order to find the right answers to some important questions.

Since Zaytuna Institute did not have the necessary accreditation to issue bachelor's degrees, unlike the present-day Zaytuna College, on completing his four-year degree this respondent returned to New York and did an undergraduate degree at New York University (2009–2013). Now enrolled in the PhD programme, he expressed no regret about spending four years at Zaytuna and not securing a formal university certificate at the end of it. He acknowledged the value of having studied the traditional texts in detail at Zaytuna Institute and of acquiring a solid foundation in the Arabic language. He also appreciated the spirit of the Zaytuna scholars, who ingrained in him an appreciation of the fact that this education was just the beginning and that he must continue higher learning, either at one of the Western universities or by travelling to study with traditional scholars in a Muslim-majority country. He had no doubt about the role that the Islamic rationalist scholars are playing in keeping young Muslims from losing their religious identity, despite the pressures of secular society. He noted how easy it is as a minority in society 'to stop attending the mosque, not pray, and stop identifying oneself as a Muslim'.

He was, however, disturbed about two developments concerning Hamza Yusuf. First, he was concerned that by taking on the role of a public spokesperson for Islam, Yusuf was increasingly talking on subjects from an Islamic perspective without specialist knowledge; second, he believed that by openly adopting a critical stance against political Islam the rationalist scholars were running the risk of creating frictions among Muslims and thereby displaying the same bigotry of which they accused the Salafis. The merits or demerits of these two critiques will be addressed fully in the light of available evidence in the final chapter, but this respondent's open expression of such concerns during the interview is important in its own right, as it demonstrates how, when modern-educated and critically aware young Muslims engage with Islamic texts, even when being very respectful towards their teachers, they do formulate independent opinions and find the confidence to express them. He could appreciate that becoming a public figure might help Yusuf to raise funds for the college, but he was of the view that by speaking on every subject his credibility as a scholar was being compromised in the eyes of some of his own students. 'There is a point to having specialisation and knowing things in depth,' he argued.

Similarly, this student had reservations about how Hamza Yusuf, and other scholars in the Islamic rationalist network, had indirectly endorsed the oppression of the Muslim Brotherhood by siding with scholars in Egypt who had supported General al-Sisi. He noted how Hamza Yusuf and other scholars within this network had promoted scholars from

Tarim, in particular Habib Ali-Jifri,[1] who associate Sunni orthodoxy exclusively with advocacy for an Ash'ari-Maturidi kalam and thus exclude mainstream Islamic groups from the fold of Sunni Islam; they had also promoted their counterparts in Egypt, such as Shaykh al-Azhar and Ali Gomma, who endorsed the killing of Muslim Brotherhood members by the Egyptian army. Clearly much closer to Imam Zaid than to Yusuf, this former student of Zaytuna Institute noted how, after the Raba Mosque operation in Egypt, when more than 800 people were killed in a military operation ordered by the al-Sisi government, Imam Zaid had publicly stated his support for the people of Raba, while Yusuf had refrained from making a similar statement. Deeply disturbed by Hamza Yusuf's indirect endorsement of the oppression of the Muslim Brotherhood, he stated that his allegiance to the rationalist scholars was not unqualified. He explained that he was particularly pushed to voice these concerns after attending the Third Peace Forum in Abu Dhabi and then attending the Revival of the Islamic Spirit (RIS) conference in December 2016. This resulted in his writing a powerful letter to Yusuf to express his disappointment with his teacher. Included as the Appendix to this book, the letter, which was sent to Hamza Yusuf in February 2017, is a fine example of the quality of scholarship of those attracted by the Islamic rationalist scholars to a serious study of Islam. The letter is extremely respectful and reflective in tone, yet highly articulate and confident in voicing the writer's concerns, thus demonstrating the spirit of early Islamic scholarship, whereby respect for the teacher was essential but so was the need to retain independence of mind and to ask questions if the teacher was perceived to deviate from Islamic ethical or moral principles.

As for the job prospects for graduates of Zaytuna College, he mentioned the challenges to securing a proper job within the religious sector, as the communities, even if they had the necessary funds, were often unwilling to pay a proper salary to the imam or give him much independence. He noted how Jihad Brown, despite being highly respected for his religious knowledge, was still struggling to find a community which could properly host him. Thus, in his experience, students of Zaytuna were often either following the chaplaincy route, teaching in Islamic schools, or pursuing graduate studies. He described how many of the young Muslims gravitating towards Zaytuna were those who felt the need to fight back against Islamophobia by presenting a more refined

---

[1] Yahya Rhodus studied with Habib Jifri and continues to be very close to him. He also often acts as his official translator; a role he has continued to play during this period.

understanding of religion, noting how the college itself also emphasised this appeal when advertising its degree course. Overall he was optimistic about what the Zaytuna graduates could achieve: 'They are trying to put out quality material. They are getting quality numbers of students each year. These were students who were accepted to good schools but then chose to go to Zaytuna to pursue Islamic education. So in terms of the calibre of the students, it is quite high.' In his own PhD programme, he was now interested in studying Abu al-Thanā' Shihāb al-Dīn Maḥmūd al-Ālūsī's (1802–1854 CE) exegesis of the Quran. Al-Ālūsī may be considered representative of the development of Islamic scholarly thought of the mid-nineteenth century[2]. He credited his interest in al-Ālūsī's scholarship to his time at Zaytuna: 'When I was studying at Zaytuna, my first exposure to al-Ālūsī was there, he was constantly referenced in the tafsir. I find tafsir quite interesting. I came into this through Zaytuna.'

A Medical Student in Edmonton Pursuing Private Learning in Islamic Science; South Asian Origin

A *hafiz*, a student of classical Islamic scholarship in private study circles, and at the time of the interview enrolled in a medicine degree at a leading university in Edmonton, represents the profile of another serious student of the Islamic rationalist scholars. I first met him during the al-Ghazali retreat at Rosales, where he was acting as a reciter during the tarawih prayer. He was exposed to this network of Islamic rationalist scholars when very young, and, as is the case for several others profiled in this chapter, through an elder sibling. His older sister, whom he described as 'almost a surrogate mother', being twelve years older, would take him and another sister along when attending MSA events; she would also play Hamza Yusuf's recordings in the car. He recalled how his childhood experiences of listening to Yusuf lament the lack of serious Islamic scholarship among contemporary Muslims made him hope that he could fill that gap. He already had a Quran teacher. In the summer of 2004, he read both the biography of Malcolm X and Fazail-i-Amaal (a major Islamic text from South Asia): 'I stayed up late and read both the books together.' Both books greatly influenced him. Later he watched a movie about

---

[2] As this student pointed out, one of the descendants of this very scholar, Dr Alousi, co-founded Zaytuna Institute with Shaykh Hamza, which preceded the Zaytuna College. Zaytuna College now has named one of its halls as the al-Ālūsī hall.

Malcolm X and recalled how he was profoundly influenced by the scene in which the FBI is monitoring him but fails to find any incriminating evidence against him, which prompts them to say, 'Compared to King, this guy's a monk.' As my respondent noted, 'I thought I should be like a monk. That resonated with me, so I said that I should also be like a monk.' His family was religious; the community was dominated by Salafi Islam, and that was the kind of Islam into which he was inducted. During this period he visited a particular website which argued that Hamza Yusuf was deviant, and that put him off Yusuf. At this stage, he was reading a lot on the internet and did not have a formal mentor.

Then he came across Masud Khan's website, which hosts all the writings of Tim Winter and also those of Nuh Keller. What they said about the importance of madhhabs and tasawwuf made sense to him. He did not associate with Salafism much, despite being exposed to it in his community. The writings of Winter and Keller really changed things for him. By then YouTube had also started to make their videos available, which enabled him to listen to these scholars online. In 2006, he enrolled on the Rihla programme. His initial motivation was a desire to meet Shaykh Yaqubi from Syria, who was teaching on the Rihla programme that year and whose scholarship resonated with him strongly. He had also intended to take bay'ah with him, although for some reason that did not come about; this experience, however, did lead him to think through the implications of taking the bay'ah. These implications were multifaceted and existential, extending even to everyday markers of identity: 'How am I going to dress. How am I going to present myself to the world?' In the lectures, Shaykh Yaqubi urged the wearing of traditional dress, but the respondent felt that this was not very practical for Muslims living in the West. He searched for options and came across Shukr Clothing, a clothing business run by followers of Nuh Keller. It offered garments that were modest but tailored in Western styles (a compromise between a *thawb*, long Muslim dress for men, and a dress shirt). He tried to conform, but with the passage of time, he decided that these options did not resonate with him.

After High School, he went to Chicago, where his father was working at the time, to memorise the Quran. In Chicago he started studying fiqh with an Islamic scholar. Here he also met Dr Umar and, although his attempts to study with him did not materialise during this period, he did start to read his writings. As part of his degree in history at the University of Alberta in 2012, a university grant enabled him to visit Rosales. It was here that he got to spend serious time with Dr Umar, who was occupying the room next door. He returned to Rosales in 2013 and 2014 and since then had been actively following the scholars within the network. Returning to Edmonton for his university education, he started to study Islamic sciences on the side with a traditionally trained Somali scholar. Most of his study of Islamic sciences had been private, informal, and part-time, and was likely to continue in the same way.

As in the case of the previous respondent profiled in this section, this respondent, being a more serious student of Islamic sciences, also shared many reflective thoughts on the contributions of the rationalist scholars, while also expressing some of the same concerns noted by the first respondent. Aware of the importance of the 1999 Leicester meeting, where Dr Umar, Hamza Yusuf, Nuh Keller, Shaykh Yaqubi, and Tim Winter had gathered with a few other scholars to discuss the way forward, he noted how, before starting their da'wah work, these scholars had actively discussed and agreed on the model of Islam that they were going to promote. In his view, that was the point of genesis of Islamic traditionalism, as the term is being used today. In line with what has been mapped in Chapter 2 about the core components of their teachings, he noted how an emphasis on following the four schools of law, Ash'ari and Maturidi 'aqidah, and then the tradition of ihsan, is core to the teachings of the rationalist scholars. Equally, he was very aware of the tension that I mapped in Chapter 2 regarding Yusuf's reluctance to endorse the formalisation of tariqahs. Hamza Yusuf's personal experience with tariqahs, he felt, was, however, complicated. He agreed that Yusuf's experience with Murabitun might explain his reservations about bay'ah, but then he noted that Bin Bayyah, whom Yusuf actively promotes and acknowledges as a teacher, is also a shaykh of a tariqah, having inherited the seat from his father. He was also very knowledgeable about the linkages among the scholars in Muslim-majority countries from whom the Islamic rationalist scholars had themselves learned.

Like the previous student profiled in this section, this respondent was wary of these scholars' frequent critique of political Islam. He also acknowledged that the Islamic rationalist scholars had promoted scholars such as Habib Ali-Jifri and Ali Gomma, who had sided with an oppressive Egyptian state against the Muslim Brotherhood. These scholars, he feared, seemed to be promoting a very exclusionary definition of ahl-sunnah w'al-jama'ah and thereby excluding all non-Sufi groups from the fold of Sunni Islam. He was similarly very aware of the controversy surrounding the conference in Chechnya which was led by Habib Ali-Jifri. He was of the view that some were perturbed by the non-political stance being advocated by the Islamic rationalist scholars, who nevertheless were endorsing scholars in the Muslim world who were promoting repressive regimes. Referring to the Chechnya conference he asked, 'Who is this Sunni community? Why are we reviewing this question? It is a settled question ... Promoting al-Azhar as the exclusive bastion of Islam. Salafis were deliberately excluded.' He recalled that Ali Gomma was invited to a retreat in 2013, only a few days before the Egyptian coup d'état. Gomma's vociferous support of the Sisi regime, including its perpetration of what the respondent believed to be war crimes, left him extremely conflicted. He described the issue as being contentious and mentioned that Tariq Ramadan had openly criticised the Islamic Society of North America and Reviving the Islamic Spirit (and indirectly Hamza Yusuf, who was influential in shaping the agenda of these two platforms, especially RIS) for promoting scholars from the Muslim world who promoted military regimes in the guise of promoting Sufism.

Finally, as I have found for most of the students of the Islamic rationalist scholars, even this student was pursuing studies with Islamic scholars beyond this network. While following the rationalist scholars, he was also aware of developments within the Deoband tradition. He was of the view that modern scholars of Deoband failed to do justice to their earlier tradition, as the tradition, in his view, was originally quite dynamic. But he listed a few Deobandi scholars who in his view were adopting dynamic approaches to engaging Deobandi teachings with modern realities. He was studying with some of these scholars.

As for his potential future contribution to spreading the teachings of the Islamic rationalist scholars, he said: 'My teachers have always encouraged me to teach. I have been teaching.' He had already been teaching at *Tarjuma* – a local Islamic platform inspired by Ta'leef Collective and covered in detail in the next chapter – where he gave public lectures on living Islam. Currently in medical school, he felt that these different aspects of his life were not compartmentalised but complemented each other: 'It was never an option to be full-time imam. I will be pursuing the tradition for the rest of my life, and the real fruit of it comes out when you can bring it all together. All the people who are your community – if one can show them the potential and the possibility of how it is a life-affirming tradition, finding ways that people can engage with it, trying to tell people that tradition is vast and you can find your niche here – that is an obligation for the scholar as well as the activist. I have my own path in this tradition, and helping others is very important to me.'

A PhD Student of Islamic Theology at Cambridge; South Asian Origin

Enrolled on a PhD programme in Islamic Theology at Cambridge, the third respondent in this section came from the United Kingdom. I learned about him while doing fieldwork in Istanbul, where a Canadian Syrian student (profiled later in this section) who also followed the Islamic rationalist scholars had mentioned him to me. They had met in Istanbul while taking classes in Islamic sciences with Syrian scholars. A British national, this respondent was at the time of the interview a PhD student of Tim Winter at Cambridge, but his exposure to the network of Islamic rationalist scholars had happened at a much younger age. Born in the United Kingdom to Pakistani parents, he spent some of his early school years in Pakistan and after spending a few years back in the United Kingdom left for Syria around 2005, where he followed the Islamic Studies programme at the Abu Nour Foundation. At the time of the interview, he was in his final stages of the PhD degree and was spending more time in Istanbul than in Cambridge, in order to pursue private studies with Syrian scholars. Interested in Islamic philosophy, especially kalam, his PhD thesis considered the theory of perception as it relates to the vision of God.

Conscious that Islamic seminary education had suffered in recent Islamic history and that the study of kalam had suffered in particular, the engagement of the Islamic rationalist scholars with kalam thus appealed to him: 'They are engaging with the concepts that are for the time, they are scholars of the time, they are relating to the time. We need to have Ibn Arabi-like scholars, we need al-Ghazali-like scholars. We need scholars who are very capable of dealing with the modern time; we need scholars who are engaged, at a very deep conceptual level. Let's not forget that our tradition is very deep. The inherent quality of kalam is that it is very adaptable.' However, he was also keen to emphasise that Ash'arism is a movement of rational theology, and not everyone is required to engage with it: 'How many great philosophy professors you need? The same is true for Islamic education.'

He recalled his mother as being very religious, while he himself did not take religion very seriously as he grew up and mainly only followed the Friday prayer and kept fast during Ramadan. But he lost his mother at a young age, and the time that he had spent with her in Pakistan did have a lasting impact on him: 'It was such a religious country, it had its impact.' He remembered being reflective from a young age. In 1998, he came across Hamza Yusuf and was immediately in awe of him:

I thought he was just a genius. I could not believe the sciences he studied and the people he studied with. Here was a good-looking young man, he spoke like a classic American Californian man and he spoke about Allah. Moreover, he was not just talking about it; he was acting on it with such a degree of sincerity. Then it became a quest for me to try to find out more, coupled with desire to think about things. Then I made it my mission to listen to all of his lectures. On my way to college, I would wear headphones and listen to Hamza Yusuf and that is what got me started on this path. I don't know anyone who is not directly or indirectly influenced by him; it is his sincerity.

Deeply inspired by exposure to Yusuf, he started to learn Arabic privately. Eventually he decided that he had to pursue study of the Arabic language properly, as only then could he understand the original texts. Knowing the language, he felt, was very important in order to establish a sense of connection with the tradition. Optimistic about the future of Islam in the West, he expressed the view that Islam was becoming indigenous in the United Kingdom and that in the next fifty years the Islamic institutions being established would have become so strong that there would be less need to travel overseas to seek Islamic knowledge. He himself had already started teaching courses at the Cambridge Muslim College, where at the time of the interview he was teaching a course on logic.

A Canadian Graduate Pursuing Private Islamic Education in Istanbul; Syrian Origin

With an introduction from Dr Umar, I met this respondent in Istanbul, where he was pursuing studies with Islamic scholars from Syria. His family had moved to Canada from Saudi Arabia when he was very young. After seven years of university education in Toronto he graduated with a business degree and worked in a managerial position for a major departmental chain for a few years, before setting out to travel overseas in search of Islamic knowledge. His inspiration for investing in this pursuit came from Hamza Yusuf. He had first heard of Yusuf when the latter began his programme on MBC TV in the 1990s and later also participated in one of the Rihla programmes. He was introduced to Dr Umar in 2003 at a lecture that the scholar was giving at the Institute of Islamic Studies at McGill University. Around the same time he also started to read Tim Winter's writings. While based in Istanbul he was also connecting with both Turkish and Syrian scholars who had relocated to Istanbul due to the crisis in Syria.

Talking about the importance of the Islamic rationalist scholars and his own spiritual journey, he commented that in the modern age many people sense a void and a lack of purpose in their lives. Whereas in the past it was acceptable to do the same job for one's entire lifetime, people now want more out of life. It is this dissatisfaction with modern life, he maintained, that is making some young people gravitate towards extremist versions of Islam. In his assessment, the followers of Dr Umar, Tim Winter, and Hamza Yusuf were all university educated and intellectually mature. He maintained that the appeal of these scholars was that they presented a much more real sense of Islamic history: 'A lot of the times we believe that Islamic civilization started to fall apart very quickly, while in reality we really started falling apart only 150 years ago. That is one of the things that all three scholars talk about.'

In his view, retaining active faith in Islam while living in Western society is a challenge for the next generation of Muslims, and creative efforts are required to stop them from abandoning the faith. The Islamic rationalist scholars, in his assessment, were playing an important role in giving young Muslims confidence in their faith and convincing them of Islam's ability to relate to their modern reality. Referring to SeekersHub, of which he was an active member when in Canada, he noted the contribution that these institutions were making to the spreading of Islamic knowledge among young educated Muslims such as himself, and by training a new generation of Western Islamic scholars, thereby reducing the dependence of Muslim communities in the West on Islamic scholars brought from overseas. He was also highly appreciative of his experiences at the other institutions linked to the rationalist network. Talking about the retreats he had attended at Rosales, he noted that its natural environment, away from the city, very effectively promoted self-reflection and that it had helped to bring like-minded people together. Similarly, in his experience, Reviving the Islamic Spirit's annual conference in Canada, attracting more than 15,000 Canadian Muslims and prominent Islamic scholars from all over the world, was a very good platform revitalising the faith of young Muslims. Conscious that these short and intensive activities acted as an 'iman boost (spiritual high)' and needed to be complemented by more systematic learning to sustain the faith, he still felt that these conferences and retreats were playing an important part in revitalising people's faith. He was of the view that to keep people committed to faith in the West it was necessary to dazzle them: 'One has to put up a show. One has to be able to say that I am not just a hafiz, I am also a philosopher. One needs to have the ability to present something which is unique.'

He was appreciative of his time in Istanbul and of the beauty of the city and at the time of the interview was considering how long he would be able to stay there. He expressed the view that Muslim communities in the West needed to institutionalise more scholarship programmes, to enable young Muslims like him to pursue longer periods of Islamic scholarship with traditionally trained scholars overseas. When I was in SeekersHub later that year, I heard that he had returned to Canada to marry one of his fellow students at SeekersHub, and the couple had subsequently returned to Istanbul with the intention of pursuing serious study of Islamic sciences for the next few years.

A Student of Mechanical Engineering at McGill University, Canada; Arab Origin

Another of the students of the Islamic rationalist scholars with potential to become a third-generation teacher within this network had graduated from McGill and at the time of the interview was pursuing a career in mechanical engineering. He was introduced to Hamza Yusuf for the first time in 2007, when his uncle, who was based in the United States, gave his mother a copy of the cassette of Hamza Yusuf's talk on purification of the heart; his mother then started to play this cassette in the car. He recalled that the first thing that struck him was Yusuf's very good command of English. This mattered to him, because when growing up in Syria it was normal to perceive anything English or French as good. Listening to Yusuf, he felt that the topics he was addressing were never raised in the mosque *khutbah*s (religious sermons). He was attracted to what he heard of Yusuf's vision of Islam; initially he did not realise that Yusuf was a convert. That year Yusuf also began to appear on the MBC TV network, and my respondent started to watch him regularly. He later also attended Rihla.

He talked in particular about the impact that Tim Winter had on him when he first met him. He found him to be the most elegant and sophisticated man he had ever met. He remembers how Winter was asked something and he replied in such fine Arabic that he was left in complete awe. Thus his first impression of Winter was as someone very elegant, intelligent, and fluent in both Arabic and English. He saw Yusuf in person finally at the Reviving the Islamic Spirit conference, which was a very important moment for him, as the scholar spoke about Islamic arts, in which my respondent was very interested. In his words: 'Another thing is that he always sees the beauty in things. He talks very honestly. When you read the Quran, it unlocks you, it opens you up. He is not trying to apologise. Just the way he says things.' He felt that he always wanted more when listening to the rationalist scholars. They impressed on him that there is more to this life than just 'the things that a young man wants'. He was equally struck by their humility. Since he did a bit of graphic designing, he became involved in making posters for some of the events at which the scholars were making presentations. For one of the events at which Dr Umar was speaking he was the assigned photographer. Just as in the case of Winter and Yusuf, he was deeply struck by Dr Umar's personality: 'I remember just being there, first of all, he looked so magnificent. That is the first impression. I had not read his work, he was talking about Muslims going to the [United States]. Then after that class, he started to talk about *bi-Allah* and *fi-Allah* (by God, and in God). I remember I was grabbed. What also impressed me was the languages he spoke: French, German, Spanish. I asked him, what part of Prophet Mohammad's life impresses him the most, he said all of the life of Prophet is beautiful to me; I asked what is his favourite verse in the Quran and he replied, all of the Quran is my favourite.'

Deeply impressed by Dr Umar, he had since tried to spend as much time as possible learning from him during his visits to Canada. He had made an effort to attend the annual Zawiyah retreat led by Dr Umar at Rosales. At the same time, like all other serious students of these scholars, he was also pursuing studies with other scholars who were not part of this network but who could offer detailed teaching of specific Islamic texts of interest to him. He was at the time of the interview studying in particular with a Syrian shaykh who gave private lessons and taught only in Arabic. As for the number of serious students like him, in his immediate circle he could think of ten individuals who were pursuing serious study with one of the Islamic rationalist scholars, and he commented that their wives were also students of these scholars. Beyond these ten, he maintained there was a wider group of sixty learners who were trying to take their studies seriously; and then there were the general audiences. About Hamza Yusuf, he said: 'I consider him to be *Wali* (friend of God).' He noted, however, that now he did not listen to him as much as he had done in the early years, partly because Yusuf was now talking about more generic things, rather than giving lectures on specific subjects.

A French Student Studying Islam at SeekersHub, Canada; North African Origin

Another interesting profile, somewhat distinct from those presented above, was of a French student at SeekersHub, Canada, whom I got to interview during my visit. His experiences demonstrate that within the Western context there is much country-level variation, with each country posing its own unique opportunities or challenges to the integration of Muslim communities. He had come to SeekersHub to pursue full-time Islamic education under the supervision of Faraz Rabbani. In France his experience of both the broader society and the Islamic scholarly platforms had not been very positive. He had found many Muslims in France to have a Salafi or *ikhwani* (of Muslim Brotherhood) mindset. On the subject of Islamic legal debates, he commented that one could normally find only a Salafi way of thinking, as there was a dearth of traditionally trained scholars who could assert authority. He also felt that the young generation of Muslims in France was completely lost, and that Salafism, due to its relative rigidity, was unable to show them a way out. He described how he had initially followed the Salafi teaching but could not bring himself to observe the strict discipline that it demanded in terms of ritual practices: 'It was too difficult, I did not have the method to implement; to be able to pray on time'. He felt that it was only once he began to read books on Islamic spirituality that he learned how to develop a spiritual relationship with God which made the performance of ritual obligations easy.

Coming from a little town to the south of Paris, he described seeing Muslims living in very difficult conditions: 'In the West, for a good part, French people make you feel that even if this is your nationality, you are not like them. So as a young man you start to ask that since life is so difficult, why do I get up in the morning, why go to school? Why should I respect this teacher who is not respecting me? I was going back to Algeria every year, a place where people were welcoming me.' It was at the age of 18 that he began to think actively about religion, but it was not until he was 27 years old that he started to look for Islamic knowledge online. He commented that in France Muslims do not feel safe searching Islamic websites, for fear that they might be assumed to be terrorists. Through his online searches he had discovered that Islam is not simple, and that there are different understandings of it, and he felt that he had been lucky to find sources in French talking about this. After reading these sources, he tried to make up his mind by himself.

Traditional Islam appealed to him more than Salafi teachings, as it is based on proof.

Initially he had wanted to study mathematics and engineering, hoping that these subjects would help him to do something productive for communities in Algeria. But once he discovered traditional Islam, he came to the conclusion that 'the most important need for our communities is to have bulk of traditional scholars'. Through his online searches he discovered SeekersHub courses and Faraz Rabbani. After some period of online learning, he was able to travel to Canada with the support of Rabbani to pursue a close study of Islamic sciences. Conscious that in the traditional system becoming a teacher requires many years of dedicated study, he noted: 'In the traditional system they won't give permission to teach unless they are satisfied with the knowledge you have acquired. But for me that is not a concern. I found it [traditional Islam] the first time when I was 29 years old, I can say I have wasted 29 years of my life before. Someone who is in this environment from 10 years old he will be a magnificent human being. In France, young Muslims are not sure whether to condemn attacks in France or not, should we go and leave France?'

He emphasised how in the traditional way of teaching the teachers take care of the direction of each student's study path. He hoped that one day he would be able to teach fiqh and the rulings related to day-to-day life. He was also conscious of the need for rulings that block the extremist understandings of today: 'All these debates are based on traditional books of Islamic law. How should we understand Islamic law? ... The only cure for this is to show what is the real level of knowledge needed to give juristic judgements; to make some taste the responsibility of doing it. This is why fiqh is so important today.'

His decision to dedicate his life to Islamic learning and teaching, however, was not easy: 'Initially, they [his parents] thought I was crazy. For my parents, I was going to be an engineer, but now I am doing this. But they are happy. For my siblings, Islam should be simple. For them and some people religion is meant to be very personal, as soon as you talk about shakyhs who are making decision[s] for you, they get worried.' He noted how the general secular mentality in France encouraged individuals to interpret everything for themselves and choose options that appeared easy to them. Noting the pressure on young Muslims in France, he was worried about the future of Islam in that country: 'To stay Muslim despite the pressure is not easy. They are not comfortable with the answers. Sometimes they are on the verge of leaving Islam.'

CONCLUSION

By presenting detailed profiles of the followers of the Islamic rationalist scholars, as well as their dedicated students, and by capturing in detail the factors that draw students to these scholars, it is hoped that this chapter has presented sufficient evidence to illustrate that the key to the appeal of these scholars is their ability to present a logical form of Islam to university-educated Muslim youth from affluent and often socially liberal families. The emphasis on teaching Muslims about the rationalism of Islamic 'aqidah and the logical reasoning underlying Islamic legal theory is what makes these scholars particularly popular among young Muslim university students. However, as noted by many of their followers and students profiled in this chapter, the fact that Islamic rationalism, as taught by these scholars, treats deep spiritual and mystical realities as part of rational human experience is what makes such a concept of Islam particularly powerful. Rationalism, then, is not just about seeking evidence or logical explanations for every Islamic ruling, but equally involves working to nurture one's inner soul through appreciating beauty in all aspects of human existence, appreciating art and culture, and pursuing other humanist endeavours.

These are young Muslims who want to be able to lead a full life – a life which is not just about work or prayers but also allows for having dynamic professions, enjoying opportunities for travel and exploration, and options for everyday relaxation and entertainment. These Muslims want to be active members of the institutions and society around them. They want to be seen as creative individuals and members of a community which has a proud history and civilisation, which can actually stand proud vis-à-vis Western civilisation and confidently engage with it, rather than being at war with it. The teachings of the Islamic rationalist scholars provide them with the necessary confidence in Islamic civilisation, and offer practical ways to engage with modern society while remaining committed to core Islamic values.

Further, the evidence presented in this chapter shows how a certain degree of affluence is common to the followers and serious students of these scholars. They generally come from families where fathers are professionals in well-paid positions. These are the Muslim youth who, due to their family background and university education, are destined to assume important positions within the diaspora Muslim communities in the West. These individuals are best placed to initiate and sustain dynamic new platforms that can harness the creative energy within young Muslims and counter the stagnant image associated with Islam and Muslim societies.

Lastly, by presenting detailed profiles of a few of the followers who are pursuing more serious training with the rationalist scholars, this chapter has presented evidence to support its main contention: the reason this Islamic rationalist revival movement will become a powerful force in the twenty-first century is that it has mainstreamed within Muslim communities. Its future is no longer tied to the commitment of a few Western converts; instead their efforts have inspired young Muslim men and women from well-to-do and often socially liberal families to invest in serious study of Islam. It is these young Muslims who are critical thinkers, are trained in leading Western academic institutions, and now are investing in serious study of classical Islamic texts that will sustain the Islamic rationalist revival in the present century. These Muslims, because of their tacit knowledge of being part of the modern Western reality are able to relate to Islamic legal and moral dictates in a way that most scholars in the Muslim-majority countries have failed to do since the colonial period. As discussed in some detail in Chapter 3, under the colonial influence Muslim societies saw societal elites abandon Islamic education platforms in favour of Western educational institutions. Consequently, the students and scholars in madrasahs in the Muslim world have in the previous two centuries come mostly from economically marginalised and often rural segments of society. The scholarship they have produced and their attempts to relate Islam to modern reality have thus been shaped by their context. By bringing modern-educated and affluent young Muslims back to serious study of Islamic sciences, the Islamic rationalist scholars have reversed one of the most damaging legacies of colonial rule in the field of Islamic scholarship. This shift in the profile of the students and future scholars of Islam will, in my assessment, play a key role in making the twenty-first century known for the revival of Islamic rationalism.

In the final chapter, I set out to share evidence of the gradual spread of these rationalist scholars' influence among the modern-educated and socially progressive Muslim youth in the urban centres in Muslim-majority countries. These young people have very similar dispositions to those second- and third-generation Muslims in the West who have been considered in this chapter. Since globalisation has ensured access to the same media outlets, mobile apps, and internet sites, young university-educated Muslims in the two contexts are actually grappling with very similar everyday realities. We also see how many creative platforms are emerging as a result of the teachings of the Islamic rationalist scholars, and how these platforms are trying to integrate Islamic values with everyday reality to produce something positive.

7

Elites and Institutional Consolidation

Why the Movement Is to Spread

In the city of Lahore, the capital of Pakistan's largest province and the country's cultural hub, a young Pakistani woman in her mid-twenties is holding a poetry recital at one of the elite secondary schools. Born into an affluent Pakistani family – as would hold true for most students in her audience – this young woman, who had grown up between Pakistan, Australia, and Yemen, where her father's corporate-sector positions took the family, had only recently returned to Lahore after graduating from a leading university in the United States. It was as a student at this university that she had first been inspired to write poetry. The poetry recitals that she was holding in the elite private schools in Lahore during her current stay, however, had a very distinct poetic expression compared with her earlier work: her current poems took inspiration from the work of Muslim Sufi masters and mystics, most notably Rumi, and not those of Western poets to whom she had turned to inspiration earlier. Further, during the current programme of recitals she covered her hair with a loose wrap. This subtle but visible transformation in her poetic expression and her appearance had begun only early that summer. Soon due to leave Pakistan again to pursue job offers in Australia, her stay in Pakistan was short and not the trigger for this shift; it was directly a result of her participation in the Rihla programme that summer. While inspired by all the scholars teaching on the programme, she had in particular been influenced by the teachings of Feraidoon Mojadedi, who taught the course on Rumi, the great Sufi master and Muslim mystical poet from the thirteenth century. A member of the network of Islamic rationalist scholars, though not formally trained, Mojadedi is better described as 'a lover of the Sufi poets' whose passion for the work of the Sufi masters comes through not just in his teaching sessions but even in ordinary conversations.[1] The teachings of Mojadedi at the Rihla led this young Pakistani woman to seek poetic inspiration increasingly from Islamic mystical sources. The decision to start loosely covering her hair, though, went beyond the influence of the teachers, although they did indeed encourage modesty in dress for men and women; what made her more confident to assert her Muslim identity was being in the company of other young Muslims with a shared and a relatively privileged socio-economic background whom she had met at the Rihla, and who like her were deeply influenced by the teachings of the Islamic rationalist scholars.

I learned about the experience of this young Pakistani woman and the difference that exposure to these scholars had made to her way of thinking and associating with her Muslim identity not through her but through her mother, Hajara, who was a fellow companion on the Sacred Caravan 'Umrah programme that I attended in 2016. That year Dr Umar, instead of Hamza Yusuf, had led the group to perform the 'umrah; Mojadedi, who from the first year of the launch of the Sacred Caravan 'Umrah programme has been part of its organisational team, was again in charge. Hajara, who had paid for her daughter to participate in the Rihla programme that year, was well exposed to this network of Islamic rationalist scholars and was herself a follower of Nuh Keller, with whom she had taken a bay'ah. The reference to Hajara's daughter had come up one night as we sat in Masjid-i-Nabawi while she awaited her husband's call to confirm the safe arrival of their daughter in Kuala Lumpur. Taking a stopover in Malaysia on her way to Australia, Hajara's daughter was to attend the wedding of a Malay friend whom she had met at the Rihla. Since this friend happened to be a Malay princess, Hajara's daughter was actually a royal guest, courtesy of the friendship formed at the Rihla.

This particular case makes a perfect opening to the final chapter of this book because it helps to support the two key contentions of this volume. First, it illustrates how the followers of the Islamic rationalist scholars are not confined to Western countries; instead, many of them are well-educated and well-travelled youth from Muslim-majority countries. Globalisation of the media, ease of travel, and improved economic opportunities for the upper-middle-income groups have facilitated increased access to Western educational institutions for young people from

---

[1] Mojadedi runs the Rumi Bookstore in Berkeley which specialises in the sale of rare Islamic texts; he is closely connected to Hamza Yusuf and Zaytuna College and thus is very much a part of the network of Islamic rationalists.

Muslim-majority countries. As students in Western universities, they are introduced to the same Islamic scholars and networks as are the second- and third-generation Muslims in the West profiled in the preceding chapter. The presence of these students from Muslim-majority countries in the retreats organised by these scholars is thus one of the main routes leading to the spread of the scholars' influence in Muslim-majority countries. When conducting fieldwork at these retreats, I have routinely found many young people from these countries in the audience; in some cases they were not even enrolled in Western universities but had learned about the rationalist scholars and the specific retreat through friends and had decided to attend.

But equally importantly, this case illustrates how understanding the significance of the elite socio-economic status of the young people influenced by the rationalist scholars is critical for an appreciation of the real potential of this movement. Although Hajara herself was pleased with the changed sensibilities of her daughter as a result of her participation in the Rihla, there was a mixed response within the family's immediate social networks as well as from the principals in schools where she performed. Hajara's daughter had mainly been invited to give her recitals because her profile was in line with the aspirations of elite or upwardly mobile families in Pakistan for their children: exposure to foreign culture, education in a leading Western university, and the recognition of their credentials by Western institutions, as Hajara's daughter had done by getting her poems published in university publications. Hosting a poetry recital by a young woman of this profile suited an elite school's progressive image and reflected its efforts to expose its students to the 'right kind' of role model. The close association between acquisition of Western cultural tastes, attitudes, and knowledge with assertion of one's elite social status, a legacy of the colonial rule as outlined in Chapter 3, remains a reality in most Muslim countries even today: fluency in English or French, the languages of the colonial rulers, and the clarity of one's accent remain critical markers of one's high social standing. Thus, with her hair covered and her Sufi-inspired poetry, Hajara's daughter received a mixed response: principals in some schools were openly critical, others were patronising and suggested that living in the West can make some Muslims excessively religious. This experience was difficult for Hajara's daughter, but with some encouragement she persisted, and the family's social networks ensured that the invitations to perform kept pouring in. Gradually, even from within these secular elite circles, many began to express appreciation for her work and saw in her a positive model for other young people.

Herein lies the importance of understanding why this volume contends that the real strength of the Islamic rationalist revival movement is its ability to attract the young members of the Muslim elites. Young people from more affluent and socially influential families are in a position to shape institutions and exert pressure on existing societal attitudes; in other words, they are in a position to trigger institutional change. Theories of institutional change recognise that change is often slow and incremental and a result of evolutionary forces (North 1990; Acemoglu and Robinson 2000; 2009), but they also recognise how individuals in positions of influence can have a major impact in setting the direction of change (Bano 2012b). At a time in history when Islamic platforms are under intense pressure to reform, the strategic efforts of young people from elite Muslim families to spread a more rationalist reading of Islam, which at one level safeguards against the rigidity of the traditional Islamic platforms and on the other questions the Western-centric views of secular elites, can in my view have a major influence in shaping the future popular expression of Islam. The failure of the more conservative Islamic movements such as Salafism or Deobandi madrasahs to relate Islamic moral and legal ethics to the demands of modernity, and their failure to offer guidance to young Muslims in how to retain their faith and be influential members of modern society, is pushing the need for change within Islamic discourse. The appeal of those conservative movements that dominated the Islamic discourse during the twentieth century is dwindling: the extreme pressure faced by conservative Islamic movements is visible in the recent developments within Saudi Arabia, the home base of Salafism as globally understood. By arguing for the need to return to moderate Islam, the Saudi Crown Prince Muhammad bin Salman has indicated the Saudi state's desire to distance itself from the rigid readings of the text associated with Salafi thinking. In such a changing context, a new Islamic discourse will come to dominate the space that Salafism occupied during the latter half of the twentieth century; opting for a very liberal secular course whereby Muslims abandon their religion in large numbers or practise Islam only nominally is one possible way forward (Devji 2017); resort to Islamic militancy to reassert the influence of conservative strands of Islam is another; and the revival of Islamic rationalism yet another. Which one of these competing options will eventually prevail in a context where pressures for change are intense is today the key question of interest for observers of Islam. This book has tried to build a case to show why the third path forward is the most likely institutional equilibrium for production of Islamic scholarship in the future, as it offers the most optimal response in the light of the changing context. By popularising the Islamic rationalist approach among the youth who are to become the Muslim elites, these scholars have reduced the likelihood of the younger generation of secular elite Muslims opting out of their religion.

The key contribution of the Islamic rationalist scholars is thus that by inspiring young Muslims from socially progressive families to appreciate the intellectual elements, the arts, the aesthetics, the deeper mysticism, and the poetry that were all an integral part of Islamic civilisation, as was Islamic law, these scholars are giving them the knowledge and the confidence to feel proud of their Muslim identity and Islamic civilisational history. The middle ground that these scholars advocate offers an alternative course between extreme religious rigidity and Western liberalism. These young Muslims come to appreciate that they need not adopt the Western moral or cultural framework in order to appear modern; instead, they come to question the legacy of colonial rule whereby modernity is equated with Westernisation, thereby putting the West always in the lead position. Such young people come to value their Muslim identity and the Islamic civilisational past with its arts, culture, poetry, and philosophy. These fields were indeed neglected by Islamic scholarly establishments during the colonial period. The need to survive in a politically marginalised context obliged most Islamic scholarly platforms to focus their energies on what they understood to be their core responsibility: protection of the basic faith and intergenerational transmission of knowledge about ritual obligations. As Ober (2008) notes in his study on democracy and knowledge creation in classical Athens, a society which loses its own identity in the process of institutional evolution is unlikely to be regarded as a success case, and nor is one which lacks the creativity to adapt to the changing context: creativity and routinisation of learning are thus both integral parts of the knowledge-creation process. Although the Islamic scholarly classes focused on the routinisation of Islamic knowledge in the colonial and post-colonial contexts, due to an external environment that made creativity and experimentation costly, changes in the twenty-first century are making routinisation a costlier option, as in this age of globalisation an ability to take advantage of the new opportunities and experiment is key to institutional success.

Thus, without having studied in elite schools and without having graduated from a leading American university, Hajara's daughter would not have had the credentials to question the prevalence of the Western-centric mind-set among the societal elites; these credentials, as noted above, were key to winning her an audience within the exclusive schools in the first place. It is also this very background which enabled her to withstand initial criticisms, persist with her approach, and yet continue to be invited to present her work. The fact that she herself was, however, able to revive confidence in her Islamic identity with relative ease, and that so did many others in her audiences, is actually a credit to the traditional mosque and madrasah networks which might not have adapted to changing contexts but whose strategy of focusing on the routinisation of learning in a period of socio-economic instability enabled the preservation and successful transmission of basic faith in Islam to the next generation. The success of the Islamic rationalist scholars in mobilising young university-educated Muslims is thus partly due to the Muslim communities and the traditional scholarly classes who have managed to preserve the basic faith relatively effectively. Thus, apparently small efforts, such as Hajara's daughter's decision to present her Sufi-inspired poetry within elite circles in Lahore in order to invoke the deeper mystical and philosophical tradition in Islam, can collectively contribute to a societal-level shift in favour of Islamic rationalism, given that elites shape societal institutions. Such efforts simultaneously put under pressure the rigidity associated with orthodox Islamic scholarly platforms, as well as the laxity of the Western-centric concept of development.

Given that the level of any individual's religious conviction is rarely stable, there is no guarantee that Hajara's daughter will remain as inspired by the Islamic poetic influences or religious faith as she was feeling a few months on from her participation in the Rihla programme. But, because retreats such as Rihla do not merely impart Islamic knowledge but also create a strong network of like-minded and dynamic young people who are well placed in society, participation in these retreats has the potential to bring about a more lasting change. In my own observation, the physical manifestations of change in one's attitudes, such as the decision to wear a hijab, are often short lived, but the deeper shifts in conviction and confidence in one's Muslim identity are often more permanent. Thus, Hajara's daughter might not continue to loosely cover her hair, or might already have stopped doing so, given that it was not her original style, but her increased confidence in her Muslim heritage and identity is likely to endure. We have seen support for this, even in the cases of many of the young persons profiled in the previous chapter who have remained inspired by the rationalist scholars in the long term. The opportunity to return to the retreats organised by these scholars, and the possibility of maintaining friendships formed through these retreats, helps in the process of sustaining the young people's commitment. It is in changing the mind-set of the Muslim elites of the next generation and restoring their confidence in the Islamic civilisation and its ability to be relevant in modern times that, I argue, lies the biggest achievement of the Islamic rationalist scholars. Elites are well placed to shape socio-economic and political institutions around them. Further, they are the ones most at risk of opting out of religion altogether under the pressures of secular influences. It is this elite profile of the followers of the network of the Islamic rationalist scholars studied in this volume that leads me to argue that this movement for the revival of Islamic rationalism will continue to gain momentum in the twenty-first century and become the dominant face of Islam in the coming decades.

Here it is also important to note that thus far we have studied only one route by which young Muslims in Muslim-majority countries are discovering the rationalist scholars: by virtue of time spent studying or working in the West, or through returning friends and family. There are other routes that are equally important in spreading the influence of these scholars in the Muslim-majority world. Apart from discovering them through YouTube videos or through articles available on websites, many young Muslims are becoming exposed to these scholars through the increasing number of visits that the scholars make to these countries. These invitations often come from individuals who might have studied with them in one of the retreats; but they also come through individuals and platforms who have discovered these scholars through the internet or the TV channels. I have found evidence of their influence in many Muslim-majority countries when doing fieldwork for my other studies (Bano 2017; 2018a; 2018b). During one of my focus-group discussions with Saudi women in Jeddah in 2017, when asked if they knew of Hamza Yusuf, these women, who worked in senior positions with a multinational company, gave a resoundingly positive response. They appreciated the role that he is playing in shaping young Muslims' understanding of Islam and they noted how he and the other scholars in this network are helping young people to rediscover the inherent mystical and spiritual beauty within Islam. Most noted being introduced to Hamza Yusuf through his TV show on the MBC channel during the 1990s. Critical of the restrictive Islamic curriculum taught in the Saudi schools, these women paid tribute to the very rich scholarly tradition of Islam. At the same time, youth in Muslim-majority countries are being exposed to these rationalist scholars through invited talks, such as the lectures given by Dr Umar at the Lahore University of Management Sciences (LUMS), the most prestigious university in Pakistan, whose graduates take on leading positions at home and get many opportunities to travel abroad both to study and to work. In March 2018, Dr Umar led a five-day retreat in Egypt which involved a cruise down the Nile from Luxor to the Aswan. Hamza Yusuf and Tim Winter similarly travel to all corners of the world.

The growing global influence of these scholars is also visible in the profiles and locations of their followers on Twitter: their Twitter followers are located not just in the West but equally in the Middle East, North Africa, and South and East Asia, as well as in Australia and New Zealand. It is thus not surprising that, while arguing for an American, European, or British Islam, these scholars are now also increasingly recognising the relevance of their teachings for Muslims from across the globe. They now acknowledge the shared experiences of modern-educated Muslim youth across different countries.

The question, then, is what is changing in the broader socio-economic and political context to stimulate the revival of Islamic rationalism (or what these scholars refer to as 'traditional Islam'). During the twentieth century, it was the puritanical Islamic scholarly strands, such as Salafism or Deobandism in South Asia, or the political Islam movements, represented by the Muslim Brotherhood in the Middle East or Jamaat-i-Islami in South Asia, that were the focus of Western policy and academic discourse, due to their global prominence. Why is the twenty-first century – which opened with the attacks on the World Trade Center – in reality leading to a revival of Islamic rationalism? The answer to this lies in understanding the changing socio-economic conditions of Muslim societies and the improved conditions of the Muslim diaspora in the West; however, it is equally an unexpected outcome of the negative media publicity given to Islam since 11 September 2001. It is important to understand these shifts in order to appreciate this volume's core argument about the relationship between knowledge production and societal conditions. Which one of the competing Islamic discourses becomes dominant at a particular point is a direct response to the societal conditions in which the Muslims find themselves. As noted in Chapter 2, Islamic scholarly platforms have demonstrated the greatest dynamism in periods of political stability and economic prosperity, while under conditions of uncertainty more literalist and conservative interpretations have exercised an appeal. With these changing trends, we can see how the explanation for the revival of Islamic rationalism in the twenty-first century is consistent with these historical patterns.

Despite the high degree of institutional path dependence whereby the state institutions or the profiles of the elites in Muslim-majority countries have shown a great degree of continuity from the colonial period, the reality is that, seventy years on, the influence of colonial institutions is weakening. In ensuring institutional path dependence, both the economic hegemony of the West and the psychological impact of colonial powers' perceived civilisational superiority played a role. With the turn of the twenty-first century, however, the West's economic hegemony and its civilisational credentials and values are under pressure. There is active discussion today in academic as well as policy circles about the risk that the West runs of losing its economic supremacy to what are being referred to as 'the rising powers': China, Russia, India, and Brazil (Destradi 2017). Further, the excessive consumerism that has come to dominate Western modernity, and the constantly changing shape of the Western family as social and sexual mores change, are making many question the Western development experiment (Bano 2017).

Within the field of development studies, increasing numbers of scholars are either arguing or noting that these perceived limitations are leading some societies to consciously opt for localised models of development, instead of adopting Western economic and social development models (Gow 2008). This process of critical reflection, not just specific to the Muslim-majority countries but visible also in other developing countries, is a product of the educational gains made by these societies in the past 60–70 years. Even when most Muslim countries, as is the case for the developing world as a whole, suffer from continued challenges to ensuring universal access to education and improving the quality of state schooling, the last 60 years have seen rapid improvements in these areas, compared with the starting point at the end of colonial rule. The majority of the children across the Muslim world do attend a school, and a quarter of the student population in the more economically stable Muslim countries proceed all the way to university education (Moore 2002). Further, in many universities female students constitute the majority (*Express Tribune* 2014; Saudi Gazette 2015). Education has thus been one of the main areas of change; but an equally important trigger for change has been the increased access to media and communication technology. Since the 1980s, with the steadily increasing ease of access to mobile phones, cable TV networks, the internet, and more recently the ever-increasing social media apps, the world has become much smaller than it was in the 1950s. This is true not just in terms of the virtual realm but also in terms of the actual physical realm: the improved aviation industry has made travel much cheaper, safer, and accessible to the middle classes and not just to the affluent few. Thus, despite facing continued challenges of governance, there has been an improvement in people's lives in the areas of education, health, and communication, due to technological advancements that have reduced the costs of provision of these services, coupled with a greater presence of private-sector initiatives especially in the areas of education and health.

Within the Muslim diaspora in the West, the story is similar: it is the improved prosperity of some among second- and third-generation Muslims in Europe and the United Kingdom that has led to the emergence of the new Islamic scholarly platforms. Better educated than their parents and more integrated in Western institutions (Cesari 2002; Abbas 2005), the young Muslims profiled in this volume who are following the Islamic rationalist scholars, and some of whom are to become the next generation of scholars, are very much a product of this improved prosperity that at least some second- and third-generation Muslims in the Europe and the United Kingdom have come to enjoy (Abbas 2005). In the United States, where, due to their professional background, first-generation Muslim immigrants enjoyed a degree of material affluence from the start, the Muslim community today is economically strong, university-educated, and socially integrated in mainstream institutions (Ahmed 2011; Grewal 2013). It is because of this material prosperity that the main institutions within the Islamic rationalist network have emerged from the United States, and it is the reason these scholars themselves emphasise the important role that the American Muslim community can play in shaping future Islamic scholarship.

While the above-noted changes are arguably reflective of the more positive developments that have facilitated the rise of Islamic rationalism associated with the emergence of a more confident Muslim identity, an apparently negative development since 11 September – the popular representation of Islam as being an inherently militant religion – has also yielded unexpected dividends. Perturbed by what they were hearing about their religion, many young Muslims opted to explore it for themselves; and, while some renounced their faith at the end of the process, the majority stayed and in the process became more convinced of its reasoning. In this process of critical self-reflection these young Muslims were helped by their engagement with Islamic scholars associated with the Islamic rationalist network, but also with other reformist scholars, such as Tariq Ramadan and Yasir Qadhi (Bano 2018b), who, though using different methodological tools, are similarly arguing for adapting Islam to Western realities. The pressure that the global community has put on Islamic institutions since 11 September has shaped not just the responses of individuals, but also those of the states. Long accused of funding global Salafi movements that inspire jihad, the Saudi royal family in 2017 made a major break from the past by announcing Saudi Arabia's 'return to moderate Islam'. During 2018, Saudi Arabia has pledged to remove many of the religiously inspired restrictions, such as the ban on women driving, and opened up the social space by making a major investment in the entertainment industry and allowing the hosting of concerts and the operating of public cinemas. How much of the call by Saudi Crown Prince Muhammad bin Salman to return to moderate Islam is a political tactic aimed at appeasing the West, and how much it reflects a genuine desire for change, can be determined only with time; however, researchers working on Saudi Arabia had in recent years been arguing that a domestic constituency in favour of liberal social change is growing, due to the increased access to higher education for both men and women and widespread use of the internet and mobile technology (Bano 2018a). The economic shock experienced by the Saudi state since the 2014 fall in global oil prices has indeed also played a role in triggering this change: the Vision 2030, led by the Crown Prince, aims to diversify the Saudi economy beyond its current dependence on oil and promote new sectors, such as entertainment and tourism; but it also places a heavy emphasis on social change. Whatever might be the ultimate factors making the Saudi state publicly argue for a movement towards moderate Islam, the weakening of Salafism within its very home base itself shows the extent of the pressure placed on conservative Islam.

Above we have considered the domestic and global shifts that are rendering the societal conditions in Muslim-majority countries and also among the Muslim diaspora in the West conducive for the revival of Islamic rationalism. It is now appropriate to look at the real-life organisational platforms inspired by this movement. The next section focuses on the creative energy on display by the young Muslims who are engaging with the rationalist scholars who teach their students to engage with the richness of classical Islamic scholarly tradition, whereby the arts, humanities, and poetic and mystical dimensions of Islam become as important as the study of Islamic law and ritual obligations.

INCREASED CONFIDENCE AND CREATIVE EXPRESSION

This chapter opened by mapping the impact of the actions of one individual student of the Islamic rationalist network; there are numerous other examples to illustrate how the students of the Islamic rationalist scholars are also establishing many collective platforms advancing new approaches. One area in which the teachings of these scholars are inspiring creative responses from among the students and the wider group of followers is that of modest dressing. Given that beauty, including physical beauty and graceful dressing, is strongly emphasised by these scholars, who themselves dress very elegantly and argue this to be the Sunnah of the Prophet Muhammad, many of their followers have been inspired to experiment with designing new ranges of clothing which blend Eastern modesty with Western aesthetics. Shukr Islamic Clothing (Shukr Islamic Clothing 2018), a chain of stores selling modest clothing that the students of Nuh Keller launched in 2001 on his advice, has become particularly popular for producing elegant attire for both men and women, in styles that observe Islamic standards of modesty and use designs and at times also fabrics from the Muslim world, but are tailored with a view to observing Western formal dress requirements. Their men's collection includes jackets, traditional Muslim caps whose use among the network's followers has in particular been popularised by Hamza Yusuf, and formal and casual shirts; the women's selection includes the 'abayah but also long skirts and shirts. While Shukr Islamic Clothing is the oldest and the most established of such initiatives, I have encountered young students of the rationalist scholars, mostly females, who had set up similar enterprises on a small scale, or were planning to do so in the future, in order to give young Muslims modest but stylish and colourful options. In the view of these women, the standard shopping outlets associate modesty with dullness, while these young women were keen to show how modest dressing can be beautiful as well as colourful. As we saw in the previous chapter, the graceful dressing of the Islamic rationalist scholars has played a critical role in impressing many of their students; by dressing elegantly, while also respecting the aesthetics of the local society, these scholars have made their students appreciate that maintaining a pleasing appearance is in itself a sign of devotion to Islam.

The other area in which creative innovation is evident is that of diet. As noted in Chapter 5, the rationalist scholars find the modified and artificial nature of modern food a highly problematic aspect of the technological development and excessive consumption of modern society. They argue for the use of organic food and advise their students to prioritise quality over quantity. This emphasis on organic food is justified not only in terms of health benefits but more importantly in terms of the Islamic obligation to protect the natural environment and all living things.

Thus, these scholars are also heavily critical of halal food suppliers who, in their view, follow the procedural process of slaughtering animals in the name of God but violate the basic Islamic ethical principles by keeping them in inhumane conditions, as does the rest of the industry, in order to maximise profits. These concerns have again initiated change in the behaviour of their students at an individual as well as collective level. For an organisational-level initiative, Willowbrook Farm on the outskirts of Oxford in the United Kingdom provides a good example of a business that claims to farm in an ethical and responsible manner (Willowbrook Farm 2018).

Run by the sister-in-law of Tim Winter and her husband, the farm has received growing attention for providing halal meat that not only conforms with procedural requirements but also aims to meet the deeper ethical principles of animal herding and farming required in Islam. While the idea of establishing this farm is entirely the founders' own, the young Muslims using the services of this organic farm are similar to those following the Islamic rationalist scholars. I myself learned about it from a young British female filmmaker of Egyptian origin whom I had met at the end of a retreat at Rosales. A regular at some of these retreats, she highly recommended a visit to the Willowbrook Farm, as in her view it shared a similar vision to that of the teachings of the Islamic rationalist scholars. The farm also provides camping opportunities and guided tours for visitors, in addition to hosting an annual music festival, normally in August, where many Muslim musical groups perform. One of these annual festivals aired a documentary by Mustafa Davis, who attended in person. In my interview with the couple, they emphasised how they aspire to revive the Islamic farming practices developed by the Muslim civilisation, which were highly developed and can inform best practice even today. Reviving the old Islamic farming practices is thus very much in the spirit of the work being done at this farm.

In the same spirit, Zaytuna College has launched a certificated course in permaculture. It aims to help young Muslims learn to preserve the best practices from the Islamic past 'to create a foundation for a better future'. The advertisement for the course notes how Muslims are required to be good stewards of the earth and pioneers in food production, and how permaculture is the application of adab, interpreted in the advert as 'putting things in their proper place' in the natural world (Zaytuna College 2018c). Through the study of permaculture the course hopes to teach the students to better preserve their material environment. The advert also draws on the work of Naquib al-Attas to argue:

'When one puts trees and stones, mountains, rivers, valleys and lakes, animals and their habitat in their proper places, then that is adab toward nature and the environment.' Clearly, putting things in their proper place requires the recognition of an order or balance.

God tells us in *Surah Rahman* that He has created everything in balance, and commands us not to 'upset the balance.' (55:9) Similarly, in *Surah A'raf,* we are commanded not to 'cause corruption on earth after it has been set in order.' (7:56) Permaculture seeks to restore balance and order on earth in a manner that is consistent with a Qur'anic worldview and in conformity with our divinely mandated function as stewards of God on earth, *khalifatul Allah fil 'ard*. (Zaytuna College 2018c)

Another area in which the influence of the rationalist scholars is becoming evident in real-life situations is architectural innovation in the design of the mosques. The Cambridge Mosque project developing under the super-vision of Tim Winter is a conscious attempt to develop a major mosque which does not simply replicate the Middle Eastern architectural style and would thereby stand out as foreign in the Cambridge landscape, but one which instead fits in with the local aesthetics, skyline, and art forms (Brown 2017). Developing mosques which draw on the beauty of the local archi-tectural style while respecting the functional needs of Islam is seen as a way to create a sense of belonging for the mosque within the local community, rather than risking its being viewed by the local residents as a foreign imposition. When discussing Islam's ability to immerse itself in different cultures and yet retain its core essence, Tim Winter and Dr Umar often talk about mosque architecture as it developed in China (Abd-Allah 2006). Mosques there reflect the architecture of Chinese temples, while retaining the direction of the Ka'bah and the *minbar,* and this embedding of mosque architecture in the local culture is argued to have helped the early dissemin-ation of Islam within Chinese society. The Cambridge Mosque project presents one of the first efforts to achieve something similar in the United Kingdom. Further, it is not just presenting a different architectural design; rather, as is the case with the permaculture course at the Zaytuna College, the mosque design has been shaped by Islamic ethical requirements to ensure the efficient utilisation of natural resources to minimise waste or harm to the environment. Thus, the mosque building is environmentally friendly. The design includes beautiful large gardens for the use of the community and draws on natural light to minimise the use of artificial light. While adapting to local aesthetics and recent scientific developments to make an indigenous style and environmentally friendly mosque, like the mosques in China, the Cambridge Mosque retains all the essential functional characteristics dictated by Islamic guidelines.

Similarly, in the area of arts and aesthetics new initiatives aimed at preserving or reviving Islamic art forms and Islamic artefacts are ongoing. Among the Spanish converts in Granada discussed in Chapter 2, many are involved in reviving Islamic-style pottery and crafts. One of the Spanish converts in Alicante has developed a beautiful garden using Islamic principles of gardening. Similarly, Adiba, one of the daughters of Abdus Samad, specialises in the preservation of old Quranic manuscripts, especially those discovered in Andalusia. She worked for a couple of years in Cairo before returning to Granada. Abdus Samad and Adiba initiated this preservation work when a conflict emerged over the treatment of the Islamic manuscripts that from time to time are discovered in the south of Spain. As they argue, each manuscript tells a story, and both the manuscript and the story need to be preserved as part of Andalusian Islamic heritage. They have over time extended their efforts to collect old Quranic manuscripts more widely, including those found in Timbuktu and Algeria. After the fall of Andalusia, many of the scholars went to Timbuktu and produced a new civilisation in the sixteenth and seventeenth centuries, creating knowledge which both Abdus Samad and Adiba are keen to preserve. They are also part of an Islamic manuscript preservation project run between Cambridge University and Leiden University.

Another area of creative expression is found in the new scholarly publications that the rationalist scholars and their students are launching to create space for the expression of new ideas. Production of periodicals, journals, and magazines is critical to the flourishing of any intellectual movement, as such publications become the platforms where new ideas are expressed and debated. Whether it is the Western Enlightenment or the women's rights movements of the 1970s, the role of the publications that expressed the intellectual ideas propelling a new course forward has been critical to bringing about a societal-level change in attitudes. Equally, works of fiction are known to play a key role in changing societal attitudes, as by taking bold story lines that challenge established orthodoxy their authors can push society to reconsider its social and moral framework. This is the potential of *Renovatio*, the magazine launched by Zaytuna College in 2017. The strength of this publication is that it is able to attract established Western academics who write proper scholarly pieces for it, but the publication does not restrict itself to being a serious academic journal; instead, in the spirit of the liberal arts college, the publication allows space for more literary and artistic pieces and for open conversations. Thus, its December 2017 issue, entitled *With God on our Side? Islam and the Question of Pluralism* (Renovatio 2017), featured scholarly articles on the issue of pluralism, but it also carried interesting pieces looking at Islamic art and aesthetics, so that the main thrust of the publication was on stimulating intellectual ideas instead of necessarily presenting the rigorous research pieces published in social-science journals. 'The Silent Theology of Islamic Art' was one such interesting piece: arguing that Islamic art can speak more profoundly and clearly to many than does the written word, its author contemplated whether Muslims would be wiser 'to show, not to tell?' (Renovatio 2017).

Last but not least, it would be appropriate to conclude this section by noting how these scholars are inspiring young Muslims in the West to create spaces for community that allow for Muslims but also their neighbours, irrespective of racial or religious diversity, to create beautiful shared moments. The two platforms encountered during my fieldwork across multiple sites that were most striking in this respect were both in Edmonton, Canada: The Green Room and Tarjuma. I was introduced to them by one of the ardent students who was profiled in the previous chapter as someone destined to join the third generation of scholars in the Islamic rationalist network while also pursuing a professional career as a doctor. Both initiatives were inspired by Ta'leef Collective, and thus Usama Canon has directly played a key role in supporting the efforts of the young Muslim men leading these two platforms. The Muslim community in Edmonton is one of the oldest Muslim communities in Canada. The Green Room initially emerged as a result of state funding made available to support voluntary associations serving minority communities. The initial efforts did not yield many results, which meant that the programme was due to be delisted in 2012; but at that time a group of young Muslims were motivated to step in and restructure it. These new young leaders of The Green Room interviewed almost one hundred young Muslims and learned that many self-identifying young Muslims in the city did not find existing institutions, especially mosques, responsive to their needs, or view them as places where they could be themselves. Inspired in part by Ta'leef Collective, The Green Room became a space where Muslims of all backgrounds could come and not feel judged; further, non-Muslims were equally welcome to join.

The new programme had a triple focus: growth, connections, and service. *Growth* involved development of leadership in Muslim youth through provision of year-long training programmes; *connections* emphasised the need to connect people through promoting social activities, such as arts events, poetry recitations, and walks through the city; and *service* involved contributing to causes that benefit the people of the city, such as serving dinner in the inner city. This three-fold programme proved particularly effective in attracting young people between the ages of sixteen and twenty-four from across the socio-economic classes. As in the case of Ta'leef Collective, the strength of The Green Room initiative, compared with most of the other platforms and retreats run by the Islamic rationalist scholars, is that it is attracting not just the Muslim youth who represent the elite segments of Muslim society but equally those from less affluent and educationally less privileged backgrounds. Only 20 per cent of the population attending The Green Room's activities have post-secondary degrees. Its membership base is thus strong, and its main events attract between 600 and 700 participants. Its Ramadan programme, which offers daily iftar, is open to non-Muslims as a way to introduce them to Islam; nearly 200 people attend each day. The Green Room has long-term funding from the provincial government and more recently has also won international funding.

While Ta'leef Collective and Usama Canon remain the main inspirations behind this platform, other scholars within the Islamic rationalist network have equally supported the platform: Dr Umar, for example, has spoken at its events. Noting how Ta'leef inspires The Green Room members to appreciate the importance of connecting people with each other, one of the members noted: 'Ta'leef means to bring things together. The inspiration for Ta'leef Collective comes from the Quranic verse where Allah says "God brought their hearts together, if you had spent all in the world you would not have brought all the hearts together" (Surah 8:63). Together The Green Room and Tarjuma [the other initiative discussed below] are bringing the hearts together and focusing on building a community.'

During my discussion with the leadership, they noted that regarding a mosque as a microcosm of Muslims is problematic. The Green Room, they argued, attracts a different demographic from the local mosques; mosques still cater primarily to the Muslims who have not spent their formative years in Canada, and they often do not provide space for women. In the leaders' assessment, the majority of mosque congregations in Edmonton are under the control of South Asian communities, and their administration is ethnically influenced. Further, mosque leadership is often transferred from one group of immigrants to the next, so that the younger generation, born and raised in the local context, are often not involved in the mosques. As one member of the Green Room commented: 'People of our generation do not last in these mosque boards. The administrative styles of those controlling the mosques are very different than those of the people who are brought up here.' Another member noted how there are very few local imams in the mosques even now, as no one is giving incentives to encourage young people to fill those roles; the communities are not willing to pay much. This member noted that although 'a ton of young Muslims have interest in getting involved in Islamic teaching within the community, it is just not financially viable'. As often noted in the interviews that I conducted with the scholars in the rationalist network, The Green Room's leadership noted how in addition to not paying enough to the imams, the mosque committees try to control the imams too strictly and allow them no autonomy. As one member argued: 'People are willing to work for 20 per cent less but don't do so, due to lack of professionalism in the mosque committees.'

The young men leading the Green Room initiative emphasised the need for the scholars to adapt Islamic rulings to the demands of the local context. As one member noted, 'The youth is conscious of the need to adapt. If it will persist, it will need to be an Islam that is relatable.' The young men leading and supporting this initiative were clear that Islam in their view does have a future in the West, but as one member noted:

It will not be the Islam of 800 years ago or Islam of that scholarly tradition ... Certain rulings that were suitable before are now not applicable. Islam needs a connection to God, because that is the ultimate reality ... However, what is fixed and what is changeable needs to be questioned. A lot of things need to be revisited. You look at fiqh rulings and they relate to very simple *ahkam* (orders), [but the] real life situation is more complex.

Tarjuma is the other platform in Edmonton with a very similar objective of increasing connectivity, both within the Muslim community and between Muslims and the broader society. *Tarjuma*, which means translations, is an Arabic word with similar connotations in Hebrew, Hindi, Urdu, Somali, and Bengali. The name itself reflects its pluralistic spirit: 'a translator is someone who converses in both the source and target languages so that he/she can render an idea from one language into another without losing its essence', explains the main founder of this platform. Of South Asian origin, he was introduced to the network of Islamic rationalist scholars through his older sister when he was only ten years old. It was at the 1997 ISNA conference that he first heard Hamza Yusuf, who left a very strong impression on him: 'he brought a public intellectualism to Islam, which other scholars lacked'. He was still in school when September 11 happened and he felt isolated by its impact. He attended the Rihla programme in New Mexico when he was fifteen, thanks to an arrangement made by his sister. Here he met Usama Canon (who himself was just twenty-five years old at that time), as well as Yahya Rhodus and Mustafa Davis. Davis and Canon, as he recalls, 'impressed him as the two singers who did the nashids'. He recalls Davis and Canon singing traditional nashids 'in Western melodies that were unique and beautiful'. The Rihla proved very significant in his life. He came back, finished high school, and left to live in Egypt to study Arabic.

Years later, he re-encountered Usama Canon through his work at Ta'leef Collective. As an organizer in Edmonton's Muslim community, he began to host Usama Canon and other Ta'leef-affiliated speakers and artists in a succession of events that generated the momentum necessary to launch a formal platform. Members of this Edmonton group meanwhile began to attend Ta'leef's 'Mu'allif Mentorship Program' (MMP) in California and fifteen members from this group undertook this training. Although they gained much from Ta'leef, it was clear to the core members that they could not use the Ta'leef template without tailoring it to the local community dynamics. 'Ta'leef's genesis is directly tied to the network of Islamic rationalist scholars – both Usama Canon and Mustafa Davis became students of Hamza Yusuf in 1996 and they continue to have links within that network,' explains Tarjuma's main founder. Given the differences between the local context in Edmonton and that of the Bay Area in California, he began to study the texts that were often referenced in discourses connected to Ta'leef Collective: 'I read Ray Oldenburg's (1989) *The Great Good Place*[2] because it was often cited as a source text for Ta'leef and initiatives like it. The book highlights the importance of the third space. But I think what was missing when it was employed in these conversations was that Oldenburg was practicing a form of observatory sociology. Namely, that "third places" are the by-product of a healthy local community. It's very difficult to do it the other way around: create a "third place" and then expect a healthy community to form. You need to start with the community.'

If in accordance with Oldenburg's reasoning a 'third place' consisting of coffee houses, bars, and shopping spaces is a marker of a healthy community, Tarjuma could not establish a 'third place' until it first did the work to establish healthy 'micro-communities' within Edmonton. Tarjuma leaders have attempted to do this by hosting regular open events

---

[2] Oldenburg demonstrates how and why these places are essential to community and public life, arguing that bars, coffee shops, general stores, and other 'third places' are central to local democracy and community vitality.

designed to connect its members to one another. Noting that Tim Winter talks about how traditional Muslim societies were built on networks of extended family, Tarjuma's founder argues, 'as those networks dissipate, if not entirely disappear, the work of Tarjuma is to find ways to connect people to one another in ways that fill the gap left by the extended family.' As we were concluding the interview, the founder of Tarjuma helped capture the distinctive contribution of Ta'leef, Green Room, and Tarjuma within the Islamic rationalist network, as opposed to its purely academic and teaching activities:

People can come to Ta'leef and say that we have come home. That's a distinct and complementary mission to that of Zaytuna as an academic institution. Ta'leef and Tarjuma's primary objective is to build community, but it is also to share Islam. Tarjuma is an attempt to translate the Zawiyah, to translate the teachings of this network into practice by actually serving each other. The tea and the coffee and the beautiful connections we build are critical to enriching the inner self.

In this section I have recorded these striking examples of the real-life impact that the revival of Islamic rationalism is having, and have shown how creating beauty is at the heart of the efforts led by the scholars as well as by the students: beauty in visual appearance, in physical surroundings, in poetic and literary expression and nurturing of the arts, and in social harmony by connecting hearts. I stumbled on these efforts by young Muslims to create beauty in its multiple manifestations often unexpectedly during my multi-sited fieldwork with the rationalists' network over the course of seven years. During all this period, I never actively sought to map the actual real-life initiatives resulting from the network; a conscious effort to map this impact will thus yield much more enriching evidence. Tracing the graduates of Cambridge Muslim College and also those of Zaytuna with a view to studying what roles they play in their communities on return will, for example, be a fascinating subject for a doctoral thesis. The results are likely to be particularly striking in the case of the graduates of Cambridge Muslim College (CMC). The students of the CMC's one-year degree programme are already graduates of the traditional dar al-'ulums; at CMC their main learning is to recognise the importance of relating their Islamic knowledge to the social context if they are to guide the Muslim youth effectively. How the one-year programme at CMC changes the engagement of these former graduates of dar al-'ulums with their mosque congregations, or the way they approach solutions to the challenges faced by Muslim communities in the United Kingdom, will in my assessment provide ample evidence of creative energy similar to what I have documented in this section. Mapping this diverse array of initiatives and activities inspired by the teachings of the Islamic rationalist network on to a canvas thus creates an exceptionally colourful pattern. It is this colour added to all aspects of life – consistent with the Prophet's saying, '*Allah* is beautiful and loves beauty' – that is the real power of Islamic rationalism and the reason classical Islam was able to inspire a beautiful civilisation with its own distinctive high culture in the first place. My contention is that the twenty-first century will be the century of the revival of Islamic rationalism and of Islamic high culture, unless the socio-economic and political shifts propelling this revival undergo some dramatic reversal, or a few challenges internal to this movement (discussed in the next section), develop into full-blown problems.

LOOKING FORWARD

This volume has so far mapped the factors and processes that have led to the spread of the movement for the revival of Islamic rationalism. In this last section I conclude by focusing on three issues that in my assessment can stall its impact if not properly managed: succession and spread; retaining scholarly credentials; and maintaining moral integrity. All three issues stem from my observations and discussions during the field-work. Below, I identify the extent and nature of the risk that each one of these three impending challenges poses to the consolidation of this movement.

Succession and Spread

The first challenge faced by the rationalist revival movement is that of ensuring successful succession: a challenge shared by all movements, given the important role that charismatic leadership plays in mobilising people. In this case, the three foundational members of the network – Hamza Yusuf, Tim Winter, and Dr Umar Faruq Abd-Allah – remain the main magnets drawing the crowds. However, the second generation scholars such as Yahya Rhodus and Faraz Rabbani, or charismatic public figures such as Usama Canon, now have a strong following of their own. Further, the previous chapter noted that the third generation of scholars being trained in this network is even larger in number, and that the trainees are mostly of Muslim heritage, rather than converts, which signals the fact that the movement has become mainstream. Thus, in reality the challenge of succession is not necessarily as severe as that faced by many other movements. However, the risks to continued expansion remain real, not due to a lack of potential of this network to produce popular figures in the next generation, but because of the continued difficulty of ensuring that positions in the religious sector in Muslim communities are financially viable. The positions of the imams in most Muslim communities in the West are funded by mosque committees consisting of members of the local community, and these committees invest in themselves the ultimate authority to supervise mosque activities. The resulting positions are thus more suitable for imams from Muslim-majority countries, who are normally of low socio-economic status and are willing to work for low wages and with limited autonomy.

The slow recognition within the Muslim communities of the need to fund scholars more generously if they want to attract the best Muslim minds to interpret and engage Islam for modern times thus poses the main practical hurdle to maximising the impact of the rationalist revival movement. The fact that these scholars are teaching the Muslim societal elites does help to initiate institutional change, as these individuals do lead socio-economic and political developments; but if the positions of the imams could become attractive enough to become a viable job option for the graduates of institutes such as Zaytuna or Cambridge Muslim College, the influence of the teachings of this network could spread much faster and make deeper inroads into the community. The importance of this challenge is noted by both the scholars and the students within the network, as also noted above in the case of the leadership of the Green Room. Similarly, SeekersHub routinely sends out e-mail requests for donations to help support particular scholars in the United States and Canada who are struggling to make ends meet for lack of support by their host community. During my fieldwork in the United States, many of the young students in the network mentioned how Jihad Brown, although an excellent scholar, is failing to find a Muslim community who could support a position that would be appropriate for a scholar of his credentials and socio-economic status. Meanwhile, Usama Canon's diagnosed condition of amyotrophic lateral sclerosis (ALS), which normally leads to rapid deterioration, and his consequent decision in December 2017 to take a one-year sabbatical from Ta'leef, suggests that Ta'leef has already become the first case to test the ability of the institutions established in this network to survive beyond the time, or active involvement, of their dynamic founders.

Public Speaking and Questioning of Scholarly Credentials

While a concern about effective succession is shared by all social movements, the second concern associated with the movement for the revival of Islamic rationalism, if proven justified, will have more serious consequences for the consolidation of this movement. Some of the students were concerned about the increasingly public role adopted by some scholars in this network, especially Hamza Yusuf. His increasing appearances on Western media channels as well as on high-profile platforms, such as the Davos Forum, are creating a concern that he might lose scholarly credibility by routinely making statements on issues about which he does not have proper knowledge of Islamic law. Hamza Yusuf's position on the need to take on a more public speaking role to defend the image of Islam is understandable, and in the view of many he is indeed very well suited to the role of promoting a more tolerant and pluralistic image of Islam in the West. However, the concern of some of his more serious students and followers is that speaking out on all issues, whether or not they fall in his area of expertise, will erode his legitimacy. In my interviews these concerns were voiced more actively by those of his own students, or by students of other scholars in the Islamic rationalist network, who were themselves undertaking specialist higher studies in Islamic sciences and thus could identify some problems with the positions taken by Hamza Yusuf on issues on which in their view he did not have the necessary Islamic scholarly expertise. In the future, the way Hamza Yusuf maintains a delicate balance across the divide between being a public spokesman of Islam willing to answer any question, and nurturing his image as a scholar, will play a key role in shaping his own credibility and that of the movement. It is also important to note that this risk of losing academic credibility by making too many media appearances is real for all scholars and not just for those representing the Islamic tradition. As a general rule, too much exposure in the media can often be detrimental to academic credentials, precisely for the same reason that is making some of Yusuf's students and followers wary: the inevitability of ending up commenting on issues on which one does not have specialist knowledge.

Political Positioning and the Erosion of Moral Integrity

Finally, the biggest challenge that the scholars leading the Islamic rationalist network face in retaining their appeal among the Muslim youth from across different schools of Islamic thought is the increasingly visible tension between them and some of the proponents of political Islam. These scholars' aversion to Salafism and to political Islam was discussed in Chapters 4 and 6. Also, many of these scholars do advise their students and followers to distance themselves from the politics of the Muslim world (primarily because they cannot do much) and instead focus on helping Muslim communities within their own immediate localities. Their emphasis on discouraging young Muslims from engaging with political causes in the Muslim world has thus been a continuing basis of concern for many, as I have found in interviews with those who do not follow these scholars, and also with some of their own followers. The stance of these scholars towards political Islam has become particularly problematic for many, especially concerning the 2013 coup in Egypt, which removed the Muslim Brotherhood from power and subjected its members to excessive state violence (HRW 2014). In this context, Humza Yusuf has been seen to provide subtle support to Islamic scholars in Egypt (Ali Gomma and the Shaykh al-Azhar) and the United Arab Emirates (Habib al-Jifri), who supported the Egyptian military's oppression of the Muslim Brotherhood. As I have found in my fieldwork, this siding with scholars whose credibility has been tainted by their providing legitimacy to a military regime against an Islamist party has slightly compromised the moral standing of Hamza Yusuf in the eyes of some.

Tariq Ramadan's strong condemnation of two North American Muslim platforms – ISNA (Islamic Society of North America) and RIS (Reviving the Islamic Spirit) – which are influenced by Hamza Yusuf is reflective of the same problem. In 2014, Ramadan made a public announcement that he would in future not attend events organised by these two platforms, because in his view they were depoliticising Muslims while at the same time acting in a very political manner. ISNA, Ramadan (2014) argued, in its desire to engage with the American authorities and win their endorsement, was avoiding critiquing domestic policies of the US government which negatively affect Muslim interests: 'Summary arrests, arbitrary prison terms, inhuman psychological torture and solitary confinement, the shadowy role of informers and the deeply troubling and unacceptable methods used by the FBI, which has provoked young people to engage in extremist actions, must be unconditionally condemned.' Critiquing the silence of ISNA's leadership on these issues, he argued that the organization appeared as 'if paralyzed by fear'; he noted that it was equally silent on foreign-policy issues linked to Muslims, such as American support for inhumane Israeli policies. Noting that Muslims cannot be forever silent, he asked: 'What kind of active and responsible citizenship does the ISNA leadership offer young American Muslims? What kind of example? That of silent, fearful sycophants – or of free, public-spirited citizens who, while defending the values of human dignity and justice, serve their country in the most sincere and critical way? That of the unconditional loyalty of the timorous, or the critical loyalty of free individuals?' (Ramadan 2014). He argued that to attend the ISNA convention would amount to endorsing the leadership's silence.

Regarding RIS, Tariq Ramadan expressed his concern that this plat-form was similarly involved in promoting political apathy among Muslim youth by focusing on Sufism. Stating that he had no problem with Sufism, he argued that for some the challenge was that in the name of supporting Sufism these scholars were in fact supporting military and authoritarian regimes: 'participants, scholars or preachers, under the guise of Sufism or in the name of avoiding partisan politics, defend highly politicized pos-itions of support for states and dictatorships' (Ramadan 2014). He argued that the silence of institutions such as RIS extended support to 'Gulf petro-monarchies and despots' such as General al-Sisi in Egypt. Many of these Sufi scholars, he argued, while claiming to be above politics, were actually taking very political positions and supporting dictatorial regimes, and then refusing to take part in panel discussions to avoid being exposed. He asserted, 'My position is that all dictators must be confronted, all injustices must be fought; we cannot be silent, or feign silence while supporting the worst regimes' (Ramadan 2014).

Emphasising that Western Muslims will in the future assume a critical role, as they are educated and live in free societies, Ramadan urged that they must 'acquire greater knowledge of their religion and become free, active and outspoken citizens, fully aware of their duties and dedicated to the defence of their rights'. He argued that Muslims in the United States, Canada, and Europe must defend everyone's human dignity and should not shy away from raising concerns due to intimidation by the state. Noting that confidently advancing the right Muslim causes and issues will be the key contribution of the young Muslims, he declared (Ramadan 2014): 'The leaders of the previous generation are too cautious, too fearful; they dare not speak freely.' He argued: 'I dream of a new feminine and masculine leadership, educated, free and bold, a leadership that does not confuse the concept of dialogue with the authorities with unacceptable compromise and intellectual surrender, a leadership that does not transform Sufism, the historical underpinning of so many liber-ation movements, into a school of silence and cowardly calculation' (Ramadan 2014).

These concerns raised by Tariq Ramadan echo the very same concerns that I have heard during interviews, especially with some of the more advanced students within the Islamic rationalist network (see Appendix) as well as among young Muslims who are critical of this network. Such evidence is not restricted just to my own fieldwork but is increasingly available in the writing of some of these young Muslims themselves. A detailed piece published in *The Middle East Eye* helps to demonstrate the growing concern among young Muslims in the West who are familiar with this network that while arguing to keep Islam and politics separate, some of these scholars themselves are taking a very political position and are giving legitimacy to authoritarian regimes (al-Azami 2017). This particular piece focused on Hamza Yusuf's active involvement in the UAE-based and UAE-funded platform, the Forum for Promoting Peace in Muslim Societies (FPPMS), which is led by Bin Bayyah, with Hamza Yusuf as its vice-president. This platform played a politically contentious role in the tension that broke out in the Gulf between Qatar and its neighbouring states of Saudi Arabia and UAE in 2017. As noted in this article, when the Gulf states of Saudi Arabia and UAE led renewed efforts to internationally isolate Qatar, the FPPMS issued a strongly worded statement against Qatar which in the view of the author confirmed its critics' view that the platform was just a religious rubber stamp for the UAE's strategic ambitions. This statement, issued on 7 June 2017, described UAE as a place of 'tolerance and peace-making' and then held Qatar responsible for creating the crisis:

The Forum has followed with extreme unease the activities of the Qatari government in ripping apart Arab ranks, rebelling against the Gulf family, and insulting the generous faith of Islam by supporting terrorist groups, inciting political instability in safe countries, and inflaming sectarian conflict. [This] has led to remedial efforts by the countries of the Gulf Cooperation Council and several Arab and Islamic countries to limit the evil that stems from the actions of the Qatari government that aim at demolishing the foundations of stability and security in the region. (al-Azami 2017)

The author of this piece, who is a young British Muslim, with a PhD from Princeton University and now teaching at Markfield Institute, noted three factors that suggested that the statement was drafted in coordination with, or even by, the UAE authorities: it was issued less than 48 hours after the surprise announcement of the boycott; its highly charged language was entirely aligned with UAE foreign policy; and the statement was published by the UAE's state-owned Emirates News Agency, before its publication by the forum (al-Azami 2017). The author went on to note that the website and social media accounts of the Forum's president, Bin Bayyah, made no mention of the statement, and he interpreted this as a sign that he himself might not have been happy with it and might have been obliged to issue it as UAE is the 'paymaster' (al-Azami 2017). Nor, the author noted, did Yusuf, as the Forum's vice president, publicly comment on the blockade, although he did join the UAE's ambassador to the United States, Yousef Al Otaiba, at an inter-faith event one week after the blockade began. This courtship of the government of the UAE, which the author argued hardly qualifies as an ideal Muslim state (al-Azami 2017), poses a challenge for the Islamic rationalist scholars.

Historically, in the Islamic scholarly tradition, the credibility of the scholar is dependent on knowledge of the text, but equally on moral uprightness; this is the model set by the Sunnah of the Prophet Muhammad, and this is what the Islamic rationalist scholars themselves also emphasise. Humza Yusuf's growing involvement with political regimes in the Muslim world, and the use of his association by the latter to legitimise unjust policies, poses a risk to the moral integrity of the entire Islamic rationalist network. There is thus a need for these scholars, especially Hamza Yusuf, to evaluate the implications of some of their positions on political Islam and the nature of their relationships with the different Muslim states. It is here also important to note that the approach of these scholars to political Islam is in reality not as rigid as alleged by some of their critics. Yusuf has been openly supportive of the AKP (Justice and Development Party) government in Turkey, which by many of its domestic critics as well as Western policy makers is perceived as an extension of the Muslim Brotherhood.

Tim Winter, who himself is very cautious about not getting close to any Muslim political regime, when questioned, could understand the concerns of those students or followers who did not want these scholars to associate too closely with the Muslim regimes in the Middle East. Acknowledging that closeness to the state does often compromise a scholar's integrity, he noted that historically some Muslim scholars did, however, defend being close to the state: these scholars argued for taking the opportunity when it became available to influence the Sultan with the view to achieve a greater good. His view was that Hamza Yusuf's growing involvement with some of the states in the Middle East might be better understood from that perspective. He was also of the view that many of these scholars in the Muslim countries have to survive under extreme political pressure and therefore it was important not to judge them too harshly for certain positions they might have had to endorse under duress.

There is thus a logic to their reasoning. The key concerns of these scholars about political Islam stem from its tendency to ignore the plurality within the Islamic scholarly tradition. This neglect, as also argued by academics such as Abou El Fadl (2007), on the one hand erodes the dynamism within the Islamic scholarly tradition and on the other (due to a merging of the religious and political authorities into one party) leads to poor governance and low accountability. Similarly, Tim Winter's explanation also has its merit. While such explanations resonate with many Muslim youth, they do leave some uncomfortable. Being truly pluralistic and accommodating of diversity within Sunni Islam, including political Islam, will facilitate the continued success of this movement in the future; failure to do so would run the risk of this network becoming labelled as just another Sufi network – a label that it has very successfully managed to avoid. The core strength of this movement has been its ability to bring together young Muslims of different dispositions and family orientations on one platform and help them to appreciate the dynamic energy within the Islamic intellectual tradition. Continuing to respect the plurality within Sunni Islam is a critical prerequisite to the movement's continued success in the future.

Appendix

A letter from a former graduate of Zaytuna Institute to Hamza Yusuf

ON SCHOLARS AND POLITICS AND THE PROBLEMATIC NATURE OF THE 'FORUM FOR PROMOTING PEACE IN MUSLIM SOCIETIES'

Dear Shaykh Hamza,

It is important from the very start to establish the point that religious scholars with their knowledge of the Islamic tradition and their piety, are also [at least in Sunni theology] fallible human beings whose judgments, perspectives, positions can be and ought to be subject to informed and balanced critiques. This is especially the case when they venture into areas that are not their areas of specialty. I believe you acknowledge this point and [it] is at the heart of your disclaimer at the Rihla and Knowledge Retreat, when you say that an analysis you offer is merely your opinion, take it or leave it, and that you are still thinking through these issues. Nevertheless, I feel it is important to underscore it, for fear that a critique of the positions of our beloved teachers and initiatives they may be involved with, may not be heard, if it is seen as an attack on their beings, or their piety and closeness to God. I have no intention of going to war with God and His Messenger by attacking those who are close to Him. That being said, as you know, the Prophet, upon him and his family be peace and blessings, invited alternative perspectives, especially in matters of strategy and planning, when they were outside the clear dictates of revelation.

There is a fair critique of exclusive focus on politics to the detriment and neglect of developing one's *imān* (belief) and one's focus on God and spirituality. But must it be stuck in such absolute terms of either one has spirituality or one is obsessed with politics? The 'metaphysical critique' you offers seems to condemn an exclusive focusing on worldly conditions, asbāb (causes/means), which you argue leads to excess 'complaining' and a demand for rights and equality and lack of humiliation, but does not see everything as coming from God. However, cannot one be attentive to the human oppression of one's people, aware of the fact that God is in control (and is not pleased with everything that humans do), and still

225

commit to struggling against injustice, in ourselves and in society? Indeed, that struggle may be obligated upon one by God.[3]

Shaykh Hamza, you are a scholar and intellectual [to] who[m] many, including myself, look up. You have undoubtedly influenced so many, including me, in our journey to God, reconnecting with historical Islamic traditions, as well as becoming more informed, educated people in the world. It is perfectly fine to have a critique of 'political Islam' or Islamism and subject it to a rigorous critique. At the Dec 2016, Reviving the Islamic Spirit Knowledge Retreat, you made an important point that it was due to the lack of adaptation by traditional religious scholars, that movements emerged in the [twentieth] century that sought to respond to the changes in society and found a wide following, especially in the context of the excesses of Sufism, tomb worship, extravagant wealth accumulation of Sufi shaykhs and pirs, which led to a backlash against Sufism. However, the main staples of the triangle in your analysis, if I am not mistaken, are basically that 'political Islam' and 'Wahhabism/Salafism' merged into al-Qaeda/ISIS/'religious anarchy'.

In your piece 'The Plague Within,' you write:

> The terroristic Islamists are a hybrid of an exclusivist *takfiri* version of the above and the political Islamist ideology that has permeated much of the Arab and South Asian world for the last several decades. It is this marriage made in hell that must be understood in order to fully grasp the calamitous situation we find our community in … this militancy… has everything to do with religion: misguided, fanatical, ideological, and politicized religion. It is the religion of resentment, envy, powerlessness, and nihilism. It does, however, have nothing to do with the merciful teachings of our Prophet, God's peace and blessings upon him.[4]

In an important article, UCLA Law School professor and scholar, Khaled Abou El Fadel, writes:

> If this highly contingent and erratic definition of 'moderate Islam' strikes someone as thoroughly political, then what does this do to the coherence of the concept of political Islam (*al-Islam al-Siyasi*) and its many terrifying spectres? In the kosher type of politicized Islam that apparently is acceptable to Sisi, Azhar, Saudi Arabia, the Gulf Cooperation Council (GCC) and their allies, the state is God – it defines and manages religion in the public space, it defines good religiosity as opposed to bad religiosity, and it tells us what God wants or does not want. Therefore, obedience to the state is a legal and moral duty, and submission to the state is a virtue … If we are being entirely honest, we would have to recognize that the very concept of political Islam is quintessentially incoherent. The very first steps towards the construction of civil coherence must be honesty in discourse. The problem, however, is that the

---

[3] This is a point that Dr Sherman Jackson articulates in *Islam and the Problem of Black Suffering*.

[4] https://sandala.org/the-plague-within/.

deployment of the label 'political Islam' is itself a politically motivated and often mendacious attempt at obfuscation.[5]

As the foreign policy commentator and analyst, James Traub, points out, the UAE and Egypt under Sisi are currently pursuing an extreme demonization of the Muslim Brotherhood by designating them as a terrorist organization.

The terrorism label increasingly looks like a flimsy rationale for authoritarian control … Both Saudi Arabia and Egypt have banned the Brotherhood as a terrorist organization. The UAE convicted 69 Brotherhood members of plotting to overthrow the state. In Egypt, it is an article of faith shared by secularists and Salafists alike that the Brotherhood is responsible, directly or indirectly, for terrorist violence and sabotage – despite the lack of evidence tying the organization to Ansar Beit's murderous campaign. The great organizing principle of the current Egyptian regime is simply this: Crush the Brotherhood.

The Gulf diplomat I spoke to was quite explicit on this score. The Brotherhood and al Qaeda, he said, 'are shades of the same thing.' The Brotherhood is 'a gateway to further extremism.'[6]

Traub, aware of America's own troubled policies with curtailing freedom in wake of a perceived terrorist threat, nevertheless correctly points out:

> It's deeply disheartening to see the dark mass of the national security state so utterly eclipse the beautiful celebration of freedom that adorned the public spaces of the Arab world only a few years ago. What's more, the brutal reaction to dissent is surely self-defeating in the long run. Killing unarmed Islamist protesters has proved to be surprisingly popular among Egyptians, but doing so is far likelier to foster terrorism than to deter it. And it undermines the new war on terror by conflating domestic political rivals with a genuine transnational threat.[7]

Khaled Abou El Fadel writes about this instrumentalization of religion and of religious scholars to support the regimes as they stand and stifle criticism and dissent in the following manner:

> Islam, its doctrines, symbolisms and linguistic constructs, are persistently utilized by the Gulf States to legitimate and maintain themselves in power. The exploitation of religion as a means to keeping a conservative and exploitative elite in power is a staple of everyday life in the Gulf countries. Every one of those countries carefully nurtures and maintains a class of clergymen with religious institutions that function as a conservative legitimating force safeguarding the *status quo*, which includes the exploitative use of foreign workers, and a hyper-form of Gulf nationalistic elitism.
>
> This Islamized and oddly pietistic Gulf nationalism often manifests itself in highly racist and ethnocentric ways, deep seated social and political inequities, entrenched patriarchal institutions, and unabashed political despotism and authoritarianism.

---

[5] www.abc.net.au/religion/articles/2015/04/23/4221874.htm.
[6] http://foreignpolicy.com/2014/09/22/the-arab-war-on-terror/.
[7] http://foreignpolicy.com/2014/09/22/the-arab-war-on-terror/.

Critical to this dynamic is that the state carefully defines, regulates and dictates religious expression and orthodoxy. Religion is also exploited to further state policies, such as antagonism towards Shi'i Iran and other Shi'i allies.[8]

Unfortunately, the majority of those who have been given a platform at the Forum in Abu Dhabi, seem to be advocates and participants of this demonization. For example, Dr. Aref Nayed, the Libyan ambassador to the UAE, in an interview on CNN, stated that 'the entire discourse of ISIS is straight out of Sayyid Qutb's *Milestones* . . . OBL belonged to the Muslim Brotherhood at one point, Ayman al-Zahiri belonged to the Muslim Brotherhood, and I believe the ISIS founder and narrative is completely Muslim Brotherhood based.'[9]

As you might know, Habib Ali and Usaama al-Sayyid have recently been promoting their new books *al-Ḥaqq al-Mubīn* and *al-Insaniyya Qabl al-Tadayyun*, where they engage in a critique of Qutb which is warranted, but further engage in creating a narrative that ties Qutb and the Muslim Brotherhood to ISIS. Their critiques of Qutb do not come out in a apolitical context, but rather their writings and rhetoric, is actively being used by the Sisi regime as well as the UAE (including through the Forum, especially the 2nd Forum, where they were both given prominent platforms) to participate in this demonization of Islamist supporters.

You have previously stated that the ulama should be 'above politics', but I wonder whether that is really possible or certainly if that is what is happening here. I find it hard to sustain the idea that Shaykh bin Bayyah, Allah preserve him and reward him for all the good he has done, is really 'above the politics,' given the above political context of the UAE and the policies it is pursuing, the panels and discussion promoted at the forum, and for example, his being quoted in the UAE newspapers as stating, 'The UAE is a model for all other nations to follow and benefit from in terms of tolerance and peaceful coexistence.'[10]

* * *

As Mufti Taqi Uthmani highlighted in the 1st Forum in 2014, we ought to have a frank conversation about the issues that are at the heart of people's' grievances against their rulers and states. It is not simply a matter of asserting the need for obedience to the rulers, and shutting off the 'Islamicity' of dissent and protest as engaging in prohibited *khurūj* (rebellion). What about Shaykh Saleh al-Ghursi's point that demonstrations and protests are not *khuruj*, but rather a type of *naṣīḥāh*? Similarly, at the 3rd Forum, to simply promote the idea that Muslims should embrace the nation-state [the topic of the 3rd forum being The Nation State in Muslim Societies], but not discuss what does that mean in terms of the rights of citizens [or 'subjects'], and freedoms that the government is supposed to ensure makes the discussion grossly incomplete; to have a panel on 'The Case Study of the UAE in the Promotion of Peace' . . . It comes off as potentially a means to justify repression and blanket submission to rulers, who are seen to be

---

[8] www.abc.net.au/religion/articles/2015/04/23/4221874.htm.
[9] www.youtube.com/watch?v=sDdUI2DQZqU&feature=youtu.be.
[10] http://gulftoday.ae/portal/ff7722f4-c429-42e6-b4b1-a04eb2b3acfd.aspx.

providing 'Islamically compatible notions of governance,' yet without affirming the right to dissent, question, or provide advice (*naṣīḥah*) to their rulers or voice their grievances.

As the University of Toronto Law School professor and Islamic legal scholar, Mohammed Fadel, writes:

> [Those who engage in a]uthoritarianism, however, are completely opposed to any kind of genuine social contract in the Muslim world, so how could they possible be advocating a discourse of peace as opposed to a discourse of pacification? Certainly, there is a difference between peace and pacification (unless we are willing to endorse Bashshar al-Asad). If there was any discussion there about a genuine social contract that would hold rulers such as those of the UAE accountable, that would certainly be a milestone worth discussing. Otherwise, count me among the cynical![11]

In conclusion, as Sherman Jackson highlights in his introduction to *Initiative to Stop the Violence*, the efficacy of the message of scholars is not simply a matter of their knowledge and piety, but also dependent upon their 'street credibility.'[12] I fear that the credibility of the scholars involved with the Forum and its policies are severely going to be damaged. I believe we must have the ability to critique the political positions of scholars, including our teachers who we look up to as our masters in the tradition, and recognize they too have political positions which are subject to critique and that the *shar'iah* and the *'ulama* certainly do not speak in one voice regarding the justification of the repressive policies of regimes in the region.

In closing, I leave this reminder from Shaykh Imad Iffat (d. 2011), who was a student and colleague of Ali Gooma, and was killed in the protests in Egypt on December 16, 2011, and wrote to his student (and my colleague at Columbia), Ibrahim El Houdaibi, in 2010:

> There are all these good words about respect for shaykhs, giving them leeway and excuses, but where is God's right to His own religion? Where is the right of the public who are confused about the truth because shaykhs are silent, and your own silence out of respect for senior shaykhs? What is this new idol that you call pressure; how does this measure to Ahmed ibn Hanbal's tolerance of jail and refusing to bend and say what would comfort the unjust rulers?[13]

---

[11] www.facebook.com/mohammad.fadel.39?fref=ts.

[12] Sherman A. Jackson, introduction to his translation of *Initiative to Stop the Violence (Mubādarat Waqf al-'Unf): Sadat's Assassins and the Renunciation of Political Violence* (New Haven, CT: Yale University Press, 2015), 47.

[13] http://theislamicmonthly.com/egypt-killed-islam-in-the-west/.

Bibliography

Abbas, Tahir. 2005. 'British South Asian Muslims: State and Multicultural Society.' In Tahir Abbas, ed. *Muslim Britain: Communities under Pressure.* London: Zed Books, 3–17.

ABC. 2004. 'Feature Interview: Tim Winter (aka Abdul Hakim Murad).' [Available Online: www.abc.net.au/sundaynights/stories/s1237986.htm; Accessed 1 May 2018].

Abd-Allah, Umar F. 2006. 'Innovation and Creativity in Islam.' *Nawawi Foundation Paper.* [Available Online: www.nawawi.org/wp-content/uploads/2013/01/Article4.pdf; Accessed 22 August 2015].

Abou El Fadl, Khaled. 2007. *The Great Theft: Wrestling Islam from the Extremists.* New York: HarperOne.

Acemoglu, Daron, and James A. Robinson. 2000. 'Why Did the West Extend the Franchise? Democracy, Inequality and Growth in Historical Perspective.' *The Quarterly Journal of Economics* 115(4): 1167–1199.

2009. *Economic Origins of Dictatorship and Democracy.* Cambridge: Cambridge University Press.

Adarlo, Sharon. 2018. 'Inside the Growing Organic Halal Movement.' *The Daily Beast.* [Available Online: www.thedailybeast.com/inside-the-growing-organic-halal-movement; Accessed 1 May 2018].

Agai, Bekim. 2007. 'Islam and Education in Secular Turkey: State Policies and the Emergence of the Fethullah Güllen Group.' In Robert W. Hefner and Muhammad Qasim Zaman, eds. *Schooling Islam: The Culture and Politics of Modern Muslim Education.* Princeton, NJ: Princeton University Press, 149–171.

Agrama, Hussein Ali. 2012. *Questioning Secularism: Islam, Sovereignty, and the Rule of Law in Modern Egypt.* Chicago: University of Chicago Press.

Ahmed, Akbar. 2011. *Journey into America: The Challenge of Islam.* Washington, DC: Brookings Institution Press.

2017. 'Muslim Converts 1: Dr Tim Winter.' *Daily Times*, 22 July 2017. [Available Online: http://dailytimes.com.pk/opinion/22-Jul-17/muslim-con verts-1-dr-tim-winter; Accessed 15 April 2018].

Ali, Abdullah bin Hamid. 2012. '"Neo-Traditionalism" vs "Traditionalism".' Lampost Education Initiative. [Available Online. www.lamppostproductions .com/neo-traditionalism-vs-traditionalism-shaykh-abdullah-bin-hamid-ali/; Accessed 1 May 2018].

Anderson, Alistair R., and Claire J. Miller. 2003. '"Class Matters": Human and Social Capital in the Entrepreneurial Process.' *The Journal of Socio-Economics* 32: 17–36.

Andrabi, Tahir, Jishnu Das, Asim Ijaz Khwaja, and Tristan Zajonc. 2005. 'Religious School Enrollment in Pakistan: A Look at the Data.' World Bank Working Paper Series 3521.

Al-Attas, Muhammad Naguib. 1978. *Islam and Secularism.* Kuala Lumpur: Muslim Youth Movement of Malaysia.

    1995. *Prolegomena to the Metaphysics of Islam: An Exposition of the Fundamental Elements of the Worldview of Islam.* Kuala Lumpur: International Institute of Islamic Thought and Civilization.

Al-Azami, Usaama. 2017. 'Gulf Crisis: How Autocrats Use Religious Scholars against Qatar.' *Middle East Eye.* [Available Online: www.middleeasteye.net/ columns/qatar-uae-forum-for-promoting-peace-in-muslim-societies-gulf-reli gious-scholars-politics-715865822; Accessed 1 May 2018].

Baddeley, Michelle. 2017. *Behavioural Economics: A Very Short Introduction (Very Short Introductions).* Oxford: Oxford University Press.

Bano, Masooda. 2008. *Islamiyya, Quranic, and Tsangaya Education in Kano.* Kano: CUBE.

    2009. 'Engaged yet Disengaged: Islamic Schools and the State in Kano, Nigeria.' *RaD Working Paper 29,* University of Birmingham [Available Online: http:// epapers.bham.ac.uk/1568/1/Bano_IslamicSchools.pdf; Accessed 19 August 2015].

    2011. 'Conclusion: Female Leadership in Mosques: An Evolving Narrative.' In Masooda Bano and Hilary E. Kalmbach, eds. *Women, Leadership and Mosques: Changes in Contemporary Islamic Authority.* Leiden: Brill, 507–534.

    2012. *The Rational Believer: Choices and Decisions in the Madrasas of Pakistan.* Ithaca, NY: Cornell University Press.

    2017. *Female Islamic Education Movements: The Re-democratisation of Islamic Knowledge.* Cambridge: Cambridge University Press.

    2018a. *Islamic Authority and Social Change, Vol. 1: Evolving Debates in the Muslim-Majority Countries.* Edinburgh: Edinburgh University Press.

    2018b. *Islamic Authority and Social Change, Vol. 2: Evolving Debates in the West.* Edinburgh: Edinburgh University Press.

Bano, Masooda, and Hilary E. Kalmbach, eds. 2011. *Women, Leadership and Mosques: Changes in Contemporary Islamic Authority.* Leiden: Brill.

Bano, Masooda, and Keiko Sakurai. 2015a. 'Introduction.' In Masooda Bano and Keiko Sakurai, eds. *Shaping Global Islamic Discourses: The Role of Al-Azhar, Al-Medina and Al-Mustafa.* Edinburgh: Edinburgh University Press, 1–20.

    eds. 2015b. *Shaping Global Islamic Discourses: The Role of Al-Azhar, Al-Medina and Al-Mustafa.* Edinburgh: Edinburgh University Press.

Beckford, James A. 1986. *New Religious Movements and Rapid Social Change.* London: Sage; Paris: UNESCO.

Berkey, Jonathan P. 2002. *The Formation of Islam: Religion and Society in the Near East, 600–1800.* Cambridge: Cambridge University Press.

2007. 'Madrasas Medieval and Modern: Politics, Education, and the Problem of Muslim Identity.' In Robert W. Hefner and Muhammad Qasim Zaman, eds. *Schooling Islam: The Culture and Politics of Modern Muslim Education.* Princeton, NJ: Princeton University Press, 40–60.

2014. *The Transmission of Knowledge in Medieval Cairo: A Social History of Islamic Education.* Princeton, NJ: Princeton University Press.

Bin Bayyah, Abdallah. 2018. 'The Official Website of His Eminence Shaykh Abdallah Bin Bayyah.' [Available Online: http://binbayyah.net/english/bio/; Accessed 1 May 2018].

Bonds, Eric. 2011. 'The Knowledge-Shaping Process: Elite Mobilization and Environmental Policy.' *Critical Sociology* 37(4): 429–446. [Available Online: http://journals.sagepub.com/doi/abs/10.1177/0896920510379440?journal Code=crsb; Accessed 15 April 2018].

Böttcher, Annabelle. 2002. '*Official Sunni and Shi'i Islam in Syria.*' *EUI Working Paper RSC No. 2002/3.* [Available Online: http://cadmus.eui.eu/bitstream/ handle/1814/1761/2002_03.pdf?sequence=1; Accessed 22 August 2015].

Brown, Raymond. 2017. 'Cambridge's New £15 Million Mosque to Open Next Year – With Donations Flooding in from across the World.' [Available Online: www.cambridge-news.co.uk/news/cambridge-news/cambridges-new-15-million-mosque-13211275; Accessed 1 May 2018].

Bulliet, Richard W. 2004. *The Case for Islamo-Christian Civilization.* New York: Columbia University Press.

Burns, Gene, and Fred Kniss. 2013. 'Religion and Social Movements.' *Wiley Online Library.* [Available Online: https://onlinelibrary.wiley.com/doi/abs/ 10.1002/9780470674871.wbespm484; Accessed 26 June 2019].

Calvert, John. 2010. *Sayyid Qutb and the Origins of Radical Islamism.* London: C Hurst & Co Publishers Ltd.

Cambridge Muslim College (CMC). 2018a. 'Four-Year Programme.' [Available Online: www.cambridgemuslimcollege.org/programmes/four-yp/; Accessed 1 May 2018].

2018b. 'History.' [Available Online: www.cambridgemuslimcollege.org/about/ history/; Accessed 1 May 2018].

Cesari, Jocelyne. 2002. 'Islam in France: The Shaping of a Religious Minority.' In Yvonne Yazbeck Haddad, ed. *Muslims in the West, from Sojourners to Citizens.* Oxford: Oxford University Press, 36–51.

Chamberlain, Michael. 1994. *Knowledge and Social Practice in Medieval Damascus, 1190–1350.* Cambridge: Cambridge University Press.

Davis, Mustafa. 2011. 'Becoming Muslim: Five Words That Changed My Life.' [Available Online: http://islamicsunrays.com/becoming-muslim-in-america/; Accessed on 1 May 2018].

Desai, I. P. 1950. 'The New Elite.' *The Economic Weekly.* [Available Online: www .epw.in/system/files/pdf/1959_11/28-29-30/the_new_elite.pdf?o=ip_login_no_ cache%3D8d83d4dc61d366ab118ed5ea48daa73d; Accessed 1 May 2018].

Destradi, Sandra. 2017. 'Rising Powers in World Politics.' Oxford Bibliographies. [Available Online: www.oxfordbibliographies.com/view/document/obo-9780199743292/obo-9780199743292-0193.xml; Accessed 1 May 2018].

Devji, Faisal. 2017. 'Conversions from Islam in Europe and Beyond.' *New York Times*, 15 August 2017. [Available Online: www.nytimes.com/2017/08/15/opinion/islam-conversions.html; Accessed 1 May 2018].

Economist. 2015. 'America's New Aristocracy.' [Available Online: www.economist.com/news/leaders/21640331-importance-intellectual-capital-grows-privilege-has-become-increasingly; Accessed 1 May 2018].

Eickelman, Dale F. 1992. 'Mass Higher Education and the Religious Imagination in Contemporary Arab Societies.' *American Ethnologist* 19 (4): 643–655.

———. 2007. 'Madrasas in Morocco: Their Vanishing Public Role.' In Robert W. Hefner and Muhammad Qasim Zaman, eds. *Schooling Islam: The Culture and Politics of Modern Muslim Education*. Princeton, NJ: Princeton University Press, 1–39.

Eickelman, Dale F., Jon W. Anderson, and Mark Tessler, eds. 2003. *New Media in the Muslim World: The Emerging Public Sphere*. 2nd ed. Bloomington: Indiana University Press.

Encyclopaedia Britannica. 2018. Al-Khwārizmī: Muslim Mathematician. [Available Online: www.britannica.com/biography/al-Khwarizmi#ref109797; Accessed 30 December 2019].

ERIN. 2016. 'Shaykh Hamza Yusuf on Gay Muslims; Scholars Issue Statement.' 13 June 2016. [Available Online: http://seekershub.org/blog/2016/06/orlan dostatement-shaykhhamza-gay-muslims/; Accessed 1 May 2018].

Escobar, Arturo. 1995. *Encountering Development: The Making and Unmaking of the Third World*. Princeton, NJ: Princeton University Press.

Esposito, John L. 1999. *The Islamic Threat: Myth or Reality?* 3rd ed. Oxford: Oxford University Press.

Estes, Yusuf, and Gary Miller. 2015. 'Bible Islam – Bible Compared to Quran.' [Available Online: www.bibleislam.com/bible_vs_quran.php; Accessed August 2015].

Euben, Roxanne L. 1999. *Enemy in the Mirror: Islamic Fundamentalism and the Limits of Modern Rationalism*. Princeton, NJ: Princeton University Press.

Express Tribune. 2014. 'Gender Ratio: More Girls than Boys Admitted at the Punjab University This Year.' [Available Online: https://tribune.com.pk/story/680524/gender-ratio-more-girls-than-boys-admitted-at-the-punjab-uni versity-this-year/; Accessed 1 May 2018].

Feldman, Noah. 2008. *The Fall and Rise of the Islamic State*. Princeton, NJ: Princeton University Press.

Gambetta, Diego. 1987. *Were They Pushed or Did They Jump? Individual Decision Mechanisms in Education*. Cambridge: Cambridge University Press.

Gambetta, Diego, and Steffen Hertog. 2016. *Engineers of Jihad: The Curious Connection between Violent Extremism and Education*. Princeton, NJ: Princeton University Press.

Gemmell, Ian. 2002. 'Injuries among Female Army Recruits: A Conflict of Legislation.' *Journal of the Royal Society of Medicine* 95: 23–27.

Al-Ghazali, Abu Ḥamid Muhammad ibn Muhammad. 1995. *On Disciplining the Soul [Kitab riyadat al-nafs] and on Breaking the Two Desires [Kitab kasr al-shahwatayn]: Books XXII and XXIII of The Revival of the Religious Sciences [Ihya' ulum al-din] [of Abu Hamid Muhammad ibn Muhammad ibn Ahmad al-Gazzali (1058–1111)]*. Trans. Timothy J. Winter. Cambridge: The Islamic Texts Society.

2001. *Al-Ghazali's Path to Sufism and His Deliverance from Error [al-Munqidh min al-Dalal]*. Trans. Richard J. McCarthy. 2nd ed. Louisville, KY: Fons Vitae.

2005. *On the Elucidation of the Marvels of the Heart [Kitab Sharh 'Aja'ib al-Qalb]: Book XXI of The Revival of the Religious Sciences [Ihya' ulum al-din]*. Leicester: Dar ul Fiqh.

2014. *On Intention, Sincerity and Truthfulness [Kitab al-niyya wa'l-ikhlas wa'l sidq]: Book XXXVII of The Revival of the Religious Sciences [Ihya' ulum al-din]*. Trans. Anthony F. Shaker. Cambridge: The Islamic Texts Society.

Gilliat-Ray, Sophie. 2010. *Muslims in Britain: An Introduction*. Cambridge: Cambridge University Press.

Gilligan, Carol. 1993. *In a Different Voice: Psychological Theory and Women's Development*. Cambridge, MA: Harvard University Press.

Göle, Nilüfer. 1997. 'Secularism and Islamism in Turkey: The Making of Elites and Counter-Elites.' *Middle East Journal* 51 (1): 46–58.

Gow, David D. 2008. *Countering Development: Indigenous Modernity and the Moral Imagination*. Durham, NC: Durham University Press.

Greer, Germaine. 2000. *The Whole Woman*. London: Anchor.

Grewal, Zareena. 2013. *Islam Is a Foreign Country: American Muslims and the Global Crisis of Authority*. New York: New York University Press.

Guardian. 2016. 'Women-Led Mosque Opens in Denmark.' [Available Online: www.theguardian.com/world/2016/feb/12/women-led-mosque-opens-in-denmark; Accessed 1 May 2018].

Hallaq, Wael B. 2009. *Shari'a: Theory, Practice, Transformations*. Cambridge: Cambridge University Press.

Hamid, Sadek. 2013. 'The Rise of the "Traditional Islam" Network(s): Neo-Sufism and British Muslim Youth.' In Ron Geaves and Theodore Gabriel, eds. *Sufism in Britain*. London: Bloomsbury, 177–196.

Hammer, Juliane. 2012. 'Activism as Embodied *Tafsir*: Negotiating Women's Authority, Leadership, and Space in North America.' In Masooda Bano and Hilary E. Kalmbach, eds. *Women, Leadership and Mosques: Changes in Contemporary Islamic Authority*. Leiden: Brill, 457–480.

Hayek, Friedrich A. 1945. 'The Use of Knowledge in Society.' *American Economic Review* 35 (4): 519–530.

Hefner, Robert W. 2007. 'Introduction: The Culture, Politics, and Future of Muslim Education.' In Robert W. Hefner and Muhammad Qasim Zaman, eds. *Schooling Islam: The Culture and Politics of Modern Muslim Education*. Princeton, NJ: Princeton University Press, 1–39.

Hefner, Robert W., and Muhammad Qasim Zaman, eds. 2007. *Schooling Islam: The Culture and Politics of Modern Muslim Education*. Princeton, NJ: Princeton University Press.

Hodgson, Marshall G. S. 1977a. *The Venture of Islam, 1: The Classical Age of Islam*. Chicago: University Of Chicago Press.

1977b. *The Venture of Islam, 2: The Expansion of Islam in the Middle Periods*. Chicago: University of Chicago Press.

1977c. *The Venture of Islam, 3: The Gunpowder Empires and Modern Times*. Chicago: University Of Chicago Press.

Hoechner, Hannah. 2010. 'Searching for Knowledge and Recognition: Quranic 'Boarding Students in Kano, Nigeria.' M.Phil Thesis, University of Oxford.

Horvat, Erin McNamara, Elliot B. Weininger, and Annette Lareau. 2003. 'From Social Ties to Social Capital: Class Differences in the Relations between Schools and Parent Networks.' *American Educational Research Journal* 40: 319–351.

Howard, Adam, and Rubén A. Gaztambide-Fernandez. 2010. *Educating Elites: Class Privilege and Educational Advantage*. Lanham, MD: Rowman and Littlefield Education.

Human Rights Watch (HRW). 2014. *All According to the Plan: The Rab'a Massacre and Mass Killings of Protestors in Egypt*. [Available Online: www.hrw.org/report/2014/08/12/all-according-plan/raba-massacre-and-mass-killings-protesters-egypt; Accessed 1 May 2018].

Hutchins, Robert Maynard. 1954. *Great Books, the Foundation of a Liberal Education*. New York: Simon and Schuster.

Ibn Khaldun. 2004. *The Muqaddimah: An Introduction to History*. Ed. N. J. Dawood. Trans. Franz Rosenthal. Abridged ed. and intro. Bruce B. Lawrence. Princeton, NJ: Princeton University Press.

Independent. 2010. 'Timothy Winter: Britain's Most Influential Muslim – And It Was All Down to a Peach.' [Available Online: www.independent.co.uk/news/people/profiles/timothy-winter-britains-most-influential-muslim-and-it-was-all-down-to-a-peach-2057400.html; Accessed on 1 May 2018].

Islamic Monthly. 2012. '10 in 10.' [Available Online: http://theislamicmonthly.com/10-over-10/; Accessed on 1 May 2018].

Israel, Glenn D., Lionel J. Beaulieu, and Glen Hartless. 2001. 'The Influence of Family and Community Social Capital on Educational Achievement.' *Rural Sociology* 66: 43–68.

Kepel, Gilles. 2009. *Jihad: The Trail of Political Islam*. Rev. ed. IB Tauris.

Keller, Nuh Ha Mim. 1995. 'The Place of Tasawwuf in Traditional Islamic Sciences.' [Available online: http://masud.co.uk/ISLAM/nuh/sufitlk.htm; Accessed 1 May 2018].

1996. 'Evolution and Islam.' [Available Online: www.masud.co.uk/ISLAM/nuh/evolve.htm; Accessed 1 May 2018].

Al-Khalili, Jim. 2012. *Pathfinders: The Golden Age of Arabic Science*. London: Penguin.

Killian, Lewis M., Neil J. Smelser, and Ralph H. Turner. 2013. 'Social Movement.' *Encyclopædia Britannica*. [Available Online: www.britannica.com/topic/social-movement; Accessed 15 April 2018].

Kugle, Scott. 2006. *Rebel between Spirit and Law: Ahmad Zarruq, Sainthood, and Authority in Islam*. Bloomington: Indiana University Press.

Kumar, Krishna. 1985. 'Reproduction or Change? Education and Elites in India.' *Economic and Political Weekly* 20 (30): 1280–1284.

Lacy, Tim. 2013. *The Dream of a Democratic Culture: Mortimer J. Adler and the Great Books Idea.* New York: Palgrave Macmillan.

Lamppost. 2018. 'Jihad Hashim Brown.' [Available Online: www.lamppost productions.com/jihad-hashim-brown/; Accessed 1 May 2018].

Lareau, Annette. 1987. 'Social Class Differences in Family–School Relationships: The Importance of Cultural Capital.' *Sociology of Education* 60 (2): 73–85.

Lever, Janet. 1976. 'Sex Differences in the Games Children Play.' *Social Problems* 23: 478–487.

Mail of Islam. 'Shaykh Usama Canon.' Biography. [Available Online: www.mailo fislam.com/eng_bio_-_shaykh_usama_canon.html; Accessed on 1 May 2018].

Makdisi, George. 1981. *The Rise of Colleges: Institutions of Learning in Islam and the West.* Edinburgh: Edinburgh University Press.

1997. *Ibn 'Aqil: Religion and Culture in Classical Islam.* Edinburgh: Edinburgh University Press.

Malik, Aftab Ahmad, ed. 2006. *The State We Are In: Identity, Terror and the Law of Jihad.* Bristol: Amal Press.

Malik, Jamal. 1997. 'Dynamics among Traditional Religious Scholars and Their Institutions in Contemporary South Asia.' *The Muslim World* 87 (3–4): 199–220.

1998. *Colonization of Islam: Dissolution of Traditional Institutions in Pakistan.* New Delhi: Manohar.

Al-Maqasid. 2018. [www.almaqasid.org/about/; Accessed 10 April 2018].

McNeal, Ralph B. 1999. 'Parental Involvement as Social Capital: Differential Effectiveness on Science Achievement, Truancy, and Dropping Out.' *Social Forces* 78 (1): 117–144.

Masud, Muhammad Khalid, Armando Salvatore, and Martin van Bruinessen, eds. 2009. *Islam and Modernity.* Edinburgh: Edinburgh University Press.

Mathiesen, Kasper. 2013. 'Anglo-American "Traditional Islam" and Its Discourse of Orthodoxy.' *Journal of Arabic and Islamic Studies* 13: 191–219.

Metcalf, Barbara D. 1982. *Islamic Revival in British India: Deoband, 1860–1900.* Princeton, NJ: Princeton University Press.

Meyer, John W. 1977. 'The Effects of Education as an Institution.' *American Journal of Sociology* 83 (1): 55–77.

Mitchell, Richard P. 1993. *The Society of the Muslim Brothers.* Oxford: Oxford University Press.

Moir, Anne, and David Jessel. 1989. *Brain Sex: The Real Difference between Men and Women.* London: Michael Joseph.

Moore, David W. 2002. 'Education Levels: Nine Predominantly Islamic Countries.' [Available Online: http://news.gallup.com/poll/6046/education-levels-nine-predominantly-islamic-countries.aspx; Accessed 1 May 2018].

Morgan, Marlo. 1994. *Mutant Message Down Under: A Woman's Journey into Dreamtime Australia.* New York: HarperCollins.

Muslim Buzz. 'Who Is Ustadh Usama Canon?' Biography, November 2015. [Available Online: http://muzlimbuzz.sg/who-is-ustadh-usama-canon/; Accessed on 1 May 2018].

Nadwi, Muhammad Akram. 2013. *Al-Muhaddithat: The Women Scholars in Islam*. 2nd rev. ed. Oxford: Interface Publications.

Nasir, Muneeb. 2014. 'Global Peace Initiative Launched at RIS in Toronto.' [Available Online: http://iqra.ca/2014/global-peace-initiative-launched-at-ris-in-toronto/; Accessed on 1 May 2018].

Nelson, Soraya. 2017. 'New Liberal Mosque Led by a Woman Opens in Berlin.' [Available Online: www.npr.org/2017/08/12/543096694/new-liberal-mosque-led-by-a-woman-opens-in-berlin; Accessed 15 April 2018].

Nizami, Farhan Ahmad. 1983. 'Madrasahs, Scholars and Saints: Muslim Response to the British Presence in Delhi and the Upper Doab, 1803–1857.' D.Phil Thesis, University of Oxford.

Nonaka, Ikujiro. 1994. 'A Dynamic Theory of Organizational Knowledge Creation.' *Organization Science* 5 (1): 14–37.

Nonaka, Ikujiro, and Ryoko Toyama. 2003. 'The Knowledge-Creating Theory Revisited: Knowledge Creation as a Synthesizing Process.' *Knowledge Management Research & Practice* 1 (1): 2–10.

North, Douglass C. 1990. *Institutions, Institutional Change and Economic Performance*. Cambridge: Cambridge University Press.

'Economic Performance through Time: The Limits to Knowledge.' [Available Online: http://citeseerx.ist.psu.edu/viewdoc/download?doi=10.1.1.113.1558&rep=rep1&type=pdf; Accessed 3 April 2018].

Ober, Josiah. 2008. *Democracy and Knowledge: Innovation and Learning in Classical Athens*. Princeton, NJ: Princeton University Press.

Oldenburg, Ray. 1989. *The Great Good Place: Cafes, Coffee Shops, Community Centers, Beauty Parlors, General Stores, Bards, Hangouts and How They Get You through the Day*. New York: Paragon House.

O'Sullivan, Jack. 2001. 'If You Hate the West, Emigrate to a Muslim Country.' [Available Online: www.theguardian.com/world/2001/oct/08/religion.uk; Accessed 1 May 2018].

Pew Research Center (PRC). 2017. Five Facts about Muslims in Europe. [Available Online: www.pewresearch.org/fact-tank/2017/11/29/5-facts-about-the-muslim-population-in-europe/; Accessed 15 April 2018].

2018. A New Estimate of the U.S. Muslim Population. [Available Online: www.pewresearch.org/fact-tank/2016/01/06/a-new-estimate-of-the-u-s-muslim-population/; Accessed 15 April 2018].

Pierret, Thomas. 2013. *Religion and State in Syria: The Sunni Ulama from Coup to Revolution*. Cambridge: Cambridge University Press.

Polanyi, Michael. 2009. *The Tacit Dimension*. Chicago: University of Chicago Press.

Qadhi, Yasir. 2018. 'On Salafi Islam.' [Available Online: https://muslimmatters.org/wp-content/uploads/On-Salafi-Islam_Dr.-Yasir-Qadhi.pdf; Accessed 1 May 2018].

Rabbani, Faraz. 2018. 'Shaykh Faraz Rabbani, Islamic Scholar.' [Available Online: www.marriagesuccess.ca/faraz/; Accessed 1 May 2018].

Rahman, Fazlur. 1984. *Islam and Modernity: Transformation of an Intellectual Tradition*. Chicago: University of Chicago Press.

Ramadan, Tariq. 2004. *Western Muslims and the Future of Islam*. Oxford: Oxford University Press.

2009. *Radical Reform: Islamic Ethics and Liberation*. Oxford: Oxford University Press.

2014. 'Why I Will Not Attend the ISNA (August 2014) and RIS (December 2014) Conferences.' [Available Online: https://tariqramadan.com/english/why-i-will-not-attend-the-isna-august-2014-and-ris-december-2014-conferences/; Accessed 1 May 2018].

Rashid, Ahmed. 2010. *Taliban: Militant Islam, Oil and Fundamentalism in Central Asia*. Second ed. New Haven, CT: Yale University Press.

Razavian, Christopher Pooya. 2018a. 'Al-Azhar, Wasatiyyah, and the Waqi'.' In Masooda Bano, ed. *Modern Islamic Authority and Social Change, Vol. 1: Evolving Debates in the Muslim-Majority Countries*. Edinburgh: Edinburgh University Press, 72–96.

2018b. 'The Neo-Traditionalism of Tim Winter.' In Masooda Bano, ed. *Modern Islamic Authority and Social Change, Vol. 2: Evolving Debates in the West*. Edinburgh: Edinburgh University Press, 72–96.

2018c. 'Yasir Qadhi and the Development of Reasonable Salafism.' In Masooda Bano, ed. *Modern Islamic Authority and Social Change, Vol. 2: Evolving Debates in the West*. Edinburgh: Edinburgh University Press, 155–179.

Razavian, Christopher Pooya, and Nathan Spannaus. 2018. 'New Deobandi Institutions in the West.' In Masooda Bano, ed. *Modern Islamic Authority and Social Change, Vol. 2: Evolving Debates in the West*. Edinburgh: Edinburgh University Press, 180–210.

Robinson, Francis. 1993. 'Technology and Religious Change: Islam and the Impact of Print.' *Modern Asian Studies* 27 (1): 229–251.

1997. 'Ottomans–Safavids–Mughals: Shared Knowledge and Connective Systems.' *Journal of Islamic Studies* 8 (2): 151–184.

1999. 'Religious Change and the Self in Muslim South Asia since 1800.' *South Asia: Journal of South Asian Studies* 22 (1): 13–27.

2001. *The 'Ulama of Farangi Mahall and Islamic Culture in South Asia*. London: C Hurst & Co Publishers Ltd.

2002. 'Islam and the West: Clash of Civilisations?' *Asian Affairs* 33 (3): 307–320.

2003. *Islam and Muslim History in South Asia*. Oxford: Oxford University Press.

2008. 'Islamic Reform and Modernities in South Asia.' *Modern Asian Studies* 42 (2–3): 259–281.

Roy, Olivier. 1996. *The Failure of Political Islam*. Cambridge, MA: Harvard University Press.

Sacred Caravan. 2015. *Visiting the House of God: Manners, Rites, and Invocations*. NA: Sandala.

Sachiko, Murata. 1992. *The Tao of Islam: A Sourcebook on Gender Relationships in Islamic Thought*. Albany: State University of New York Press.

Saliba, George. 2011. *Islamic Science and the Making of the European Renaissance*. Cambridge, MA: MIT Press.

Sandala. 2018. 'Recommended Books.' [Available Online: www.sandala.org/ favorites; Accessed on 1 May 2018].

Saudi Gazette. 2015. 'More Women than Men in Saudi Universities, Says Ministry.' [Available Online: https://english.alarabiya.net/en/perspective/features/ 2015/05/28/More-women-than-men-in-Saudi-universities-says-ministry.html; Accessed 1 May 2018].

Scott, Korb. 2013. *Light without Fire: The Making of America's First Muslim College.* Boston: Beacon Press.

Selin, Helaine. ed. 1997. *Encyclopaedia of the History of Science, Technology, and Medicine in Non Western Countries.* Boston: Kluwer Academic.

Shukr Islamic Clothing. 2018. 'About Shukr.' [Available Online: www.shukr.co .uk/about-shukr; Accessed 1 May 2018].

Spannaus, Nathan. 2018a. 'From "Islamization of Knowledge" to "American Islam": The International Institute of Islamic Thought (IIIT).' In Masooda Bano, ed. *Islamic Authority and Social Change, Vol. 2: Evolving Debates in the West.* Edinburgh: Edinburgh University Press, 97–122.

2018b. 'Transforming Islamic Reform: Tariq Ramadan and the Center for Islamic Legislation and Ethics (CILE).' In Masooda Bano, ed. *Islamic Authority and Social Change, Vol. 2: Evolving Debates in the West.* Edinburgh: Edinburgh University Press, 123–154.

Spannaus, Nathan, and Christopher Pooya Razavian. 2018. 'Zaytuna College and the Construction of an American Muslim Identity.' In Masooda Bano, ed. *Islamic Authority and Social Change, Vol. 2: Evolving Debates in the West.* Edinburgh: Edinburgh University Press, 39–71.

Stewart, Devin J., Joseph Lowry, and Shawkat M. Toorawa. 2004. *Law and Education in Medieval Islam: Studies in Memory of George Makdisi.* Cambridge: Gibb Memorial Trust.

Ta'leef Collective. 2018. 'About Ta'leef Collective.' [Available Online: https:// taleefcollective.org/; Accessed 1 May 2018].

Taylor, Charles. 2007. *A Secular Age.* 1st ed. Cambridge, MA: Harvard University Press.

UNDP. 2014. *The 2014 Human Development Report – Sustaining Human Progress: Reducing Vulnerabilities and Building Resilience.* New York: Oxford University Press.

Van Bruinessen, Martin, and Stefano Allievi, eds. 2011. *Producing Islamic Knowledge: Transmission and Dissemination in Western Europe.* London: Routledge.

Walbridge, John. 2011. *God and Logic in Islam: the Caliphate of Reason.* Cambridge: Cambridge University Press.

Wilcox, Clyde, and Greg Fortelny. 2009. 'Religion and Social Movements.' In James L. Guth, Lyman A. Kellstedt, and Corwin E. Smidt, eds. *The Oxford Handbook of Religion and American Politics.* Oxford: Oxford University Press. [Available Online: https://onlinelibrary.wiley.com/doi/abs/10.1002/ 9780470674871.wbespm484; Accessed 20 April 2018].

Willowbrook Farm. 2018. 'Willowbrook Farm in the News.' [Available Online: https://willowbrookfarm.co.uk/http%3A//www.willowbrookorganic.org/ News; Accessed 1 May 2018].

Winter, Tim. 2009. 'Why I Converted to Islam (Timothy Winter) Part 1/2.' BBC Radio 3 interview with Joan Bakewell. [Available Online www.youtube.com/watch?v=GGfc6Ob1UAY; Accessed on 1 May 2018].

2010. 'Reason as Balance: The Evolution of 'Aql.' Cambridge Muslim College Paper No. 3. [Available Online: http://cambridgemuslimcollege.org/down load-papers/CMCPapers3-ReasonAsBalance.pdf; Accessed 20 April 2018].

2013. 'Ramadan in Istanbul.' [Available Online: www.lastprophet .info/ram adan-in-istanbul; Accessed 15 April 2018].

2014a. 'British and Muslim.' [Available Online: http://masud.co.uk/understand ing-the-four-madhhabs-the-problem-with-anti-madhhabism/; Accessed 15 April 2018].

2014b. 'Understanding the Four Madhhabs: The Problem with Anti-Madhhab- ism.' [Available Online: http://masud.co.uk/understanding-the-four-madh habs-the-problem-with-anti-madhhabism/; Accessed 15 April 2018].

2018. 'Boys Will Be Boys.' [Available Online: http://masud.co.uk/ISLAM/ahm/ boys.htm; Accessed on 1 May 2018].

Worth, Robert F. 2009. 'Crossroads of Islam, Past and Present.' *New York Times*. [Available online: www.nytimes.com/2009/10/15/world/middleeast/ 15yemen.html; Accessed on 1 May 2018].

Yusuf, Hamza. 2004. *Purification of the Heart: Signs, Symptoms and Cures of the Spiritual Diseases of the Heart*. NA: Starlatch, Llc.

2006a. *The Alchemy of Happiness* [audio]. Alhambra Productions.

2006b. 'A Time for Introspection' [Available Online: www.masud.co.uk/ ISLAM/misc/shhamza_sep11.htm.; Accessed 1 February 2018].

2007. 'Islam and the West.' Part 1. [Video] YouTube. [Available Online: www .youtube.com/watch?v=7ttcA9Kto9M; Accessed on 1 May 2018].

2009. 'Women's Rights in Islam.' [Video] YouTube. [Available Online: www .youtube.com/watch?v=yDIAN4IowBA&feature=youtube_gdata_player; Accessed 1 May 2018].

2011a. 'The Concept of Ihsan.' Foundations of Islam series. [Video] YouTube. [Available Online: www.youtube.com/watch?v=SLhogmk-Wug; Accessed 1 May 2018].

2011b. 'The Critical Importance of Al-Ghazali in Our Times.' Lecture, Decem- ber 2011. [Available Online: www.youtube.com/watch?v=lJezFjbn-6M; Accessed 1 April 2018].

2011c. 'Fair Trade Commerce for a Better World.' RIS Talks. [Video] YouTube. [Available Online: www.ristalks.com/details.php?v=10; Accessed 1 May 2018].

2011d. 'Success in This World and the Next.' [Video] YouTube, 28 December 2011. [Available Online: http://youtu.be/ldvz6LZ6BdU; Accessed 1 May 2018].

2011e. 'Transcript for What Happened to Poetry.' (Lecture, transcribed). [Available Online: http://shaykhhamza.com/transcript/what-happened-to- poetry; Accessed 1 May 2018].

2011f. 'When the Social Contract Is Breached on One Side, It's Breached on Both Sides.' Sandala. [Available Online: https://sandala.org/when-the- social-contract-is-breached-on-one-side-its-breached-on-both-sides/; Accessed 1 May 2018].

2011g. 'Women, Shari'ah and Islam.' [Video] YouTube. [Available Online: www.youtube.com/watch?v=4EpINIaobdo; Accessed 1 May 2018].

2012. 'Men and Women (In Islam).' [Video] YouTube. [Available Online: www.youtube.com/watch?v=H8PrFABsVcQ&feature=youtube_gdata_player; Accessed 1 May 2018].

Yusuf, Hamza. 2013a. 'Follow a Madhab or Follow a Wahabi/Salafi? 2013/2014.' [Video] YouTube. [Available Online: http://youtu.be/S-01WsNKNAE; Accessed 1 May 2018].

2013b. 'Islamic State and Shariah Law Are Fantasies.' [Video] YouTube. [Available Online: www.youtube.com/watch?v=dUe5OsGbhMo; Accessed 1 May 2018].

2013c. 'Prohibitions of the Tongue, Session 2' [Video] YouTube, 24 November, 2013 [Available Online: www.youtube.com/watch?v=XVNFnaJxeRc; Accessed 10 August 2016].

2013d. 'Reading "Ozymandias" with Hamza Yusuf.' [Available Online: www .youtube.com/watch?v=Bz80Sl5A36s; Accessed 1 May 2018].

2013e. 'The Unofficial Biography of Shaykh Hamza Yusuf.' Footnote XII. [Available Online: http://shaykhhamza.com/biography/2; Accessed 1 May 2018].

2013f. 'The Unofficial Biography of Shaykh Hamza Yusuf.' Footnote XXII. [Available Online: http://shaykhhamza.com/biography/2; Accessed 1 May 2018].

2013g. 'The Unofficial Biography of Shaykh Hamza Yusuf.' Footnote 11. [Available Online: http://shaykhhamza.com/biography/2; Accessed 1 May 2018].

2013h. 'The Unofficial Biography of Shaykh Hamza Yusuf.' Footnote 20. [Available Online: http://shaykhhamza.com/biography/2; Accessed 1 May 2018].

2013i. 'The Unofficial Biography of Shaykh Hamza Yusuf.' Footnote 21. [Available Online: http://shaykhhamza.com/biography/2; Accessed 1 May 2018].

2013j. 'The Unofficial Biography of Shaykh Hamza Yusuf.' Footnote 22. [Available Online: http://shaykhhamza.com/biography/2; Accessed 1 May 2018].

2013k. 'The Unofficial Biography of Shaykh Hamza Yusuf.' Footnote 31. [Available Online: http://shaykhhamza.com/biography/2; Accessed 1 May 2018].

2013l. 'The Unofficial Biography of Shaykh Hamza Yusuf.' Footnote 32. [Available Online: http://shaykhhamza.com/biography/2; Accessed 1 May 2018].

2013m. 'The Unofficial Biography of Shaykh Hamza Yusuf.' Footnote 34. [Available Online: http://shaykhhamza.com/biography/2; Accessed 1 May 2018].

2013n. 'The Unofficial Biography of Shaykh Hamza Yusuf.' Footnote 38. [Available Online: http://shaykhhamza.com/biography/3; Accessed 26 June 2019].

2013o. 'The Unofficial Biography of Shaykh Hamza Yusuf.' Footnote 43. [Available Online: http://shaykhhamza.com/biography/2; Accessed 1 May 2018].

2013p. 'The Unofficial Biography of Shaykh Hamza Yusuf.' Footnote 44. [Available Online: http://shaykhhamza.com/biography/2; Accessed 1 May 2018].

2013q. 'The Unofficial Biography of Shaykh Hamza Yusuf.' Footnote 46. [Available Online: http://shaykhhamza.com/biography/2; Accessed 1 May 2018].

2013r. 'The Unofficial Biography of Shaykh Hamza Yusuf.' Footnote 48. [Available Online: http://shaykhhamza.com/biography/2; Accessed 1 May 2018].

2014a. 'Global Tawbah.' [Video] YouTube: 28 August 2014 at Merdeka Hall, Putra World Trade Centre, Kuala Lumpur. [Available Online: www.youtube.com/watch?v=jwGeWE9zPVo; Accessed 1 May 2018].

2014b. 'Higher Education for a Higher Purpose.' [Video] YouTube. [Available Online: www.youtube.com/watch?v=8NCM97NOp7g; Accessed 1 May 2018].

2014c. 'Interview IKIM FM.' 4:41–6:17. [Available Online: www.bing.com/videos/search?q=Hamza+yusuf+interview+IKIM+FM&view=detail&mid=7BEC2661585E67F554017BEC2661585E67F55401&FORM=VIRE; Accessed 1 May 2018].

2016a. 'A Good Father.' Blog post, 18 April 2016. [Available Online: https://sandala.org/a-good-father/; Accessed on 1 May 2018].

2016b. 'On the Passing of my Mother, Elizabeth George Hanson.' Blog post, 10 August 2016 [Available Online: https://sandala.org/on-the-passing-of-my-mother/; Accessed 1 May 2018].

2018a. 'A Time for Introspection.' [Available Online: www.masud.co.uk/ISLAM/misc/shhamza_sep11.htm; Accessed 1 May 2018].

2018b. 'Transcript: Vision of Islam.' [Available Online: http://shaykhhamza.com/transcript/Vision-of-Islam; Accessed 1 May 2018].

Zaman, Muhammad Qasim. 2010. *The Ulama in Contemporary Islam: Custodians of Change*. Princeton, NJ: Princeton University Press.

2012. *Modern Islamic Thought in a Radical Age: Religious Authority and Internal Criticism*. Cambridge: Cambridge University Press.

Zaytuna College. 2014. *Zaytuna College Catalog 2014–2015*. Berkeley, CA: Zaytuna College.

2017. *Annual Report from the President*. Berkeley, CA: Zaytuna College.

2018a. 'Mission.' [Available Online: www.zaytuna.edu/; Accessed 13 December 2018].

2018b. 'Perennial Inspiration.' [Available Online: https://zaytuna.edu/mission/perennial-inspiration; Accessed 17 March 2018].

2018c. 'Permaculture Design Certificate.' [Available Online: https://zaytuna.edu/extendedlearning/permaculture-design-certificate; Accessed 1 May 2018].

2018d. 'Renovation.' [Available Online: https://renovatio.zaytuna.edu/essays; Accessed 1 May 2018].

Zeghal, Malika. 2007. 'The "Recentering" of Religious Knowledge and Discourse: The Case of al-Azhar in Twentieth-Century Egypt.' In Robert W. Hefner and Muhammad Qasim Zaman, eds. *Schooling Islam: The Culture and Politics of Modern Muslim Education*. Princeton, NJ: Princeton University Press, 107–130.

2008. *Islamism in Morocco: Religion, Authoritarianism and Electoral Politics*. Princeton, NJ: Markus Wiener Publishers

Index